THE
CURIOUS
STORY OF
MALCOLM
TURNBULL

THE INCREDIBLE SHRINKING MAN IN THE TOP HAT

ANDREW P STREET

ALLEN&UNWIN
SYDNEY • MELBOURNE • AUCKLAND • LONDON

First published in 2016

Copyright © Andrew P Street 2016

Allen & Unwin
83 Alexander Street
Crows Nest NSW 2065
Australia
Phone: (61 2) 8425 0100
Email: info@allenandunwin.com
Web: www.allenandunwin.com

Cataloguing-in-Publication details are available
from the National Library of Australia
www.trove.nla.gov.au

ISBN 978 1 76029 488 5

Set in 13/17 pt Adobe Caslon by Midland Typesetters, Australia
Printed and bound in Australia by Griffin Press

10 9 8 7 6 5 4 3 2 1

CONTENTS

INTRODUCTION
THE BLIGH MUTINY
(2015 REMIX)

*In which your humble narrator shakes his head and confesses
he's just as baffled by recent Australian politics as you are*

The definition of insanity, the old saying goes, is doing the
same thing over and over and expecting a different result.

It's a really stupid definition.

For a start, it's wrong on a number of levels. A quick check
of any reputable dictionary will reveal that insanity is actually
defined as 'the state of being mentally ill', and is a rarely used
blanket term regarding very specific clinical symptoms which,
in turn, determine the manner and level of treatment of the
person in whom said symptoms manifest.

Also, 'doing the same thing over and over and expecting a different result' is the mark of unbiased research, as
well as a characteristic of assiduous practise at any skill—a
fact known to anyone whom Dame Fortune has playfully
decreed should rent an apartment adjacent to an aspiring
saxophonist.

Yet it still gets thrown about as being some deep insight, normally along with an attribution to Albert Einstein (who not only didn't say it, as best anyone can ascertain, but who was also a theoretical physicist rather than a psychiatrist or expert in human behaviour, and therefore not especially likely to have a particular opinion on the matter, nor any qualification that would suggest his insights were sought upon it).

What this old saying means to contend is this: It is foolish to do an objectively foolish thing again, having observed the consequences of the objectively foolish thing being previously done. Which isn't quite as punchy, admittedly, but should take off once it's been printed on a few posters under a picture of Gandhi.

The gist of it is that history and experience are generally reliable guides to what is to come, whether that's in terms of embarking on ill-starred relationships, eating cheese late at night, or knocking off an elected prime minister via an internal coup and then heading to the polls in the hopes of skating over the line before all one's popularity evaporates.

In any case: welcome to the story of the first term of Australia's twenty-ninth prime minister, the Honourable Malcolm Bligh Turnbull.

———

No Australian PM since the colourful and tragic figure of Kevin Rudd has come to power with such expectations riding on him. After all, Turnbull had spent years featuring in the nation's fevered imaginations as their prime ministerial lust object.

Sure, people had been prepared to endure Abbott or perhaps even put up with Labor leader Bill Shorten, if they absolutely had to—but the whole time, they were thinking about Malcolm. He was the one, as poll after poll after poll confirmed, whom Australia would totally leave their current PM for . . . but then, when it happened, it turned out that the commanding leader about whom Australia had fantasised for so long wasn't quite the red-hot legislative lover they'd imagined.

All those fantasies—hard, fast action on climate change; passionate commitment to science and education; even making an honest nation of us with marriage equality— turned out to be nothing but empty promises by a timid fuddy-duddy who, it turned out, was too terrified even to mention renewable energy in case his housemates heard any suspicious turbines buzzing.

It took years for Rudd to reveal his limitations. Turnbull managed it in weeks. However, he wasn't alone: like his predecessor Captain Abbott, he was supported in his increasingly fraught journey by a coterie of power-seekers, superannuated time-servers, factional warriors and straight-up duffers, a rogue's gallery of clowns, yes-men and fuming factional enemies determined that no-one would save the electoral fortunes of the Liberal Party of Australia and escape unpunished.

But despite the supporting cast, the story is that of Turnbull himself: the son of a single father who rose from the privations of harbourside middle-class origins to become a multi-millionaire, a man of undeniable talent and intelligence who assumed that'd be enough to persuade everyone to fall in behind him; a leader with the confident ambition of someone who got halfway through *Macbeth* before tossing it aside and going, 'I bet this all ended up fine'; and a PM who promised a new, modern, respectful, articulate sort of Australian politics, and immediately pissed all that away in favour of tribal populism when the promise wasn't quite as easy to fulfil as he'd assumed.

Now it's tempting to point out parallels with his middle namesake: William Bligh, the New South Wales governor and former captain of the *Bounty*, a man who knew a thing or two about keeping the aspirational classes on side (Turnbull's ancestor John swore to give all male Turnbulls the middle name Bligh in recognition of the governor's generosity toward Hawkesbury-region landowners),[1] and who was to find himself twice tossed from power by lesser rabble: once in the legendary mutiny that made him globally infamous, and once during the Rum Rebellion, when his crackdown on the sly grog trade turned his own army against him and he was sent away in ignominy.

And an unkind author could make some snide allusion to the Liberal leadership challenge of 2009, in which Malcolm was hurled overboard by the party's own Fletcher Christian— a chap named Tony Abbott—and then wonder if, like Bligh, he would eventually be found hiding under his bed as his own party began marching upon him in the wake of the 2016 double dissolution election. But that would . . . Okay, that's pretty much the rest of the book.

But if Bligh seems a little on the nose, there's perhaps a better comparison to be made.

---

1   One assumes that Bligh would look upon the Coalition's position on negative gearing and see that his legacy of currying favour with the landlord classes was alive and well.

In Annabel Crabb's glorious 2016 portrait of Turnbull, *Stop At Nothing*, she revealed that the doting Malcolm would frequently read his children his favourite Roald Dahl short story, 'The Enormous Crocodile'. It's a remarkably illustrative tale, in which the titular reptile makes unsuccessful attempts to eat various jungle beasts before deciding that he'll devour the pupils at a nearby school.[2] And despite the various attempts of the aforementioned animals to thwart the crocodile's child-gobbling ambitions, he keeps coming back with ever more elaborate schemes to get his way, all the while declaring: 'I've thought up secret plans and clever tricks!'

Turnbull, too, as you will learn in these very pages, rose to power thanks to secret plans, and managed to wrong-foot his foes with clever tricks. However, like the crocodile he so admired, the result he desired remained elusive.

It's worth pointing out that no matter the number of secret plans and degree of clever tricks at his disposal, things don't work out all that well for the Enormous Crocodile. And that brings us to the central question being asked by pundits, journalists and the public alike, on all points along the political spectrum: will Malcolm ultimately be thrown into the sun by Trunky the Elephant?

Let's begin.

---

2 An illustrative apt description of the future PM's approach to funding the Gonski education reforms? You be the judge!

1
BE CAREFUL WHAT YOU WISH FOR ...

*In which we meet the man in the top hat and his
hand-picked coterie of ministerial superstars*

Tuesday, 15 September 2015[1] dawned crisp and bright in
Canberra as the nation prepared to welcome its twenty-eighth
prime minister—or, to use another scale, its fifth since 2010.[2]
And ...

Actually, maybe we should step back a little and remember
where things were in 2015 as the Coalition government of
Tony Abbott moved from Acute Care to being covered in
signs reading 'Do Not Resuscitate'.

———

Having swept into power with a comprehensive victory in
September 2013, the Abbott government enjoyed mere weeks
of popular approval before things started trending down-
wards. That was less because of the inevitable compromises

———

1   Specifically, it was a maximum of 22 degrees with a bit of cloud.
2   ... although two of them were Kevin Rudd.

a government needs to make once it has achieved power, and more because the newly elected PM barely drew breath in the job before baldly reversing many of his most celebrated election promises.

The sheer effrontery of this strategy might have been less breathtaking if not for the fact that so many of those promises had been very publicly pledged the night before the election when Abbott told SBS TV, live from Penrith Stadium, that there would be 'no cuts to health, no cuts to education, no changes to pensions, no changes to the GST, and no cuts to the ABC and SBS'.[3]

By the end of 2014 Abbott's government was suffering badly in the polls following its failed attempts to cut Medicare coverage and university funding—literally the first two things the PM had specifically promised not to cut. To add insult to injury, his government's embarrassing attempts to legislate for a GP co-payment and the deregulation of uni fees had been blocked in the Senate.

Attempts to raise the age at which Australians would be eligible for pensions and an aborted shot at beginning a 'national discussion' about the GST followed, while significant and ongoing cuts to both the ABC and SBS were announced. Abbott cast a proud eye over all this in December as he celebrated what he un-ironically declared had been a

---

3 There remains no sensible answer as to why the actual hell Abbott chose to make that promise. It was the night before the election; there was zero doubt that the Coalition was going to win, and any rational leader would presumably realise that making such an unambiguous statement could only hurt them down the track while doing little, if anything, to affect his electoral chances a few hours hence— especially since Abbott was presumably aware that said promise would not reflect his policies in power. It still beggars belief.

'year of achievement'. Meanwhile, his increasingly terrified looking government observed Abbott's tumbling approva rating and the Opposition's easy election-winning lead i the polls and hoped for a miracle.

And that miracle was sitting there, front and centre, witl a smile of affluent self-confidence: Abbott's long time bête noire, Malcolm Turnbull.

———

There had been a lot of history between Tony 'n' Malc. Both grew up in Sydney (Turnbull was born there in 1954; Abbott, born three years later, had emigrated to the city from London with his family in 1960), both attended exclusive private schools (Sydney Grammar for Turnbull, St Ignatius' College for Abbott), both were subsequently alumni of Sydney University, and both had been Rhodes scholars (Turnbull in 1978, Abbott in 1981).

However, despite these similarities, there were serious differences between the two which were to define the nature of their subsequent relationship.

Turnbull was the epitome of the small-l Liberal, socially progressive but with a keen interest in the unfettered operation of capitalist markets, while the pious, had-a-bash-at-seminary Abbott was a throwback to the more religious-flavoured conservatism that was less characteristic of the Liberal Party than the Democratic Labor Party under B.A. Santamaria.

The best illustration of the differences between the men was that they had been on opposite sides during the contentious 1998 Constitutional Convention, Australia's ultimately

stillborn push to become a Republic,[4] when Abbott was leader
of the Australians for Constitutional Monarchy and Turnbull
led the Australian Republican Movement. Here the contrast
in their personalities was beautifully encapsulated, with one
of them desperately attempting to hold back the inexorable
march of history out of sheer bloody-mindedness, while the
other man demanded that the nation fall into line, without
much bothering to bring the people with him. Their very
different personality traits would later come to characterise
their respective stabs at leadership.

While Abbott was a true believer in conservative politics
from an early stage, Turnbull had been rather more promis-
cuous in his affiliations. He'd been a Liberal Party member
in his youth, even running for preselection (unsuccessfully) in
Wentworth, his eventual seat, in 1981; but that uncharacteristic
failure seemed to break Turnbull's spirit. He let his membership lapse in the aftermath while he pursued other professional
challenges, which saw him develop an international profile as
a barrister, distinguishing himself through the high-profile
Spycatcher case,[5] and become a multi-millionaire via business
ventures both successful (such as his canny investment—and

---

4   Abbott clearly learned well, since the strategy used by the monarchists (including then-PM John Howard) was to push for a public vote but then ensure that the
question being put was one that the public would reject. Ring any bells regarding
any plebiscite of marriage equality?

5   It's a far larger story than can be adequately explained here, but the crib notes
are these: the UK government wanted to prevent the publication of a memoir by
Peter Wright, a former MI5 agent, on the grounds it would breach the Official
Secrets Act. Turnbull successfully defended the right of the publishers to publish in
Australia, where the Act didn't apply. That the book was later exposed to be almost
entirely a fabrication didn't hurt its sales—and in 1988 it was finally published in
Britain since it contained no secrets, official or otherwise.

cannier divestment—in early local email company Ozemail) and otherwise (an investment in an environmentally dubious palm oil company in Borneo was to prove both financially disappointing and politically embarrassing, and an initially promising investment in a Russian goldmining operation fell over with subsequently embarrassing repercussions).

There had also been a brief flirtation with Labor during his Australian Republican Movement era, during which he worked closely alongside senior Labor figure Gareth Evans. NSW Labor powerbroker John Della Bosca (a former Special Minister of State under Premier Bob Carr) had even made a semi-official attempt to recruit Turnbull to the party, but it ultimately came to nothing.

This failure of ideological purity guaranteed that there was little love lost between Turnbull and Abbott when Malcolm reactivated his membership of the Liberal Party and set his sights on a parliamentary seat. Indeed, when Turnbull ran in the hotly contested preselection for Wentworth in 2004, Abbott spoke up on behalf of the sitting Liberal, Peter King, declaring that 'the party should not reward someone who described the prime minister [Howard] as having broken the nation's heart' in the aftermath of the Constitutional Convention.

And it didn't get any easier after Malcolm won preselection. While Wentworth was (and is) one of the safest Liberal seats in the country, his battle against Peter King split the local branch, with long-time staffers resigning in disgust. One particularly galling consequence was the collapse of the local fundraising apparatus—which became a big deal six months later, when a

still-smarting King announced plans to run against Turnbull as
an independent candidate at the 2004 election.[6]

Without much of a local war chest, Malcolm ended up
spending $600,000 from his own pocket to win the seat. But
win it he did, surviving a swing against him and consigning
King to history and himself to the blue-ribbon Liberal seat.[7]

Thus Turnbull was a controversial, divisive figure among
the conservatives within the party from the very beginning—
despite his preselection being loudly welcomed by the likes of
The Australian's Janet Albrechtsen and the Institute of Public
Affairs' new director (and Malcolm's long-time friend) John
Roskam. However, the conservative wing of the returned
Howard government made sure that Turnbull knew where he
was placed on the parliamentary totem pole. He was allocated
a shitty office (unlike the lovely view offered to fellow new
boy, future trade minister Andrew Robb, whose victory in
Goldstein had been a low-fuss, non-party-rending affair) and
sent to the backbench to learn his place.

Even so, it wasn't long before he was given a ministerial
berth: first as parliamentary secretary in 2006, then as John
Howard's Minister for the Environment and Water Resources

6 In case the personal nature of King's doomed vendetta was lost on people, he
used parliamentary privilege to relate how Turnbull had warned him to step down
and allow Malcolm to walk into the seat unchallenged. More specifically, King
claimed that Turnbull instructed him to 'fuck off and get out of my way'.
7 King was a genuinely popular local member and there was a decent ground-
swell of support for him as an independent—he was still far and away the preferred
candidate before he'd even announced his nomination—and going by the numbers,
there's a case to be made that had King preferenced Labor's candidate, David Patch,
ahead of the Liberals (i.e. Turnbull), then he might have ended up squeaking over
the line. Then again, to have so obviously thrown a preferencing-tanty against his
former party would almost certainly have reduced his primary vote.

in early 2007.[8] The gig ended abruptly in November when Labor won power in a historic landslide, with Howard retiring from politics in humiliating defeat having lost both his government and his seat of Bennelong, which he'd held for thirty-three years.[9]

But that didn't slow Malcolm down. The day after the government's loss he announced he'd be standing for the now-vacant Liberal Party leadership, after former treasurer and presumptive leader Peter Costello decided to abandon his leadership ambitions and head to the backbench, where he remained until his abrupt resignation in October 2009.

Turnbull was considered the favourite, but then lost by forty-two votes to forty-five to former Australian Medical Association president Brendan Nelson: a result that sat badly for Malcolm, if not especially for the former PM.[10] Turnbull was somewhat placated by being made shadow treasurer, but he was far from satisfied with the political equivalent of a participant's ribbon from a primary school sports day.

Thankfully, he didn't have long to wait for a rematch.

---

8   That was the same year he was trumpeting the use of untested, implausible and—as it turned out—utterly bogus Russian 'technology' that promised to 'trigger rainfall from the atmosphere'. For a man later to be praised for his respect for science, this was an odd misstep.

9   Actually, that's a bit unfair. Howard knew he was hanging on to his seat by increasingly slender margins, having only fallen over the line thanks to preferences in both 1998 and 2004, despite being the sitting prime minister on both occasions. In 2007 the victor was former ABC journalist Maxine McKew, but her tenure was short: after having been one of Kevin 07's loudest and most loyal spear-carriers, in 2010 she was defeated easily by the current Liberal MP, John Alexander.

10 John Howard's memoir rather sulkily mentions that Turnbull had advised him to resign in August 2007, predicting that he'd lose his seat. The book implies this was disloyalty rather than, say, impressive prescience or unambiguously good advice.

In what might look a little like foreshadowing, Turnbull was consistently well regarded by the public as his party's actual leader stumbled. By August 2008 the media was speaking of a two-horse leadership race between Turnbull and Costello, with Nelson's removal regarded as a foregone conclusion.

Even so, it ended up being a closer contest than most expected: when the spill occurred in September, Costello declined to run and Turnbull defeated Nelson forty-five to forty-one.

No-one thought Malcolm's leadership would be uncontroversial, but few guessed it would last a scant fourteen months. A strong start attacking Labor's 2009 budget—handed down in the wake of the Global Financial Crisis—evaporated when Turnbull went after Rudd and Treasurer Wayne Swan over suspected improper dealings with a Queensland car dealer, John Grant. This supposedly smoking gun was revealed to Malcolm by a Liberal-sympathising staffer in the Treasury named Godwin Grech.

Grech's bombshell hinged on an email asking Treasury to obtain preferential treatment for Grant's business, which prompted Liberal senator Eric Abetz to convene a Senate inquiry in June 2009. Following Grech's evidence, Turnbull declared: 'The prime minister and the treasurer have used their offices and taxpayers' resources to seek advantage for one of their mates and then lied about it to the parliament.' He called for their resignations.

'And what a triumph it would have been had the terrifically unwell Grech not made the whole thing up.

It all unravelled rapidly, with Grech admitting he'd forged the email. But the real victim was Turnbull, who was political toast. His approval rating went into freefall, while Rudd's hit fresh new heights. Then Malcolm's attempt at rational bipartisanship over the government's Carbon Pollution Reduction Scheme in November 2009 caused the climate-change-sceptical conservatives within his own party to lose patience. Many—including Abbott—quit the shadow Cabinet in protest. Clearly a challenge was coming.

And then, on 1 December, it came.

The first round was a three-way battle between Abbott, Turnbull, and an ambitiously ill-prepared Joe Hockey, who was swiftly eliminated from the running, garnering twenty-three votes to Turnbull's twenty-six and Abbott's thirty-five.[11]

Round two was much closer, but definitive: Abbott beat Turnbull for the leadership by a single vote, forty-two to forty-one.[12]

———

Turnbull, it's fair to say, did not take this defeat entirely graciously.

After spraying venom at the new leader—memorably declaring him a 'front stabber'—and cursing the party's gutlessness for its pitiful stance on climate change mitigation, Turnbull

---

11 Madonna King's endlessly entertaining 2014 biography, *Hockey: Not Your Average Joe*, reveals that the future treasurer was so certain of easy victory that he didn't bother to call MPs and lobby them for their vote, as Abbott and Turnbull were doing. King quotes an unnamed 'senior Liberal' as saying: 'That feeds the view that [Joe] has this destiny thing where he should get things easily.' It transpires that Hockey was convinced neither Abbott nor Turnbull was going to stand, despite Turnbull having explicitly declared his intention to defend his leadership on television two days earlier, and despite Abbott having resigned his front bench position in what was a clear precursor to a challenge.

12 You might notice those numbers don't add up. This is because there was one mysterious informal ballot, appropriately reading 'no'—in Hockey's handwriting, presumably.

announced that he'd had enough. Having been removed as leader, he declared, he would not contest Wentworth at the 2010 election.

Three weeks and a chat with John Howard later, he changed his mind. Turnbull would remain. He would return to the backbench. He would support Abbott's leadership. He would be a team player.

And there, on the windowsill of his opulent Point Piper mansion, sat a lovely dish of revenge, gradually cooling.

2
THE CAT IN THE TOP HAT
COMES BACK

*In which Turnbull makes his move, while creating exciting
and dynamic problems for his future self*

When Captain Abbott began what one roguishly handsome commentator has inspiringly called his 'short and excruciatingly embarrassing reign',[1] he appointed Malcolm as his Minister for Communications. Why exactly, you may well ask, did the captain do that?

The answer is twofold. Communications wasn't exactly a glamour portfolio—indeed, it would be a difficult one in which to shine—but it was an area in which the party had been dangerously weak in the recent past. Indeed, the previous shadow Communications spokesman, Tony Smith, had fractured his somewhat optimistic hopes for leadership after failing to win hearts and minds with the party's broadband

---

1 Street, AP, *The Short and Excruciatingly Embarrassing Reign of Captain Abbott* (2015), 'A piece of political portraiture shot through with an antic, larrikin spirit'— Richard King, *The Australian*. The perfect gift for very specific occasions!

strategy, and Abbott supposedly blamed his mishandling of the portfolio as being one of the major reasons Labor squeaked to victory at the 2010 election.[2] And while Abbott can't possibly have been unaware of the risks associated with giving Turnbull a ministerial berth, assigning it to the man celebrated for having become a millionaire thanks to his savvy involvement in Ozemail gave the party some much-needed new-economy authority.[3]

The PM was probably also aware that even if a Cabinet berth gave Turnbull plenty of plausible opportunities to maintain a strong public presence, the chances of his great rival positioning himself for a successful challenge would have been somewhat hampered by the fact that in 2013 the communications minister's greatest responsibility was to hobble the National Broadband Network, one of the most high-profile and consistently popular Labor-era policies.

2   In what looked awfully like a portent of the leadership vote Abbott was shortly to face, Smith was made Speaker of the House in August 2015 when Bronwyn Bishop finally stood down after the escalating scandals over her use of travel allowances. Smith, predictably, was not Abbott's choice for the gig—he backed Russell Broadbent—but the Scott Morrison-supported Smith easily won the day. Insert ominous 'Bum-bum-BAAAAH!' here.

3   There are plenty of myths about Turnbull's involvement with Ozemail, so it's worth clarifying a few things. One, Turnbull didn't found the company—he was part of a group of people who refinanced it through his merchant bank, Whitlam Turnbull & Co, in 1994. Two, the innovation that he applied to it was listing the company on the US NASDAQ exchange, thereby attracting international investment attention, rather than innovating through anything especially technical. And three, the moderately successful company would still probably have gone under due to the economics of all Australian ISPs having to bid to use Telstra's infrastructure had there not been a fortuitous sale to World.com subsidiary UUNet in 1999 for $520 million. That timing was especially handy since it happened less than a year before World.com collapsed in a massive book-cooking scandal, so Turnbull's skill was that of a very lucky merchant banker rather than a savvy tech mogul.

However, all this was to underestimate both Turnbull's charm and the general public's inability to intuitively grasp differences in bandwidth and upload/download speeds between the similar-sounding fibre-to-the-node and fibre-to-the-premises schemes, and other conveniently vague terms distinguishing the Coalition's national broadband strategy from that of Labor.

The upshot was that Turnbull wasn't castigated for over-seeing an inadequate network that was mightily over budget and behind schedule, using technology that would require replacement within years—at least, not outside the specialist press—until he was out of the portfolio, running for election and being celebrated by respected tech site Delimiter as being Australia's worst-ever communications minister.

It helped that his ministerial brief also covered the ABC and SBS, both of which were facing swingeing funding cuts and didn't want to give the minister further motivation to hurt them by suggesting he might be doing a terrible job. Ultimately, in January 2015 there was a brief furore when former ABC tech journalist Nick Ross—whose reports on the NBN, and particularly on the Coalition's plan to use Telstra's existing and arguably inadequate copper wire network, had been both forensic and damning—claimed he'd been 'gagged' from reporting on these matters by ABC management in the months prior to the 2013 election for fear of incurring the wrath of the incoming Coalition government.

However, to the general public Turnbull seemed the smart, relaxed, articulate yin to Abbott's increasingly blustery, slogan-eering yang. He attended the annual Sydney Gay and Lesbian

Mardi Gras parade along Oxford Street, in his Wentworth electorate. He spoke encouragingly about green technologies while the PM and treasurer were describing wind turbines as 'offensive'. He caught public transport often—even pointedly tweeting about his $12 train fare from Melbourne to Geelong in July, while pressure built on then-speaker Bronwyn Bishop over her billing the public $5227.27 for a helicopter charter over the same distance to attend a party function.

And in August, following Abbott's announcement that the Coalition would not allow a free vote on marriage equality—despite the fact that the cross-party bill to recognise same-sex marriage had been spearheaded by LNP MP Warren Entsch—and would instead hold a plebiscite on the matter, Turnbull was unambiguous in his lack of support for the plan, if careful with his phrasing.

'One of the attractions of a free vote is that it would have meant the matter would be resolved in this parliament one way or another in a couple of weeks,' he told reporters the day after the announcement. 'The reason I haven't advocated a plebiscite after the next election is that it would mean . . . that this issue is a live issue all the way up to the next election.'

The message was clear. Abbott didn't support climate change mitigation, same-sex marriage rights or public transport infrastructure—things in which Australians were strongly in favour. Unless either the leader or the leader's staunchly held opinions changed, and changed soon, these issues were likely to become dangerous electoral liabilities.

However, since the failed spill motion against Abbott in February 2015 Turnbull had kept his head down, knowing that he didn't yet have the necessary support as leader—but was reassured that the numbers indicated a level of support for his ghostly shadow. Even without an actual challenger, and with the front bench forced by convention to vote for the current leader, the result in February had been sixty-one votes to thirty-nine.[4]

And so began what must have been an excruciating seven months for the sixty-one-year-old Turnbull, wondering if events had moved beyond him, with the entire nation knowing that the other shoe was going to drop any second.

Just in case that hadn't been made adequately clear, in April Turnbull was on the nation's newsstands as the cover star of *GQ* with the oh-so-coy headline: 'Primed Minister. Malcolm Turnbull: A man on the move. Next stop the Lodge. Maybe.'[5]

———

But while certain other critically praised books have focused on Abbott's activities during the autumn of his prime minister-ship,[6] Turnbull was no less busy as circumstances congealed around him in 2015.

---

4 According to *Shirtfronted*, the five-part feature by Peter Hartcher published by Fairfax late in 2015, Turnbull had calculated in advance of the spill that the result would be 40 against Abbott and 62 for him. With one absentee vote and one abstention, he'd at least have been chuffed that his intelligence-gathering was on the money (www.smh.com.au/interactive/2015/Shirtfronted).
5 The photo shoot was actually from 2013, because the story had been done in such haste that there had been no opportunity to do a new shoot. Why might there have been such a rush to ensure that the story got out asap? That, friends, is for us each to consider in our own heart of hearts.
6 Street, AP, *The Short and Excruciatingly Embarrassing Reign of Captain Abbott* (2015), 'A well-researched call of bullshit ... bravely written with the cliff of defamation at the author's back'—Anson Cameron, *Sydney Morning Herald*. Why not buy two copies, just in case? Who's it going to hurt?

There are two schools of thought regarding Turnbull's strategy in the seven months between the ghost spill of February and the challenge in September, and they're not mutually exclusive.

One is that Turnbull confidently assumed that people realised there was only one serious leadership alternative, thereby allowing him to sit back and let support come to him without actively soliciting it since that would have meant risking open warfare before he knew he had the necessary numbers.

The other is that Turnbull genuinely didn't have a winning majority and was unsure about the wisdom of a challenge, and therefore did nothing to rally support from the party—especially since thirty-nine parliamentarians had evidently volunteered for a life on the backbench by backing the failed spill motion against Abbott in February.

According to Fairfax's *Shirtfronted* series, Turnbull had discussed the leadership situation with Julie Bishop the day before the leadership spill in February, and the pair had called Scott Morrison (who was driving at the time, but put the call on speakerphone), at which point the suggestion that Morrison might fancy being treasurer was raised—and though it wasn't accepted, neither was it rejected outright. Both Bishop and Morrison would deny they betrayed the PM when the axe came down seven months later—for one thing, both were pondering the virtues of making their own potential leadership tilts—but they certainly knew that a challenge was eventually coming. To be fair, so did pretty much everyone else in the country.

While nothing happened in February, by August Turnbull knew the time for a move was coming, reportedly telling colleagues: 'This guy has got to go, and it has to happen before Christmas.' And if the challenger had been wise to hold fire in February, events conspired to force his hand in September.

First up, Rupert Murdoch—vocal Abbott supporter, media plutocrat and humanity's closest manifestation of an actual comic-book supervillain—took to his Twitter machine on 3 September to opine about the ghastly state of politics in his former country. His run of invective against the partisan discord his empire had largely created ended with: 'Seems capture of federal Labor leadership by corrupt violent unions. Govt must push on with reforms for sake of all sides or hold snap poll'—a stirring sentiment that confirmed the idea of an early election was being widely considered, and also that Murdoch thinks Twitter works the same way as dictating a telegram.

And while Murdoch's hold on the national imagination had slipped somewhat, compared to the glory days before Darth Vader threw him down that bottomless shaft on the second Death Star, this last thought bubble terrified the Turnbull team—not least because a) Abbott took Murdoch's opinion inexplicably seriously, and b) they knew that Abbott had been considering calling a double dissolution election as early as March, despite having begged his colleagues only weeks earlier for a clear six months in which to turn the party's fortunes around.

Thus Turnbull and an increasingly large subset of the Liberal Party were growing justly concerned that the PM would be willing to detonate the government in the hopes of protecting his leadership—an opinion which solidified when

Murdoch's *Daily Telegraph* reported on 10 September that Abbott was considering a cabinet reshuffle.[7]

Had the story run in any other paper it might have been shrugged off as heated speculation, but the fact it was in the *Tele* gave the news an authenticity only slightly below that of an official statement from the Prime Minister's Office. With these movements afoot and parliament set to rise on 17 September—with a by-election to be held two days later for the Western Australian seat of Canning, necessitated by the tragic and sudden death of Liberal MP Don Randall— Turnbull realised that the window for a challenge was rapidly closing.

It was time for a nice dinner.

———

On Sunday, 20 September there was a lovely light supper spread out at the house of Peter Hendy, member for Eden-Monaro, in order that he might entertain Malcolm Turnbull and a few other carefully chosen guests.

One was key Liberal figure Arthur Sinodinos,[8] who had been assistant treasurer to Abbott until the increasing drama surrounding his involvement in matters under investigation by the NSW Independent Commission Against Corruption forced him to step down.

---

7   The report itself made interesting reading. On the one hand it came from Simon Benson, a reporter with close ties to the prime minister's office who had been privy to a number of pro-Abbott exclusives. On the other hand, it also claimed that Abbott would retain Hockey as treasurer yet likely cut other badly performing but outspoken allies, such as Eric Abetz and Kevin Andrews. The consensus was that it was a 'Credlin special', mainly on the grounds that if it had come from the Turnbull camp—as some believed—there would have been a swift response from the PMO.

8   ... about whom you shall hear much, much more in the chapters to come. Get excited!

The fact that a man of Sinodinos's experience—both as John Howard's chief of staff and in high-flying financial gigs with the federal Treasury, Goldman Sachs and the National Australia Bank—had originally been made assistant to Joe Hockey in Abbott's original line-up had seemed at the time like an unambiguous slap in the face from the PM, but Arthur had evidently taken his assignment on the chin. However, his relationship with the PM was torched once and for all in December 2014.

Sinodinos had been implicated in a scandal regarding the NSW Liberal Party—of which he had been finance director—and the company Australian Water Holdings, of which he had been a director and which was now under investigation by ICAC. He had therefore decided in March 2014 to step aside temporarily as a minister while the investigations were undertaken, in order to prevent mud sticking to the shiny new government. The timing was terrible for the still-new Abbott team, not least because Hockey was frantically working towards what was to be his catastrophic first budget and clearly needed as much expert help as he could get.

By December 2014 it was clear that ICAC wouldn't call Sinodinos until March 2015 at the earliest and it was agreed that he would resign from the ministry and let matters blow over. The plan had been for Sinodinos and Abbott to make this announcement together, in order to eliminate any suggestion that Sinodinos was being dumped by the PM. But the story mysteriously leaked to the media—spun as Abbott having asked Sinodinos to step down—in what an apoplectic Sinodinos interpreted as a deliberate act of sabotage by Abbott as punishment for failing to save Hockey from himself.

This interpretation of the leak as being an act of high-handed vengeance against out-of-line ministers by the Prime Minister's Office was shared by Abbott's communications director, Jane McMillan, who accused Abbott's chief of staff Peta Credlin of having leaked the story; when Abbott backed Credlin over McMillan, the furious McMillan went on leave and never returned.[9]

Regardless of whether it was the result of carelessness or deliberate vindictiveness, the PM had created a powerful and unnecessary enemy. And this would be key to what was to follow.

Also enjoying a light supper on this brisk Canberra evening was Queensland senator James McGrath, who had been calculating Turnbull's numbers for the challenge, and Mitch Fifield—a Victorian senator who had actually resigned from the shadow cabinet under Turnbull in protest at the then-leader's zeal for emissions trading, but who had subsequently come around to the idea of supporting Malc as the leader under whom he was least likely to be slaughtered at the polls. And in the great tradition of politics, that survival-based calculation had proved far more seductive to Liberal parliamentarians than any great love for Turnbull's actual policies or perceived philosophies.

---

9 In case that sounds chillingly ominous, we should clarify it was the PMO to which she never returned: by May 2015 she was reportedly in a new gig at Snowy Hydro as general manager of corporate affairs. It's not like she vanished under mysterious circumstances or anything.

Hendy had similarly been a staunch and vocal Abbott supporter until the power of very basic mathematics made him acutely aware that Labor's 8 per cent lead in the polls over the Coalition under Abbott in September 2015 would inevitably consign him to unemployment as MP in the bell-wether marginal seat he'd wrenched from Labor by a 1.2 per cent margin. And, in the great tradition of the Liberal Party, he was committed to the utilitarian notion of enlightened self-interest—or, at least, the Randian concept of rational self-ishness[10]—and had changed his allegiances accordingly.

A similar calculation had been made by Victorian senator Scott Ryan, who had been an outspoken critic of Turnbull in the past. However, he'd also been third on his state's senate ticket in 2013 and presumably didn't fancy being handed his marching papers if an Abbott-led double dissolution came to pass.

Also present were Queensland MPs Mal Brough and Wyatt Roy, who had both been implicated in the growing scandal regarding the removal of Gillard-era Speaker of the House Peter Slipper, and who had already flagged their loyalty by support-ing the spill motion against Abbott in February. Also present was their fellow LNP rep Senator James McGrath, a former pollster and strategist with Crosby Textor whose very presence suggested considerable confidence in Turnbull's chances.

One figure in the room wasn't a parliamentarian: Murray Hansen, Julie Bishop's chief of staff. Presumably he attended in her place in order to provide plausible deniability when the

---

10 Boom! Ayn Rand joke! Yes, dear reader, it's yet another glorious manifestation of the unending gifts garnered by undertaking a Bachelor of Arts degree. Stay in school, kids!

deputy was inevitably accused of disloyalty to her leader. But if so, it didn't work: the presence of Hansen guaranteed that Bishop's card was marked by Abbott loyalists, despite her limp insistence that she only found out there would be a challenge when Hansen told her on Monday morning.

The group went over numbers. They went over them again. They were certain they had enough.

And the next day, down the shit would go.

———

On the Monday morning Bishop called Abbott, who was in Adelaide at the time, and told him that she needed to see him as soon as he returned to Canberra. When he did so, at 11.55 am, she reportedly told him: 'As your deputy, this is a conversation I never wanted to have, but I have to tell you you've lost the backing of the majority of the party room and the majority of the Cabinet.'

She didn't specifically say that Turnbull had already planned a challenge until Abbott asked if she thought he would do so, at which point she presented him with three options: call a challenge and get it over with, which would have the advantage of the PM being seen to take things into his own hands; wait it out and see if it's all a bluff; or just let matters take their course. She also refused to tell Abbott who was involved in the plot, insisting it wasn't her job to 'dob people in'.

The meeting, by all accounts, did not go well.

Parliament sat that afternoon as usual, despite the growing tension in the corridors. As soon as it rose at 3.30 pm, Turnbull made a beeline for the PM and asked to speak with him. During the subsequent meeting he announced his plan to challenge for the leadership. Abbott gave him an opportunity not to do that, and to shut up and stay in the ministry instead. This meeting, by all accounts, went similarly not well.

At 4 pm Turnbull strode into the courtyard of Parliament House and delivered a stinging speech explaining why he was challenging for the leadership:

> It is clear enough that the government is not successful in providing the economic leadership that we need. It is not the fault of individual ministers. Ultimately, the prime minister has not been capable of providing the economic leadership our nation needs ... And we need a different style of leadership. We need a style of leadership that explains those challenges and opportunities, explains the challenges and how to seize the opportunities. A style of leadership that respects the people's intelligence, that explains these complex issues and then sets out the course of action we believe we should take and makes a case for it. We need advocacy, not slogans. We need to respect the intelligence of the Australian people.

This was damning, but what Turnbull was promising was impressively unambiguous: sensible and clear policy, articulated clearly and presented to the public, eschewing the easy point-scoring of Abbott's beloved three-word slogans. Who would have guessed how hard it would be to keep this promise in six months' time?[11]

> Now if we continue with Mr Abbott as prime minister, it is clear enough what will happen. He will cease to be prime minister and he'll be succeeded by Mr Shorten ... [who] is utterly unfit to be prime minister of this country and yet so he will be if we do not make a change. The one thing that is clear about our

---

11 Foreshadowing!

current situation is the trajectory. We have lost thirty Newspolls
in a row. It is clear that the people have made up their mind about
Mr Abbott's leadership.

To be fair, it had actually only been twenty-nine Newspolls,
but Turnbull's point was clear: to continue with Abbott's
leadership would be to embrace electoral oblivion—and,
secondarily, also be a bad thing for Australia's economy.

Abbott called the ballot for 9.15 pm, adding: 'and I expect
to win'.

You already know how that worked out.

———

The Coalition had a new, electable leader after two years of
what amounted to a collective federal face-palming. There
was a sense of glorious optimism in the air, and everything
seemed like it was going to be alright forever again.

But the night before had been rough. The leadership ballot
had been counted and called at 9.50 pm, but it wasn't until
10.40 pm that Turnbull fronted the cameras to give his victory
speech, flanked by deputy Julie Bishop, gazing up at him with
rapt attention in a manner that guaranteed no Abbott loyalist
would ever trust her again.

It transpired that the long gap was because Turnbull was
giving Abbott a chance to concede with dignity, and Abbott
had no intention of doing so. It would later transpire that
he'd got a fair whack of drinks in and he, his staff and the
parliamentarians loyal to him were having a spirited knees-up
in his office.

So spirited a bash was this that Jamie Briggs, who had
managed to injure himself crash-tackling the now-shirtless

deposed PM, turned up for work the following morning in a wheelchair. There were also questions raised about the breaking of a marble table and later, during Senate estimates hearings, it was revealed that this was the work of Joe Hockey, who may or may not have done a spot of exuberant breakdancing on it. Abbott ultimately paid for the damage, and bits of smashed marble were retained by loyalists as souvenirs.

After a drawn-out drive around the suburbs of Canberra— a journey followed by media helicopters—Abbott turned up at Parliament House to deliver his final speech as PM. He hadn't tendered his resignation in person to Governor-General Peter Cosgrove; he had done so via fax, possibly because it had been a dusty sort of morning.

The subsequent concession speech was . . . well, perhaps not as dignified as it could have been.

Along with a recap of the Greatest Hits of the Abbott Era (stop the boats, scrap the carbon tax and hollow claims about repairing the deficit), he was also adamant that this was not his fault, you guys: 'I am proud of what the Abbott government has achieved. We stayed focused despite the white-anting. Of course, the government wasn't perfect. We have been a government of men and women, not a government of gods walking upon the earth. Few of us, after all, entirely measure up to expectations.'

But in case that sounded a little like a straw man argument (did anyone ever mistake Abbott for a god walking upon the earth?), he switched blame from his colleagues and the public to the other group that had disappointed him: the media.

'The nature of politics has changed in the past decade. We have more polls and more commentary than ever before. Mostly sour, bitter, character assassination. Poll-driven panic has produced a revolving-door prime ministership, which can't be good for our country. And a febrile media culture has developed that rewards treachery. And if there's one piece of advice I can give to the media, it's this: refuse to print self-serving claims that the person making them won't put his or her name to. Refuse to connive at dishonour by acting as the assassin's knife.'

And even as the febrile media reflected on their knife-themed connivations, it seemed that every journalist homed in on one promise the PM made that sounded, on previous form, a little unlikely.

'There will be no wrecking, no undermining and no sniping,' he promised, before making the patently inaccurate claim that, 'I've never leaked or backgrounded against anyone and I certainly won't start now.'

And, as one, a nation joined together and said, 'Um ... okay, let's see how that works out.'

———

With Turnbull in place as leader, it was clear that there would be some challenges ahead. That was not least because his win would involve working with a lot of people with whom he had no shortage of history—and Turnbull may have been popular with the electorate, but he'd burned a lot of his colleagues along the way. Similarly, as the make-up of his inner circle neatly demonstrated, those supporting him now were largely doing so for reasons of personal survival, not fervent belief in his leadership. And as the Abbott epoch had illustrated, political grudges in Australia cast exceptionally long shadows.

3
GOOD GOVERNMENT STARTS TODAY (SLIGHT RETURN)

In which we look at the freshly minted government that would definitely fix everything—and the Liberals and Nationals embark on the political manifestation of the old adage 'Marry in haste, repent at leisure'

If the new PM was planning to hit the ground running, he was somewhat hampered by the fact that Abbott's staff were feeling less than entirely determined to move out of the PM's digs, thereby forcing Turnbull to make do with his suddenly expanded office staff inside his relatively small ministerial accommodation.

Also, it was revealed, Abbott's loyal staff went on a bit of a shredding spree, presumably just to tidy the place up and definitely not in a mean-spirited attempt to make life more difficult for Turnbull's team to work out where things were at with regards to upcoming appointments and reappointments, or much less unimportant things like outstanding Freedom of Information requests.

With the Liberal leadership in the bag and the prime ministership of Australia finally under his belt, Turnbull turned to
his remaining unresolved responsibility: the leadership of
the Coalition.

This required the junior party to sign off on its approval of
Turnbull, which most observers thought of as the equivalent
of wielding a rubber stamp. After all, it wasn't as though the
Nats were going to split off if they didn't like the Libs' new
leader; they were, after all, sitting at the kids' table at the
dinner party of federal politics.

But—like children in a shopping centre food court realising that new and exciting toys were just one screaming
tantrum away—the Nationals held all the leverage in this
particular negotiation. This is because the Coalition shouldn't
be pictured as a team so much as a lifelong union sealed by
marriage, which can't be severed without a long, complicated,
expensive divorce. So, in return for the renewal of vows now
required of them, the Nats were uniquely poised to upgrade
their pre-nup arrangements.

While the two parties are separate—indeed, rivals—in
states like Victoria and Western Australia, in Queensland there
is no such thing as a Liberal or a National: since 2008 there
has only been the Liberal National Party. And that important distinction extends to the federal party as well: there are
no Liberal or National MPs or senators from Queensland, as
they all ostensibly represent the LNP.

The upshot of this was that, with only a ten-vote buffer
within the Liberal Party, Turnbull was in no position to

negotiate with the Nationals when it came to getting their approval for his leadership of the Coalition.

Since a split between the parties would be so difficult—indeed, doing it quickly or cleanly while in power would be fundamentally impossible[1]—the grim fact was that if the Nationals hadn't agreed to recognise Turnbull as leader of the Coalition, it wouldn't have meant splitting the parties somehow; it would have meant changing the leader again.

Fortunately this humiliating possibility was avoided when the Nationals enthusiastically endorsed Turnbull as leader of the Coalition just before the first sitting of parliament on Tuesday, 15 September.

There were just a few teensy, tiny conditions attached.

———

It's fair to say that the Nationals had more than a few fairly considerable reservations about a Coalition under the leadership of Malcolm Turnbull.

Since it is a party containing strong social conservatives, with a solid religious streak and a terror of climate science in particular and egghead book-learnin' generally, it had a lot in common with Abbott. Its members were far less comfortable with this fancy-pants inner-city millionaire, whose electorate included Sydney's gay-culture-heavy Oxford Street, than they were with Tony Abbott, whose faith in slogans, heterosexuality and Catholicism they could easily understand.

---

1 It would actually be pretty straightforward to work out which parliamentarian was a member of which party if the Coalition was rent in twain, since current convention dictates that federal LNP MPs and senators opt to attend either the Liberal or National party room, but never both. That said, separating the infrastructure, intellectual property and internal finances isn't something that could realistically happen quickly or bloodlessly.

Turnbull also had a less than entirely convivial relationship with the Nationals' deputy leader Barnaby Joyce, which
suggested a bumpy road ahead, since it was well known that
the party's leader, Warren Truss, was itching to retire. Tell-
ingly, it was Joyce who made the announcement that Turnbull
would have to adhere to a series of 'key values' in order to
garner the Nationals' support.[2]

Immediately after the spill the Nats were making their
displeasure known. Senator Matt Canavan criticised Turnbull's
failure to give the party a shout-out in his victory speech,
while unnamed party members were giving anonymous
sledges to the ABC of the flavour: 'These clowns [the Liberal
Party] are making us look like a failed Pacific Island state.
Why would we want to immediately associate ourselves
with them?'

Furthermore, time was not on the new Turnbull's side.
With parliament sitting, a deal had to be hashed out before
the new PM could call Question Time, and so a 'side
letter' was swiftly agreed upon between Truss and Turnbull
beforehand.

Like all arrangements made in desperate haste, with one
party in a superior negotiating position, the rapidity with
which the vows were renewed boded ill for the happiness they
hoped would follow.

For starters, the Nationals wanted the Water Resources
portfolio, which included control of the Murray–Darling Basin
Plan. That went to Joyce, who already held the Agriculture

---

2   To be fair, this announcement was made at a press conference at 11.30 pm on
the night of the spill, well after Truss's bedtime.

portfolio and thereby gave some indication of what the priorities were going to be in that area.[3]

The plan also committed the government to addressing mobile phone black spots in rural Australia, and to about $4 billion of promises in portfolio areas of particular interest to the party—such as extra benefits for families with stay-at-home mums, which seemed a little off-message for a government vocally encouraging greater female participation in the workforce.

And then there were more controversial items, like Turnbull's promise to consider the introduction of an 'effects test' to prevent large corporate players from using their commercial power to drive out smaller operators, which smacked of an economic protectionism completely at odds with the Liberal Party's open support of the free market. Regardless, this was quietly introduced in March 2016.

More problematically for a leader attempting to break with the Abbott era, the deal insisted that there be no change to the current plans or targets around emissions reduction, and that the Direct Action strategy for climate change mitigation would continue. Also, the government would maintain its explicit support for mining, which the Nationals had seemingly started endorsing over its historical heartland interest of farming.

The agreement also, perhaps most damagingly of all, laid out in no uncertain terms that there would be no suggestion

---

3   This might not have seemed to be that huge a concession, except—as Annabel Crabb outlined at length in 'Stop At Nothing'—Turnbull was obsessed with water and hydrology. Handing over something that he was genuinely expert in to someone who was, um, maybe not *quite* so across the complexities of the science would have been a serious blow.

of a free vote in parliament to ratify same-sex marriage; the government would persist with its support for the plebiscite that had been Abbott's Hail Mary pass—in both the sporting and religiously metaphorical sense.

By agreeing to inaction on marriage equality and climate change mitigation, Turnbull made two important statements: he sent a message to his own party and his Coalition partners that he was prepared to put his own pet passions aside and lead Australia's conservative parties. It also sent a message to the Australian people that he was perfectly fine with abandoning matters of principle.

But this also raised an awkward parallel with the political trajectory of Julia Gillard, another leader who had overthrown an elected PM and who had reversed her emissions-based policy at great political cost, and whose consistent and vocal support for same-sex marriage had similarly evaporated for reasons of political expediency.[4] In 2012 this had led to questions about whether the electorate would ever see the 'real Julia', who they thought they'd elected in 2010; but presumably everyone was confident that this about-face on definitive principles wouldn't lead to any such question about the 'real Malcolm'.[5]

But these compromises were the results of considerable wisdom and experience, and there was no reason to think there would be any negative consequences from them that

---

4 Gillard herself has attempted to argue that her opposition to same-sex marriage was actually due to her distaste for the archaic institution of marriage altogether—which was an awfully unconvincing gambit given that the question under conversation was 'Should a suite of genuine legal and civil rights with real-world consequences be extended to all adults?' rather than 'Hey, how's about we eliminate marriage altogether?'
5 Foreshadowing!

would create a series of completely avoidable problems for the rejuvenated government. After all, the polls were up, the future looked bright, and Malcolm Turnbull was determined to enjoy one full year of strong, bold leadership without resorting to any grubby nonsense such as, for example, calling an early double dissolution election like certain other, perhaps less honourable, prime ministers had once reportedly been canvassing.

'I'm expecting it to be about this time,' Turnbull replied to the ABC in November 2015, when asked about the timing of the next federal election. 'Well, perhaps November is getting a bit late. I would say around September, October next year is when you should expect the next election to be.'

As it happens, those expectations were not met.

———

The first order of business was selecting the ministry, which posed a few immediate challenges. Most people assumed that the ministerial line-up would be a series of rewards to those who switched allegiance to Team Turnbull. Not least among those making such an assumption was South Australian senator Cory Bernardi, who got downright biblical in the press, declaring: 'Those who've taken their thirty pieces of silver will be very obvious when the new ministerial line-up is announced . . . This is treachery of the highest order.'

That wasn't to be the case—at least, not explicitly. Julie Bishop comfortably won the ballot for the deputy leadership by seventy votes to thirty, defeating joke candidate Kevin Andrews,[6] and also held on to her portfolio of

---

6   The mere fact that Andrews—*Andrews!*—got thirty votes is a sobering reminder of the size of the conservative rump in the Liberal Party. It's like a 30 per cent vote for cancer: no-one's voting for it because it's in any way a sensible idea; they're merely attempting to make a point in the most provocatively silly way possible.

Foreign Affairs. The deputy leadership was a party vote and therefore wasn't something that Turnbull could have revoked even in the event he'd wished to do so. However, it was nonetheless spun as proof that Bishop had been rewarded for her perfidy as questions were raised about the degree to which she had known about the likely challenge ahead of time and whether or not she'd been sufficiently loyal to Abbott. When it became known that her chief of staff had attended the fateful party held by the Sunday Night Coup Team, the former PM wasted no opportunity to imply that he'd been betrayed by his treacherous number two.

This was damaging, not least because Bishop had been considered one of the stars of the Abbott cabinet. But her claim that she had kept the former PM apprised of what was going on—advising him that Turnbull and Scott Morrison had discussed the latter being treasurer in the Turnbull government, warning him to promote more women to the front bench, telling him that Turnbull was planning a challenge—were all denied by Abbott.

Following an interview with Bishop on Channel 9 in December 2015, Abbott got in contact with Fairfax: 'The claim that Julie Bishop made on Channel 9 that she told me about the conversation between Malcolm Turnbull and Scott Morrison that she witnessed is false. The suggestion that Julie Bishop lobbied me to get Marise Payne and Sussan Ley into cabinet in September 2013 is false. The suggestion that Peta Credlin opposed that is also false.'

With the matter descending into a he-said-she-said farce, Bishop held her tongue. But, despite her doomed attempts to appear non-partisan, her fate was now very much tied to that of her shiny new leader.

———

If Bishop was seen as an ally of Turnbull, Scott Morrison, the man who was named treasurer, had always been perceived as a keen supporter of Tony Abbott. He had become the darling of Australian conservatives for taking a hard line—or, more accurately, an unnecessarily cruel line—against asylum seekers as immigration minister, and former Indi MP Sophie Mirabella had publicly and pointedly declared him 'our next conservative prime minister' during a fundraising event for her campaign for re-election in May 2015.

As the then-director of the NSW Liberals during Turnbull's 2003 campaign to unseat Peter King from Wentworth, Morrison had had to reprimand the challenger for buying on-air endorsements from Alan Jones at $5000 a throw, as well as being forced to wade through some egregious branch-stacking by the frontrunners.[7] Bridges had clearly been mended in the interim, but Morrison knew first-hand just how wilful the new PM could be when he decided he had a strategy to deploy.

Yet, while Morrison was a shrewd choice for treasurer, in that he was beloved by the more right-wing sections of the media, he was rather more respected than actually loved. His prodigious political ascent had left more than a few figures

---

7 Both Turnbull and King enrolled amazing numbers of new members during the campaign: according to Paddy Manning's book *Born to Rule*, King had apparently inspired a staggering 1800 new members to join the Rose Bay branch of the party, while Turnbull had drawn in 1500 to the Point Piper branch. Why they didn't follow Joe Hockey's supposed trick in the 1996 preselection battle for North Sydney, as laid out in *Hockey: Not Your Average Joe* by Madonna King, and just sign up dead people is not entirely clear.

feeling as though they'd been clambered over along the way, such as Michael Towke, who'd won Liberal preselection for the seat of Cook in 2007 after the retirement of Bruce Baird. He was set to take the federal seat until a controversy broke out over his credentials and eligibility, the upshot of which was that the executive had refused to endorse him. He now made public his claim that he had been heavied into making way for Morrison, who had only come third originally.

Furthermore, the degree to which Morrison was loved by the right of the party was delivered a serious blow by what had appeared to be his betrayal of Abbott. While Morrison had voted for the deposed leader in the spill, it was said that he'd not rallied his supporters to follow suit. Things got even messier when, mere days after being made treasurer, Morrison asserted that it wouldn't have mattered who had won the leadership ballot: he'd have been treasurer regardless.

According to Morrison, Abbott had offered him the Treasury portfolio ahead of the spill—proving that Abbott's patience with his gaffe-prone Joe Hockey had a limit after all—but he, Morrison, had refused to 'throw Joe Hockey under a bus'.

While defending his position to an unusually pushy Ray Hadley during their regular weekly chat on 2GB, Morrison insisted he knew nothing about the offer before it was made to him. 'I didn't understand why he wanted me to pick a fight with Joe Hockey,' he said, adding that he'd declined because he didn't think the offer had been 'well thought through . . . Obviously it had been brought together in haste, given the events. Mr Abbott had expressed absolute confidence and loyalty to Joe Hockey, so why would he have changed?'

Hadley wasn't convinced, though, and asked Morrison to swear on a Bible that he hadn't betrayed Abbott, which the profoundly religious Morrison declined to do. He also claimed to not be able to find the Bible that was inexplicably stored in the studio (although Fairfax photographers had no problem identifying it), before telling Hadley: 'If that's what you need, then we don't have the relationship that I thought we had.'

Abbott, predictably, was incensed at the very suggestion that he'd have dumped Joe Hockey and replaced him to save his own skin—and, to be fair, he'd been advised to do that more or less continuously for the previous seven months and had failed to do so. He assured the media that the claims of a treasury offer was 'not true, not true'.

While this controversy hurt Morrison's standing with the conservative wing of the party, it gave Turnbull a needed boost. By strapping himself to Morrison, Turnbull had the advantage of a palatable deputy (since his actual deputy, Bishop, had dropped out of view among cries of 'Judas!'). However, it also meant that he was potentially creating a future rival. After all, if Morrison did well as treasurer, that made him a threat; if he did badly, he would fatally wound Turnbull's hopes of hanging on to the leadership.[8]

---

8 There's a pervasive theory that the rising public profile of Morrison was one of the reasons Abbott moved him from the Immigration portfolio to Social Services. The argument at the time was that it was the largest department with the greatest budget and therefore needed strong oversight—which was a backhander to the ineffectual previous minister, Kevin Andrews—but there was also the suggestion that Social Services was a ministry in which it was all but impossible to shine and this would take the ambitious minister down a peg. The fact that Abbott's buddy Andrews was also given Defence, the ministry for which Morrison had often publicly expressed a desire, adds weight to this interpretation.

Still, that was a problem for later—and things were moving fast!

———

There were plenty of dramas when it came to selecting the rest of the front bench.

Turnbull also had a history with conservative Tasmanian senator Eric Abetz. The hard-right powerbroker had been a supporter of Turnbull during his previous leadership era and had played a key role in attempting to bring down Prime Minister Kevin Rudd and his treasurer Wayne Swan via information passed on by the party's mole in the Treasury—that Godwin Grech fellow mentioned earlier. It was a humiliating debacle, bringing Turnbull's leadership of the party to an early close and making Abetz look like an utter fool in the process.[9]

Any residual fondness Abetz might have had for Turnbull was not enhanced when he became one of the most high-profile ministers to be now given the heave-ho, both as employment minister and leader of the government in the Senate.

Abetz made no secret of his bad feelings, using a Fairfax profile to declare that Turnbull had made a mistake in dumping him. Resignation wasn't on the cards, though: his state branch confirmed that he would still be number one on the Tasmanian senate ticket for 2016, ensuring he wasn't going anywhere.

———

9 Although, weirdly, Abetz still cited his questioning of Grech—in which he asked questions fed to him by Grech and based on non-existent evidence—as being proof of his legal skills and political acumen in a 2016 *Good Weekend* feature: 'If I might say, [the cross-examination of Grech] was nearly faultless. Most people thought it was exceptional, and Malcolm was full of praise for my capacities and abilities, etcetera' ('Senator Eric Abetz: Why dumping me was a big mistake', *Sydney Morning Herald*, 26 March 2016).

Another dumped minister had more of a history of opposing Turnbull: Kevin Andrews had followed his undistinguished stint as human services minister with an ill-starred shot as defence minister before Turnbull sent him to the backbench. Kevin had also starred in an earlier clash with Malcolm: before the leadership challenge that installed Abbott as leader in 2009, there had been a spill motion in which Andrews had acted as a stalking horse—and while he'd not expected to win (and didn't: Turnbull won forty-eight votes to Andrews' thirty-five), the mere fact that he'd won any votes at all at that time illustrated just how shaky Turnbull's grasp on the leadership had become and how likely it was that he'd be deposed the second he met with a halfway acceptable challenger.

Andrews didn't take his replacement as defence minister by NSW senator Marise Payne—previously in the outer ministry with the Human Services portfolio—at all well, holding an impromptu press conference after the announcement to opine about how he'd been wronged. 'Can I say that I'm disappointed that Mr Turnbull did not accept my offer to work with him . . . Frankly, my remaining in this job was not about me. It was all about the stability of our defence force in Australia and its leadership.'

His unwavering commitment to the stability of the defence force and its leadership was soon to be made very, very clear. He was to spend his first few months on the backbench issuing statements about defence matters, often before Payne had an opportunity to give an official response.

———

Turnbull made other changes to his ministry, including the promotion of several of the people who'd supported his challenge.

First up, Queensland MP Mal Brough was made Special Minister of State, responsible for ensuring the government maintain scrupulously high standards of ethical behaviour in office, and Queensland's Stuart Robert became Minister for Human Services, among other responsibilities,[10] and Arthur Sinodinos was made a parliamentary secretary. Sure, these appointments might have looked a wee bit like payment for support rendered by key factional allies but, as time went on, there were to be, well, other consequences.[11]

And there was also the decision to cut a bunch of ministers loose, without fear or favour. While some of them had been active opponents of Turnbull, like Andrews and Abetz, others had been actually supportive of the new PM, such as small business minister Bruce Billson, who took the demotion as a hint that he should retire from politics altogether.

Another person who had supported Turnbull but was denied a guernsey in the ministry was Ian Macfarlane, a former Howard and Abbott minister. Macfarlane took this betrayal hard—to the point of attempting to leave the Liberal Party altogether and join the Nationals instead. The argument was that, as a Queensland MP, he was technically a member of the Liberal National Party rather than one or the other—all that would change would be which party room he would attend. But after a lot of behind-the-scenes wrangling the Queensland LNP state executive decided not to allow the

---

10 Robert was one of the bloc of MPs aligned with Morrison who swapped their support to Turnbull in the spill, and the *Daily Telegraph* speculated that it was Morrison who saw Robert rewarded and also initially insulated from the fallout from the China trip that . . . actually, we'll get to that in a bit.

11 More foreshadowing! *Moreshadowing!*

switch to proceed, and Macfarlane announced that he too would leave parliament rather than bother to stand again.[12]

There were, however, some odd survivors.

Both environment minister Greg Hunt and immigration minister Peter Dutton had been outspoken Abbott supporters—indeed, Dutton had been particularly scathing about Turnbull in the press—and naturally assumed they'd be for the long drop. Yet both retained their portfolios.

There are numerous theories as to why this was, and they're not mutually exclusive. A popular one was that they represented a sop to the pro-Abbott team, to signal that the Liberal's new daddy would be firm but fair. Another was that both mandatory offshore detention for refugees and the Direct Action climate plan were areas in which Turnbull couldn't easily change direction and were also clearly going from bad to worse, and that leaving Abbott's appointees in place would reduce Turnbull's direct culpability when they inevitably crashed and burned, as well as freeing Malcolm to appoint some efficient new broom to sweep up the mess and build new, saner policies.

Other ministers who kept their gigs included George Brandis (who kept the Attorney-General portfolio but had the Arts ministry snatched from him and handed to a surprised-looking

---

12 There's some confusion as to what Macfarlane was hoping to achieve with the switch. The general assumption is that, as an ex-frontbencher, he'd have immediately become a high-profile Nationals member and probably been able to finagle a ministerial portfolio denied him as a Liberal. But there's another fun conspiracy theory which posits that the whole thing was actually orchestrated by Nationals leader Warren Truss and Turnbull himself in order to provide a more palatable leadership option than Barnaby Joyce when Truss stood down. Regardless, neither plan worked.

Mitch Fifield) and a couple of outspoken Abbott supporters: Mathias Cormann stayed on as finance minister, Josh Frydenberg kept a ministry berth as Minister for Resources, Energy and Northern Australia, and Abbott-supporting South Australian MP Jamie Briggs was promoted from the junior ministry to a new gig as Minister for Cities and the Built Environment.

One other minister who kept his gig was trade minister Andrew Robb, and his history with Turnbull was nothing if not complex. Robb had entered parliament at the same time as Turnbull and had been shadow climate spokesman until stepping down for a few months in 2009 after revealing he was struggling with serious depression. Watching the negotiations between Labor and the Coalition over an emissions trading scheme—with Labor's Penny Wong and Robb's replacement, Ian Macfarlane, hashing out a plan—with increasing concern, he decided that the deal needed to be attacked with an axe. Claiming to be tired from his medication, Robb asked Turnbull if he could speak early at a shadow cabinet discussion about the ETS—and tore it to shreds.

Turnbull was stunned and furious, ringing Robb to give him an unambiguous serve. However, Robb had articulated a growing anti-climate change attitude within the Liberals (one propagated by the likes of South Australian senator Nick Minchin and the on-the-rise Tony Abbott) that was to scuttle any hopes of the bipartisan ETS plan. Robb was to benefit handsomely, being appointed trade minister in the Abbott government.

By February 2016, Robb decided he'd had enough and announced that he was leaving the front bench—he was replaced by the pugnacious Steven Ciobo—and would not stand for his seat at the next election.

And then there was the question of what to do with that shop-worn previous treasurer . . .

———

Joe Hockey had supported Turnbull in the 2009 ETS stoush, even publicly castigating Robb for his disloyalty; but, according to Madonna King's biography *Hockey: Not Your Average Joe*, he never forgave Turnbull for running in the leadership challenge that installed Abbott, despite Turnbull still being leader of the party at that point and having shown no sign that he was about to go quietly.

Bizarre though it seems in retrospect, Hockey was assumed to be a shoo-in by most of the party—until he backed a conscience vote in the parliament on the ETS, which was seen by his colleagues as a wishy-washy compromise that was nowhere near good enough for anyone. He was therefore shocked and humiliated when he was knocked out of the running in the first ballot.

Going by the version of events outlined in King's book, Hockey felt betrayed by both Turnbull and Abbott—which ignores some inconvenient facts, including that Turnbull had publicly staked his leadership on the need for action on climate change, and that Abbott had resigned from the shadow front bench in what was clearly a precursor to running for the top job.

The relationship between Hockey and Turnbull never really recovered—at least, according to Hockey. Unlike Abbott, he didn't need any time to consider what his future might hold. Unsurprisingly, he quit.

Not only did he quit, he did so with taking-my-toys-and-going-home alacrity. None of this sticking-around-until-the-next-election nonsense for Joe: he was upping stumps and causing a by-election in North Sydney, in order to take the most popular failure-prize for superannuated also-rans that the party needed to get out of their hair: ambassador to the USA.[13]

The by-election in Hockey's seat of North Sydney was held on 5 December 2015 and Liberal candidate Trent Zimmerman won easily—although that bald statement doesn't capture the drama inherent in the whole shemozzle. For a start, the election was closer than expected and cost the public over a million dollars—a heck of an avoidable sum to accommodate the ambassadorial aspirations of the man who had bleated about 'the end of the age of entitlement' throughout his storied and rich-in-error term. Dropping seven figures so Joe could get a sweet new public service gig did a lot to get the fiscally conservative voters of the electorate offside.

It also mightily annoyed the party members themselves, who considered the entire preselection process a fix to give the safe seat to the man who had worked with, and was clearly something of a protégé of, Hockey. This, of course, was conspiracy-mongering nonsense: two other candidates stood against Zimmerman, although there were all sorts of unusually onerous restrictions on how many members would be allowed to vote in each Liberal Party branch, plus a suspiciously short voter registration process (emails were sent out

---

13 In doing so he walked in the footsteps of such august failures as Labor leader Kim Beazley and Liberal leader Andrew Peacock, in what was basically a note-for-note cover of the second episode of the bitingly satirical series, *The Hollowmen*.

on a Thursday evening with instructions to complete and return them by midday Friday). However, these rules had been decided upon by the NSW Liberal Party, which was at the time under the steady hand of its acting president . . . a fellow named T. Zimmerman.

The seat was recognised as such a safe Liberal seat that Labor didn't bother fielding a candidate and, with excitement over Turnbull's leadership still fizzing, it was assumed that Zimmerman winning was basically an annoying and expensive formality. However, for the first time in two decades, the Liberals only won the seat on preferences: Zimmerman's primary vote was just over 48 per cent—solid, but a huge drop from the 61 per cent primary that Hockey had enjoyed in 2013.

With no Labor challenger, with the Greens candidate being a rank outsider and most of the independents seeming to be running just for the sheer thrill of the attention, the threat to Zimmerman had come from one man, Stephen Ruff: an independent loudly endorsed by Hockey's predecessor, Ted Mack. Mack was a legend on Sydney's North Shore. He'd been a councillor and mayor, a member of the NSW parliament and, in 1990, had run for the federal seat of North Sydney. As with literally every other election he'd contested at any level, he won easily. He'd remained staunchly independent throughout his political tenure—even weathering the brickbats of being the only MP to vote against Australia's involvement in the Gulf War—without seeing any serious damage to his level of popularity. He retired in 1996, at which point Hockey won North Sydney safely for the Liberals.

Despite enjoying nearly twenty years of Joe, North Sydneyites clearly had long memories: Ruff only won just under 19 per cent of the primary vote but, with just about every other candidate preferencing him over Zimmerman, it ended up a far closer race than anyone could have predicted. Yes, the Liberals won with 60 per cent of the two-party-preferred vote, but a Liberal candidate in North Sydney should never have had to stoop to preferences to win his seat.

It was the first sign that maybe the Turnbull government's honeymoon period was going to be rather more truncated than observers had predicted. More evidence was to come.

———

If the names on Turnbull's enemies list were a problem, at least he had his friends.

Christopher Pyne had definitively swung in behind Turnbull just before the leadership challenge, following the party's contentious support of a plebiscite on same-sex marriage rather than a free parliamentary vote. Indeed, he was the only frontbencher other than Turnbull to attend the reading of the doomed bill for a free vote co-sponsored by LNP MP Warren Entsch and Labor MP Terri Butler, after Abbott had deliberately arranged a competing announcement which conveniently required him to miss the reading.[14]

---

14 The incredibly important thing that Abbott simply couldn't miss was an announcement about the dangers of ice addiction at 'an Australian Federal Police training facility'—presumably the very one at which Abbott was living at the time. Among the vital information imparted was the key takeaway that the then-PM's priority was 'jobs, growth and community safety'. Clearly this was thrilling, urgent stuff that absolutely could not have been expressed at another time, or done via a press release, or perhaps not even done at all.

Pyne was useful both in terms of being a high-profile minister and as an influential figure in South Australian Liberal circles. When the vote came down for Turnbull, the level of South Australian support for the challenger could be largely attributed to Pyne. He did, however, have some serious liabilities of his own, the largest of which was South Australia itself.

Under Abbott the state had been gutted by the government's refusal to provide any more subsidies to the manufacturing industry generally and the motor industry in particular. It was heading towards massive levels of dangerously localised unemployment, especially in the north of Adelaide and in the Eyre Peninsula centre of Whyalla, which was facing ghost town status if its steelworks were closed.

The ABC's Adelaide television studios had also been shuttered as part of the cuts that Abbott had promised were not going to happen. This led to the sorry sight of Pyne actively campaigning against his own government's policy. And it wasn't hard to see why: the ABC's Adelaide headquarters is in Collinswood, making it part of the electorate of Adelaide—but a leisurely five-minute drive eastwards puts one in Pyne's neighbouring electorate of Sturt.[15]

The extraordinary popularity of local independent (and former Liberal Party member) Nick Xenophon was also turning from an annoyance to a direct threat when the Nick Xenophon Team (NXT) was established in the face of the likely changes to the Senate ballot. Along with forming

---

15 That's the sort of local knowledge that only decades of living in A-town can offer. You're welcome!

an official party, Xenophon announced plans to run more candidates in South Australia and beyond, in both houses of parliament.

With Xenophon polling almost a quarter of the primary vote in his own right, this raised terrifying possibilities for the Liberals. South Australia contained eleven federal electorates, split more or less down the middle between the major parties; the NXT vote turned reasonably safe seats like Mayo (held for the Liberals by Jamie Briggs) and Adelaide (held by Labor's Kate Ellis) into marginals reliant on preferences. Even Pyne's seat of Sturt would be at risk, under the reasonably safe assumption that NXT and the Greens would preference one another over the Liberals.

Then there had been the disastrous process of tendering for the building of Australia's next generation submarines, which Abbott seemed set to confirm would happen in Japan. That changed fairly dramatically as time went on—but let's not spoil that chapter-to-come just yet!

And, finally, Pyne had been somewhat implicated in the burgeoning scandal surrounding the removal of former Speaker of the House Peter Slipper during the Gillard government's tenure. Slipper's resignation in the wake of travel scandals and sexually charged messages to a staffer had been controversial enough at the time, but questions were now being raised about whether or not laws had been broken by a number of Coalition parliamentarians.

An investigation by the Australian Federal Police was already rumbling into life, looking at the involvement of Pyne and two of Turnbull's other big supporters: Queensland MPs

Mal Brough and Wyatt Roy. Still, that wasn't anything to worry about. Seriously, how bad could it be?

———

And then there was the elephant in the room. The one wearing red speedos and a look of angry disbelief.

Tony Abbott had returned to the backbench following his promise that there would be, as he put it in his final speech as prime minister, 'no wrecking, no sniping, no undermining' going forward.

He didn't, however, confirm whether or not he would stay in parliament, offering only that he'd make a decision in December.

And then the sniping began.

4
NO SNIPING, NO UNDERMINING; OR THE RETURN OF THE CAPTAIN

In which the previous prime minister promises to support the man who betrayed him, and it works out about as well as you'd expect

On 15 September 2015 Tony Abbott gave his final speech as prime minister, conceding that he had been removed as the Liberal Party's leader by Malcolm Turnbull the previous evening. He rather pointedly didn't mention the new PM by name at any point, but to be fair, it was a rough day.[1] That speech, as you'll recall from chapter two, did contain the breathless declaration that, 'There will be no wrecking, no undermining and no sniping. I've never leaked or backgrounded against anyone and I certainly won't start now.'

---

1 And, as reports of the ensuing raucous, table-smashing, leg-injuring party attested, a rough night as well.

And while part of the reason for Abbott's removal was that he failed to be as good as his word with regard to his election promises, this claim was at least partially true.

After all, as any military expert can tell you, sniping requires one to sit still and keep quiet.

———

Everyone knew exactly what Abbott was going to do after losing the leadership: he was going to quit parliament and maybe become Australian High Commissioner to the United Kingdom or something equally fancy-sounding, power-free and far away. And, almost certainly, he would busy himself writing political thrillers in which smooth-talking but traitorous millionaires were neutralised by patriotic men of action who looked just as good in military fatigues as they did in red speedos.

After all, the general view was that deposed party leaders should take their political revolver and retire to their parliamentary tent to do the decent thing, not least because leaders that hung around had a history of becoming dangerously destabilising for their party. This had been amply demonstrated by the events of 2010–13, when Julia Gillard welcomed the newly deposed Kevin Rudd to a place in Cabinet with the Foreign Affairs portfolio, which turned out to be the perfect vantage point from which he could exact his revenge on his former deputy. Indeed, Liberal MPs might have pointed out, Malcolm Turnbull had decided to quit politics after being bested for the opposition leadership by Abbott in 2009 and had to be sweet-talked into staying in parliament, eventually returning to the ministry—and how did *that* work out?

Perhaps recognising this, Turnbull made no move to give Abbott a portfolio in his comprehensive ministerial reshuffle, leaving Tony on the backbench, where he'd presumably take the hint and follow Joe Hockey out into the political tundra.

Except . . . he didn't.

The only comment Abbott made regarding his future was that he'd be making a decision by December as to whether or not he'd stand for preselection in his electorate of Warringah.[2] And this seemed like a bold move: after all, Hockey had read the writing on the wall—especially the bit that said that both Abbott and Turnbull had been willing to cast him to the wolves and replace him with Scott Morrison—and if anything the ex-PM was even less popular than his treasurer had been.

But Abbott, fighting the urge to turn to the sympathetic media in a self-serving attempt to stroke his ego and vent his bruised and bilious spleen, maintained a dignified public silence for almost three whole weeks.

On 1 October he was on Neil Mitchell's show on 3AW, mixing his metaphors to explain that 'there has been a lot of dirty water under the bridge' and that he would 'exercise the former prime minister's prerogative of silence' regarding the new PM. He also pleaded with listeners not to abandon the party, and reiterated that he would definitely have led the Coalition to victory at the 2016 election—which, given that the polls were showing his government on 46 per cent versus Labor's 54 in two-party-preferred terms two days before he

2   It's generally assumed that Abbott was genuinely balancing up his options and speculating about his future, but if you're of a more conspiratorial bent then you might speculate as to whether this was to discourage the new PM from holding an election during his salad days. Then again, not even Abbott would have expected the honeymoon to sour quite so much within three months.

was rolled as leader, seemed a somewhat optimistic assessment of his chances.

Abbott's words of comfort to the masses defecting from the party had been spurred by Tasmanian senator and close supporter Eric Abetz, who had some time on his hands after being dumped from the Employment portfolio. Eric decided to reach out to Liberal Party members with a syntactically clumsy letter that entreated loyalty but nonetheless drew public attention to what sounded like enormous internal dissatisfaction: 'With calls for the formation of a new party and hundreds of resignations from the Liberal Party, I call on members to remain as members of our party.'[3]

Abetz's dedicated attempt to staunch the wound (and, presumably, raise people's spirits by saying 'party' as much as possible) was admirable, even though Tasmanian Liberal president Geoff Page clarified Abetz's numbers by pointing out that the 'hundreds of resignations' Eric was lamenting could be more precisely calculated as 'seven', a loss that had been offset by the eight new people who had signed up since Turnbull took the reins.

Abbott's Hurt Feelings Tour then took off on its UK leg with a performance at the annual Margaret Thatcher Lecture in London on 27 October, where he went through some of his most-loved classic hits, plus a little something new for the fans.

The first problem that Europe faced, Abbott made clear, was that it was insufficiently harsh on refugees, and this 'misguided altruism' was 'leading much of Europe into catastrophic error'.

---

3 As it happened, the formation of a new party was already underway, as Abetz well knew. But we'll get to that!

And the answer? 'Turning around boats [and] denying entry at the border for people with no right to come. It will require some force, it will require massive logistics and expense; it will gnaw at our consciences,' he explained with little evidence of any gnawing going on, 'yet it is the only way to prevent a tide of humanity surging through Europe and quite possibly changing it forever.' Because, as he made clear, mercy is the enemy of justice and 'too much mercy for some necessarily undermines justice for all'.

Abbott's speech also criticised the too-soft approach that western military forces were taking in Syria and Iraq against the fundamentalist Islamist terror organisation known as Islamic State of Iraq and the Levant (aka ISIL, or Daesh, or any number of other abbreviations)—a point that was correctly interpreted as a slight against the new PM and his recently appointed defence minister, Marise Payne, and their failure to commit Australia to joining the (arguably illegal) air strikes within the borders of Syria. 'It's a pity that the recent UN leaders' week summit was solely about countering violent extremism,' he sighed, 'and not about dealing much more effectively with the caliphate that's now the most potent inspiration for it.'

Turnbull saw the red cape waving furiously, but chose not to charge. 'Tony has given a speech. I will leave others to run the commentary on it,' he said with a shrug, before adding pointedly: 'He has obviously had a remarkable career in public life, including two years as prime minister. We owe him a great debt for that.'

That was the first salvo, but it obviously wasn't to be the last. And a terrible justification for Abbott's continued hammering

of the military priorities of the new regime was just around
the corner.

—

On 13 November Paris reeled under a series of coordinated
attacks by extremists affiliated with ISIL, leaving 130 people
dead and hundreds wounded. The Australian prime minister
was in Berlin for the G20 meeting as the news broke and was
therefore not able to jump onto 2GB and offer up a knee-
jerk response to the unfolding horror; along with other world
leaders, he was embroiled in finding out what was actually
going on.

Fortunately the former PM was on hand to give an opinion,
demanding that Australia immediately commit troops to
Syria and Iraq and casting sly aspersions on the motivations of
Muslims generally and Australian Muslims specifically. (It's
worth noting that Abbott had been wanting to get Australian
forces onto the ground for months. He had approached the
US government in June 2015 and asked for an invitation for
the RAAF to assist in air strikes—to which the somewhat
surprised US military responded, 'Um, sure, if you want?'—
which was proudly spun in August as being Australia heeding
the call from our allies to enter the Syrian theatre of war. The
United Nations be damned.)

'What we do need, I think,' Abbott told Alan Jones, 'is a
movement inside Islam which makes it absolutely crystal clear
that anything that smacks of death to the infidel is wrong.
I certainly think that this latest atrocity—on top of other
recent atrocities—does indicate that we do need to do more
to tackle this toxin at its source. This ISIL caliphate—it can't
be contained, it has to be defeated. It's not going to go away

just by wishing it to go away. It's only going to be defeated if people take very strong steps against it.' He also called for 'a revolution in Islam' similar to that of the Reformation.

This message was at odds with the statement from the actual prime minister when he spoke to the media several hours later.

After condemning the attackers and emphasising that 'the home of freedom has been assaulted by terrorists determined to attack and suppress freedom not just in France but throughout the world,' Turnbull declared: 'Protecting Australians, protecting freedom, is a global struggle for freedom against those who seek to suppress it and seek to assert some form of religious tyranny.'

However, then his rhetoric became dangerously reasonable.

'Ultimately, there will have to be a political solution. The military angle is very important. It is very important that Daesh is confronted and defeated militarily but, longer term, the stability that will enable those millions of refugees to return to their homes will depend on a political solution.'

Foreign minister Julie Bishop was even more forthright, telling Sky News on 17 November: 'As Tony Abbott well knows, Australia does not act unilaterally. We need to have a legal basis under international law to send our forces into other countries, for their own protection but as well because Australia plays by the rules and we are not going to expose our soldiers to international consequences should we be acting unilaterally.'

Defence minister Marise Payne also seemed to feel that a wild, emotional retaliation was perhaps not the greatest idea.

'We will take advice from the chief of the [Australian] Defence Force and senior officials to determine the best way forward. And I think it's very important to say we don't do that in isolation, we do that in consultation with the people we are already working with, and most particularly with the Iraqi government—because this is, after all, about the self-defence of Iraq.'

This dangerous and unfamiliar outbreak of reason went down unexpectedly well with the Australian people, who seemed to like the thought of having a bit of a ponder before risking Australian lives in the Middle East and were charmed by the discussion of strategy being made in terms of military objectives rather than Abbott's painting of the matter as a zero-sum ideological battle against a 'death cult'.

And this was the point at which Abbott decided to muse aloud about why, exactly, the immigration minister wasn't on the National Security Council.

After making clear that appointments to the NSC were the exclusive preserve of the prime minister, Abbott popped onto Sky to point out to his good buddy Andrew Bolt that 'the Minister for Border Protection is, in my judgement, a significant part of our national security machinery'.

This was the moment for the Abbott backing singers to snap immediately into sweet, sweet harmony.

'When you think about the border protection and border control implications of making sure you are letting humanitarian entrants in, rather than people who it appears on this occasion slotted into a highly complex and coordinated attack in Paris, then my view is that further reinforces the necessity for Mr Dutton to be permanently appointed to the NSC,' huffed Andrew Nikolic—the Tasmanian MP who had been dropped as government whip by Turnbull in the recent reshuffle—on the ABC.

'The immigration minister was a member of the NSC in the past and should be now,' echoed dumped former defence minister and failed challenger for the deputy leadership Kevin Andrews, speaking to Fairfax. 'In my experiences as a past member of the NSC, the immigration minister brings a valuable and critical perspective to the decisions about our security. It is artificial to separate immigration issues from national security.'

The National Security Council had several permanent members: Turnbull, Payne, Bishop, the deputy PM and Nationals leader Warren Truss, Attorney-General George Brandis, Treasurer Scott Morrison and cabinet secretary Arthur Sinodinos, plus the odd bonus minister when the need arose. Notably, however, none of these people were pals of Abbott and his sudden concern seemed less about ensuring that the NSC had access to the sage counsel and boundless intellect of Dutton and more about having his own guy on the inside.

Just in case this point was somehow lost on the general public, the media was conveniently informed about what appeared to be an unofficial 'resistance movement' holding lunchtime meetings each Tuesday while parliament was sitting. Named after the location in which said meetings were held—the 'monkey pod room' at Parliament House, which boasted a table made from the tropical timber—they consisted of the party's most ardent conservatives and Abbott supporters. And there were a few familiar faces.

Organised by Dutton and including such hard-right stars as Abbott, Andrews and Nikolic, as well as Michael Sukkar, Angus Taylor, Zed Seselja, Natasha Griggs, Craig Kelly and Ian Goodenough, the group got very cranky when it was accused of being some sort of organised government-in-exile. Its members insisted it was just a casual group of like-minded Liberal Party members who would, occasionally, eat chocolate cakes that Abbott brought along, baked by former chief of staff Peta Credlin.[4]

In December, as promised, Abbott announced his political intentions: to not make a decision about his political intentions until April.

'I'm too young to retire and I certainly want to have some kind of role in our public life in the years to come,' he told *The Australian*, 'but precisely how I might give effect to that is something I will decide in coming months.'

If this continued postponement suggested indecision, the former PM was nonetheless focused on bringing the new political regime into question. And as ministers fell in December and January, it seemed a good time for the former leader to show an overdue talent for delegation in debating Marise Payne's authority as Minister for Defence

4   This is true, as was the fact that Abbott was living in Credlin's Canberra house at the time. Griggs was particularly incensed about this being discussed by journalists and got on Facebook to declare: 'So having lunch with colleagues is now newsworthy—get a life!' *Zing!*

Hence Andrews did what he did so well: acted as a stalking horse for his fallen leader,[5] taking to the ABC airwaves in January to criticise Payne's decision not to commit extra Australian troops to the war zone in Syria.

'She has information before her that I obviously don't in making the decision,' he conceded, 'but my general in-principle view is that if the Americans have made a reasonable request of us, then we should be giving it the most favourable consideration. We are a long term, decades-long alliance partner with the US and we should therefore be starting with a favourable consideration of what the US request of us. Because at the end of the day, the US have come to our aid on occasions when we've needed them.'

While that was going on, the former PM decided that now would be a grand time to confirm that April be damned—he'd definitely be standing once again to contest the seat of Warringah, just as the preselection process for the seat began. 'It has been a great honour to serve the people of Warringah for twenty-two years and I hope to retain their trust and confidence.'

Various Liberal figures leaped up to praise the decision, including Greg Hunt and Eric Abetz, while former Queensland premier Peter Beattie took to Twitter to rejoice that 'Tony Abbott staying on in politics is good news for Bill Shorten and the Labor Party'. Turnbull's office, meanwhile, commented that they would not be commenting.

---

5 Some truths can only be expressed in typos, preserved in URL addresses: the *SMH* spoke for the entire nation on 20 September 2015 when it ran a headline that ended 'exits', but the original headline, preserved in the web address for the story by David Wroe, evidently ran: 'First female defence minister Marise Payne hailed as Kevin Andrews exists'.

While Turnbull and Morrison stumbled badly over various options for tax reform—which will get a whole chapter of its own, because everyone loves tax reform!—the newly re-energised ex-PM started to flex his muscles and wrote a series of self-serving columns for right-wing magazine *Quadrant*.[6]

His opening salvo, with extracts published in the rather-more-widely read *Australian*, was a classic of the genre. In the four-thousand-word screed he defended the 'fundamentally fair' 2014 budget,[7] declaring that he was confident that the Abbott government 'could have won the 2016 election with a program of budget savings and lower tax'.

This was followed by a curious recasting of his 2013 election victory as having demonstrated public support for the Coalition's promises 'to abolish the schoolkids bonus and the low-income supplement, to delay employer-provided super-annuation benefits and to reduce Labor's promised funding boost to schools and hospitals beyond the next few years', which was . . . let's say an *idiosyncratic* interpretation of events.

Then there was a genuinely weird moment on 25 February, when the occasional Member for Fairfax, Clive Palmer, popped up in Question Time to suggest that there was a

6 In a bleakly hilarious piece of ideological displacement, *Quadrant* was informed in May 2016 that it would no longer be receiving grant money from the Australia Council as the arts budget had been massively slashed under successive Coalition budgets, leaving a much-reduced arts funding pool. In a scathing piece published on 15 May, editor and alleged historian Keith Windschuttle fumed that this was not the work of the government fulfilling the precise policies *Quadrant* proudly espoused but was 'a brazen political decision intended to devalue our reputation and demonstrate that it is the Left which runs and controls the arts'. Oh, bless! The piece also confirmed that *Quadrant*'s sales figures are 'over 6000'. Just for comparison, *The Monthly* sells five times that amount.

7 Fundamentally fair or not—and let's be clear: it wasn't—at the time of writing (July 2016), the 2014 budget was still yet to be passed.

secret Abbott/Turnbull leadership deal in place. Palmer asked the PM: 'As Australia's third-oldest prime minister, if you are still prime minister after the election, will you serve a full term in parliament or will you retire to your unit in New York and do a switcheroo with the member for Warringah, sustaining yourself with innovation and growth opportunities your investments have provided for the people of the Cayman Islands?[8] It has never been a more exciting time to be a Cayman Islander. Are you a seat warmer?'

Turnbull laughed at the question, assuring Palmer that he was in rude health. Unkind observers might have thought that Palmer was just angling for a distraction from his crumbling business empire and the growing revelations about the degree to which his companies had been donating money to the Palmer United Party even as they approached receivership, but the idea that there existed some sort of Bob Hawke/Paul Keating or John Howard/Peter Costello transition arrangement had a certain conspiratorial appeal— although, given those examples, the fact that Turnbull did actually become PM would seem to disprove the existence of such a deal.

Speaking of former prime ministers, on 2 March both Abbott and Turnbull were at the same table for a special dinner celebrating the twentieth anniversary of the election of John Howard. At the beginning of his speech on this illustrious occasion, Turnbull attempted to hand an olive branch

---

8 The embarrassing revelation that Turnbull had involvements in companies that used offshore tax shelters in the wake of the global scandal surrounding Mossack Fonseca should really have become a bigger deal, but at least Clive got a parting joke out of it.

to his vanquished foe; when praising the near-superhuman magnificence of the Howard-era MPs and senators,[9] he made a point of adding: 'In particular, I want to acknowledge my predecessor as prime minister, Tony Abbott. Tony was a vital, powerful part of the Howard government, but as leader he led us back into government and ended the shocking dis-illusionment and catastrophe of the Rudd–Gillard–Rudd years. Thank you, Tony.'

The most recent ex-PM did not, it's fair to say, seem entirely placated.

———

However, a classic electoral issue, dear to the heart of Abbott, then reared its head once again: submarines, and the building thereof.

Ever since former defence minister David Johnston insisted he wouldn't trust the Port Adelaide-based Australian Submarine Corporation to 'build a canoe', much less the future fleet of defence vessels, the question of whether the government would continue to build submarines in South Australia had become a marvellous carrot to wave under the state's nose in order to get local support, before going to back to ignoring the state generally regarded as being the least electorally important.[10]

Abbott had deployed his promise-fleet back in February 2015 as a way of getting the support of SA senators and MPs ahead of the vote on a possible leadership spill against him. SA senator Sean Edwards was given the thumbs-up to announce

---

9 One of whom, you might notice, was Turnbull himself.

10 That was to change dramatically in 2016, but we don't want to spoil the surprise!

on 7 February that ASC would be putting in a tender for twelve submarines to be built there, keeping much-needed jobs in South Australia. This was true right up until the spill motion was defeated on 9 February, at which point Edwards and his SA colleagues were told that actually, nah, questions about construction would be a decision for the probably Japanese submarine companies to make, most likely in Japan, since there wouldn't be an open tender after all—at least, not one that involved ASC.

This resulted in one of the most magical interviews in Australian politics, as Sky News' David Speers asked Edwards on 10 February why he had announced there'd be a tender, when there would in fact be a 'competitive evaluation' process, which would not include ASC.

The correct answer was: 'Because I have been deliberately manipulated and then left to twist in the wind, because what was I going to do about it?' But that would have suggested that Abbott was a fibber and Edwards was a goose, so instead Edwards went for a more politically palatable option: spouting complete gibberish.

'The assurance that I asked of the prime minister and that all of my South Australian colleagues to the best of my knowledge have asked for is for them to be included,' the elected official in a position of authority said to a professional journalist on television. 'You know, you never get a second chance to ask your uncle to your wedding. You've got to go through life having not asked your uncle to come to the wedding. Now, this is something that they [Australian shipbuilders] want to be involved in.'

While the question of whether or not Edwards' uncle had RSVP'd remained an open question, the landscape had changed dramatically in the year and a bit since that interview. Now, in the first months of 2016, the sub-building deal that many people foolishly believed Abbott had hashed out with Japanese prime minister Shinzo Abe was on the backburner and it looked as though France was going to get the gig instead. This was pretty humiliating for the former leader, not least since the $50 billion eight-sub deal with the Japs was reportedly agreed upon verbally in 2014, before any sort of assessment or tendering process had taken place.

However, on 2 March there was a mysterious leak of a classified Defence white paper claiming that there would be a potential ten-year delay in rolling out the new-generation submarines, and thus the current fleet of Collins-class subs would need to remain operational until the early 2030s.

The question being asked was how exactly this confidential paper could possibly have ended up at *The Australian*, in the hands of Abbott's old pal Greg Sheridan and accompanied by a comment from no less an authority than submarine enthusiast and former prime minister Tony Abbott, who said he was 'flabbergasted' by the news regarding Australia's 'fragile capacity' to defend itself.

The swiftness of the timing—almost as though the leak and the response had come out simultaneously!—provoked unkind speculation that perhaps the former PM was the culprit. However, he'd specifically said that he had never leaked or backgrounded against anyone and he certainly wasn't about to start now, so obviously it was pure, magical coincidence.

It was also revealed, by another magical coincidence, that a draft of the classified white paper had been received by Kevin Andrews four days before he was replaced by Marise Payne, although he told the press: 'I am advised that the relevant documents were returned or destroyed.'

It was also pointed out by the government that Abbott's then-defence minister David Johnston had as long ago as 2014 informed the then-PM that the new subs wouldn't be operational until 2031 at the earliest, which suggested that Abbott was significantly exaggerating the amount of gast to which the news had exposed his flabber.

Turnbull had already put up with a lot of undermining, but this time he didn't mess around. 'I can confirm that the secretary of the Department of Defence has advised me that he has initiated an investigation, which will obviously be conducted by the Australian Federal Police, into the apparent leak of these classified documents that were referred to in the newspaper,' he announced that same day, indicating that he was getting mighty tired of this shit.

Two days later he continued to call bullshit, declaring that Abbott 'made some remarks during the week about submarines which were commented on and in fact contradicted by the Chief of the Defence Force and the secretary of the defence department. I respect Tony's right to speak his mind and he should continue to do so, but it's very important that, as prime minister, I set the record straight.'

However, Abbott would not be cowed. He now began to assert throughout March, both in the party room and the wider world, that 'there are some changes, but fundamentally the

Turnbull government is seeking re-election on the record of the Abbott government', as he put it on Sky News. It was a line that Labor would have been wise to use for their election campaign.

This didn't go down well with Liberal Party members keen on the return of the Turnbull government, with former Howard-era minister Peter Reith scolding the former PM in editorials that bore unambiguous titles of the flavour of 'Tony Abbott has no mandate to undermine Malcolm Turnbull'.

But Abbott had no intention of backing down. 'I intend to defend the legacy of the Abbott government and, as a former prime minister, I will speak out in defending that legacy. I will speak in the party room on issues where members have a right to put their views.'

But then something came along more potent than criticism: ridicule.

———

March also saw the publication of the much-anticipated book by veteran political journalist, *Australian* columnist and former staffer to Howard's treasurer Peter Costello, Niki Savva. *The Road to Ruin: How Tony Abbott and Peta Credlin destroyed their own government* was only one in a number of books that had come out in the previous six months examining the collapse of the Abbott experiment,[11] but with Savva's incomparable insider access it promised to have the most dirt. And while it didn't answer the question that Australia seemed most curious about—so, were Abbott and Credlin doin' it or what?—it at least confirmed that everyone in the party was just as baffled by what was going on as was the rest of the nation.

---

11 Ahem.

The timing was terrible for Abbott, since he was clearly attempting to reposition himself as the ex the nation had dumped too soon, but Savva's book was a potent reminder of the dysfunction and aggressiveness that had forced the party to move against him. Excerpts were published in the papers, Savva was widely interviewed, and the government made half-hearted tut-tutting noises about how dreadful all this attention into the ex-PM's relationship with his chief of staff was. Simply dreadful. Disrespectful of such a widely revered figure with so much to offer in public life. Who would even read this tantalisingly scurrilous nonsense, especially that bit on page 145. Etcetera.

In response, Abbott published another *Quadrant* essay in April, in which he gave a qualified *mea culpa*—which, technically, was more of a *tua culpa*.[12]

'I can't let pride in what was achieved under my leadership blind me to the flaws that made its termination easier,' he generously wrote, 'even if claims were exaggerated or exploited in self-serving ways.'

The mistakes cited included initially appointing a total of one woman to the front bench, trying too hard to bring in his generous parental leave scheme, sticking to his decision to reintroduce knights and dames, and failing to devote more time to appearing before the media in order that 'voters see more personality and less adversarial sparring'.

Other than that, he levelled the blame at the real culprits who were responsible for the end of the Abbott government: literally everyone else.

---

12 'Your fault.' Stay in school, kids!

First up, he chided the voting public for not graciously accepting that they'd need to suffer more in order to return the budget to the mythical surplus. Mainly, however, the blame rested with his colleagues in the Liberal Party who clearly felt 'under-appreciated' by their loving but distant leader. In short, if blame for the end of the prime ministership of Tony Abbott needed to be shifted to people who weren't Tony Abbott, he was courageous enough to do so.

———

By the time the 2016 federal election campaign came along and started in earnest, Abbott more or less kept his head down, campaigning mainly in the electorates of his support- ers, like Kevin Andrews and George Christensen, rather than wasting his time in his own seat of Warringah. At least, until former *Australian Idol* co-host James Mathison announced he was running as an independent and started to attract a bit too much local attention.

However, a few eyebrows were raised in the matter of party unity when a fundraiser in Brisbane was cancelled on the very day it was supposed to be held, because local party organisers were reportedly 'embarrassed' by Abbott and didn't want him to attend.[13] Then Peter Dutton speculated, apropos of nothing, that Turnbull should put Abbott in the Defence portfolio just as reports began to emerge that the party would be pressuring for the ex-PM to be given a Cabinet post in the event of a win.[14]

---

13 Officially the reason for the cancellation was that the fundraiser was set to lose money. However, organiser Mark Chapman was expelled from the party as a result of this storm in a Speedo.

14 Abbott's response to this stirring message of support from his factional ally was: 'I am not expecting to go back into the ministry and I'm not going to speculate on speculation', which is several light years away from 'no'.

But Abbott showed remarkable restraint in mid-June when Andrew Bolt attempted to goad him into contradicting Turnbull over whether or not Indigenous inhabitants would have considered European settlement to be an 'invasion'.

'I certainly wouldn't use the word *invasion*,' Abbott responded on 23 June. 'The terminology I use is settlement. If that's too benign, fair enough, say Australia was *occupied*, if you like.'

Still, there was a flash of the old Tony when he confirmed to Bolt that, sure, he'd rather like the chance to serve in the Defence portfolio if, say, the PM was to decide to bring him back to the front bench. He would be prepared to let bygones be bygones.

'Let us suppose that someone has done the wrong thing, for argument's sake,' he hypothesised, when Bolt raised the question as to whether Liberal voters would deliberately not vote for a Turnbull government due to their still-fermenting fury at the loss of their beloved figurehead. 'Do you want to hurt the country in order to punish someone? Now I don't think that's a very sensible thing to do. You never try to get even with an individual if that means hurting the country.'

———

At the Coalition's election campaign launch—which happened six days before the federal poll, after seven weeks of official and about eighteen months of unofficial campaigning—Abbott didn't make any attempt to crack a smile as he watched the man who betrayed him declare that only a Turnbull Coalition government could offer the nation the stability it so desperately needed, while the media hammered the message home that the likely return of the

Coalition was possible only because their dud of a leader had been dumped back in September.

There he stood, the only 'party elder' other than John Howard to attend, his jaw set and his expression pained, as Turnbull praised Howard, declaring that he had 'set the gold standard, leading the most successful and effective government. Your reforms set up Australia for the longest period of prosperity in our history.'

Abbott, by contrast, was congratulated on winning the 2013 election against the fatally wounded Labor while being issued what seemed a backhanded warning to keep his head down: 'You remain a dedicated advocate for our cause.'

That Abbott's much-photographed handshake with his party's leader wasn't accompanied by a swift left hook to the jaw was a master class of self-control. Occasionally the tongue snaked out for a quick lap, but otherwise he remained stony-faced, his eyes shining and sharp. Among the tired, middle-aged men of the party sitting around him, he looked like something very different. A lizard, maybe—watchful and still.

After all, lizards are excellent stealth hunters.

5
THE RISE OF THE DELCONS

*In which Turnbull's internal enemies make their
presence felt*

The triumphant emergence of Malcolm Turnbull had not been entirely popular within the Liberal Party, much less the Coalition. His ten-vote victory over Abbott had left a lot of his own party seething, most notably the man he deposed, and there were some very passionate Turnbull-not-likers who had no intention of letting the new PM go about his business unhindered.

This group was known by many names—the Abbotteers, Team Australia, the Monkey Podders,[1] the Extreme Right of the Liberal Party That Would Rather Have Lost Under Abbott Than Won Under Turnbull—but the name that stuck was coined, somewhat unexpectedly, by News Corp columnist Miranda Devine: the DelCons, short for 'delusional conservatives'.

---

1 Remember that group of conservatives who supported Abbott? They met in the 'monkey pod room' in Parliament House. Honestly, it was only last chapter.

The group were, as per Devine's definition, members of the party unshakably committed to the fantastic belief that the government would have somehow pulled off a resounding victory under Tony Abbott and that the leadership change was not merely unnecessary, but downright damaging to the Coalition brand.

Senior among the DelCons were the former ministers Eric Abetz and Kevin Andrews, both strong Abbott allies who had been dumped by the incoming regime. They'd had little love for the new leader before, and they certainly weren't enamoured of him now.

While most of the incoming ministry were those who'd backed Turnbull, there hadn't been a complete changing of the guard. Very vocal Abbott fan Greg Hunt kept the Environment portfolio, and Peter Dutton maintained his ministerial responsibility for Immigration and Border Control—the same Dutton who was also the unofficial leader of the Monkey Pod group that was absolutely, definitely not some sort of clandestine resistance movement, that's for darn sure.

And while the Podders were eating Credlin-baked cakes and absolutely not plotting anything (why do you even ask?), there was also a handful of loose-cannon conservatives who couldn't even be bothered to pretend to hide their contempt for the new leader and who were especially outspoken in their determination to maintain a strong line against anything that smacked of creeping progressiveness. And their definition of what that included was impressively broad.

———

Kevin Andrews had long been Abbott's right-hand man, possibly because he knew that he himself wasn't a politician whom the public found particularly inspiring. Even *The Australian*, in an otherwise quite flattering profile in May 2014, accurately described him as 'an ordinarily waxen figure', a term befitting a man whose main political triumph was largely achieved by not going anywhere, geographically or professionally.

The devoutly Catholic former lawyer was one of the longest-serving MPs in parliament,[2] having first appeared in 1991 when the former deputy Liberal leader (and fellow deeply conservative lawyer) Neil Brown stepped down as MP for the Victorian seat of Menzies. Labor didn't even bother running a candidate in the by-election for the safe Liberal seat, and thus Andrews made his spectacular parliamentary debut without any challenger of note. So talented did he prove at sitting quietly on the backbench that he proceeded to do exactly that for the next ten years.

However, in 2001 he became the Howard government's Minister for Ageing before graduating to the portfolio of Employment and Workplace Relations. Here he oversaw the introduction of Howard's disastrous WorkChoices industrial relations program, before being plucked out to oversee the Department of Immigration for the government's final nine volatile months. He helped to keep things spicy in his new role by making a controversial statement bemoaning the failure of African refugees to assimilate into Australian society, before the government was unceremoniously booted out of office.

A lesser politician might have been somewhat shamefaced at having been directly responsible for two of the departmental

2 After the retirement of Philip Ruddock at the 2016 election, Andrews became the 'father of the House' as the longest-serving MP.

areas most responsible for the end of the Howard epoch, but
Andrews blithely soldiered on. And his patience was rewarded:
while both Brendan Nelson and Malcolm Turnbull justly
overlooked him for inclusion in their shadow ministries, the
conservative wing's growing fears that an emissions trading
scheme was going to become a reality under Turnbull meant
opportunity was about to knock for climate change sceptics,
who knew how to do what they were told by the more confident
boys, such as hardline conservative SA senator Nick Minchin.[3]
Abbott's leadership victory in December 2009 was a mighty
triumph for Andrews, who was rewarded with the Social
Services portfolio in the Abbott government after it won the
2013 election, at which point he was able to enact his biggest
policy change: offering the Australian people $200 relationship
counselling vouchers, budgeted at a handsome $20 million.

Andrews was a big fan of relationship counselling—indeed,
he and his wife Margaret merrily told *The Australian* that they
had a 'check-up' every few years. His 2014 book *Maybe 'I Do':
Modern marriage and the pursuit of happiness* contained the
deathless statement that the greatest threat to stable society
was 'not the continuing financial crisis. Nor is it the threat of
radical Islam. The greatest threat is within. It is the steady,
but continuing breakdown of the essential structures of civil
society—marriage, family and community.'

So the Andrews were big fans of marriage and marriage
counselling. What they didn't mention quite so much at the
time was that they had more than a casual interest in the subject.

---

3   It never, ever, EVER gets less weird that Nick is the uncle of comedian, musician
and notoriously outspoken lefty Tim Minchin. Families, huh?

As journalists swiftly discovered, Andrews' register of parliamentary interests revealed that he listed his membership of Marriage Education Programme Inc., a company that offered marriage counselling services (at $240 a pop: a bargain, especially with a voucher!). It was subsequently announced that Kevin and Margaret had resigned from the company in December 2013—a few months after Kevin took on the Social Services portfolio—although Margaret seemingly continued to work as a marriage counsellor there,[4] according to her husband's updated 2013 register of interests.

The controversy burned out quickly, however, and in any case the scheme was a flop. Only 7785 of the 100,000 vouchers were taken up (at a total cost of $2.5 million, according to a report tabled in Senate estimates) and Andrews' replacement, Scott Morrison, scrapped the scheme altogether in February 2015. Morrison also had to deal with the fallout of Andrews' attempted cuts to welfare spending—specifically, the removal of funding for services tackling homelessness, his bungled attempt to impose a six-month wait on all unemployment benefits for people under thirty, and his laughable plan to force unemployed Australians to apply for up to forty jobs a week in order to remain on benefits.

This short-lived folly drew howls of protest from social justice groups, who understandably saw this as a punitive measure designed to punish those unable to find a job. More importantly, as far as the Abbott government's priorities were concerned, it was also vehemently opposed by business

4 Indeed, in the 2014 honours she was awarded an OAM 'for service to the Catholic Church in Australia through a range of marriage education programs'.

groups who had given the matter more thought than Andrews evidently had done and realised that they'd be inundated with endless applications from unqualified applicants being forced to make up the numbers. After a few tense weeks, that plan was quietly shelved.

Given Andrews' less than stellar performance in Social Services, in December 2014 he was moved into the traditional portfolio for bumbling ministers past their use-by date, Defence—and it was an announcement that was met with as much enthusiasm in the military as it was by Andrews himself.[5]

On the first day in the job he was the subject of mockery by Neil James, the executive director of the Australian Defence Association, who claimed that Andrews had told him he had 'no interest in defence issues' during a conversation years earlier. James added: 'Defence is getting very, very tired of receiving ministers who are really in their last term or two in parliament. What we need is younger and more able ministers with a future ahead of them.'

Meanwhile the Defence Gay, Lesbian, Bisexual, Transgender and Intersex Information Service expressed concern that its progress in having the military adopt more inclusive policies might be made far more difficult under a minister who'd expressed disdain for marriage equality and had been booked to speak at the virulently anti-gay World Congress of Families, before he bowed to public pressure and pulled out.

---

5 That's no reflection on the importance of the role itself, just to be clear: I'm merely pointing out that both Labor and the Coalition have often seen the portfolio as a clearinghouse for superannuated politicians about to be led behind the shed. Of the six Defence ministers before David Johnston (Andrews' predecessor), four—Stephen Smith, John Faulkner, Robert Hill and Peter Reith—held it as their last post before leaving politics.

Andrews had been given the job of sorting out the dog's breakfast that were the new contracts for Australia's fleet of twelve shiny new submarines,[6] a job that everybody had once assumed would go straight to the Australian Submarine Corporation in Port Adelaide until the announcement in parliament by Andrews' predecessor, David Johnston, that he wouldn't trust the ASC 'to build a canoe', thereby ending his ministerial career. Andrews also had to deal with the newly independent former Palmer United senator Jacqui Lambie, who was threatening to vote against all government legislation unless defence personnel received a full pay rise instead of the one offered to them, which was 1.5 per cent below inflation.

Had this not been tricky enough, the whole issue of the submarine contracts, as we've seen already, was to prove vital to Abbott in terms of retaining the support of South Australian parliamentarians. The failure of a leadership spill motion against Abbott in February 2015 was due, in part, to assurances the PM gave South Australian MPs and senators, particularly Senator Sean Edwards, that the submarine contract was on the table for ASC—a state of affairs that lasted right up until the spill didn't go ahead and Abbott didn't need Edwards' support anymore.[7]

---

6 Which were, as independent senator David Madigan declared during an appearance on ABC TV's *Q&A* in February 2015, 'the spaceships of the ocean'. Which isn't true for a bunch of reasons, most notably that submarines need to withstand massive external pressure while spaceships face the opposite problem of their internal atmospheres pushing out to the vacuum of space. But, importantly, this is easily the most adorable thing Madigan said during his political career.

7 Or so he thought: it's reliably estimated that Edwards, along with all but four of South Australia's eleven Liberal senators and MPs, voted against Abbott in the eventual leadership spill. Whoops!

The problem with suggesting there could be a contract with ASC was that Abbott had already made a handshake deal with Japanese prime minister Shinzo Abe to have his nation build the submarines. Clearly, this had been a delicate situation which would have required a silver-tongued orator with a masterful grasp of rhetoric, a good deal of media savvy and above-average levels of personal charisma if it was going to be elegantly smoothed over without the media, the opposition, the defence industry and the people of South Australia all piling on.

The day after the leadership non-spill—10 February—an uncomfortable-looking Andrews fronted a gaggle of reporters in Adelaide to correct Edwards' statement that there would be 'an open, competitive tender', explaining this would instead be a 'competitive evaluation' that would be 'careful, cautious [and] methodical'.

A shrewder operator—Turnbull, say—might have casually delivered the line in such a way as to imply that this was merely a choice of synonym rather than a deliberate and badly veiled attempt to do a complete about-face, but Andrews' halting diction and obvious, perspiring discomfort telegraphed to the press that they should definitely ask the minister to explain the difference between a tender and this 'competitive evaluation' thing. So they did.

Again, this was a situation that called for charm, eloquence and maybe a bit of humour. Andrews, however, went for annoyance, nervousness and a refusal to answer questions—an interesting decision, given the circumstances.

'I'm not going to get into all sorts of definitions and what's a definition and what that is,' he declared to the increasingly entertained press. 'I'm saying, as the Australian defence minister, this is the approach that we are taking.'

This managed to make the situation a lot worse, drawing attention to the fact that shady deals were being done and that Andrews was woefully out of his depth. It effectively killed the Japanese deal and, once the dust settled, Australia was committed to building eight submarines (not twelve) in Germany (not Australia) with the electronics and maintenance happening in Port Adelaide: a deal that managed to combine all the inconvenience and political cost of spending taxpayer money offshore with the vastly inflated expense of working with ASC, while also enjoying the inefficiencies of the job being done by two separate companies on opposite sides of the world.

However, the one thing Andrews was utterly competent at was loyalty, and when the leadership challenge happened in September 2015 he didn't flinch at the chance to challenge for the deputy leadership, scoring thirty votes to Julie Bishop's seventy—suggesting that fourteen of those who supported Abbott over Turnbull still couldn't stomach the idea of Andrews being anywhere near the leadership.

Still, although Turnbull sent him packing in September 2015, that didn't stop Andrews weighing in on military matters—issuing statements contradicting decisions made by his successor Marise Payne and agitating for greater involvement in the Middle East—but now he was basically a figure of fun, which explained why the media went hard in April 2016 when he implied he might be preparing for a run at the top job himself.

'It has never been my burning ambition to be the leader of the party,' he began, 'but if circumstances arose, which they did in both of those instances, where I thought there should be a change or a contest, I am prepared to do it.' And in the context of the discussion—the situation was clearly theoretical, not a shot across the bows—the very idea of Andrews challenging Turnbull was irresistible, and just about every media outlet trumpeted that this was a warning to the current leadership rather than an incautious comment on a different subject.

Still, Andrews was—as he himself put it—something of an 'intellectual leader' in the conservative wing of the party, and there would shortly be a chance to rally some support.

———

While some DelCons were merely interested in supporting the Liberal Party, Cory Bernardi had been long determined to present himself as the one true voice of Australian conservatism. The South Australian senator had been preselected for the vacancy created when then-defence minister Robert Hill resigned from Howard's cabinet and parliament in 2006, taking up a new gig as Australia's ambassador and permanent representative to the United Nations.

Hill had been a liberal sort of Liberal, which had been predictably unpopular in the Howard era. He and the PM had clashed while Hill was defence minister: so much had Howard interfered with the portfolio that Hill had taken to calling himself 'the minister assisting the Prime Minister for Defence' in public, and the UN appointment was largely assumed to be a way for Howard to move him on without any embarrassing public confrontation. And his replacement was certainly not about to do anything like, for example, openly support the legalisation of 'abortion drug' RU486 in Australia, as Hill had boldly done.

Despite being the son of staunch working-class Labor supporters, Bernardi had been a Liberal Party member since youth (even though he might have accidentally given John Howard tuberculosis just before the 1996 election campaign).[8] He'd been groomed by a powerful mentor, South Australian conservative senator Nick Minchin, and became the president of the South Australian Liberal Party in 1998 and vice-president of the federal party in 2005. With that sort of influence, he could ensure that he had the unassailably safe number one position on the SA senate ticket in 2007 (ahead of the moderate, future Turnbull-era education minister Simon Birmingham), just in time to be thrown into opposition in the Ruddslide election.

His hold over the state party meant that he would stay at the top of the ballot in 2013, making him electorally immortal: few parliamentarians needed to do less to curry favour with the electorate than Bernardi. And that was good, because he did nothing to ingratiate himself to the wider community.

---

8   Bizarre, but supposedly true! According to Bernardi himself on ABC TV's *Kitchen Cabinet*, he and his hotel-owning father had dined with Howard and Christopher Pyne in 1996, just before Howard's first election win. Bernardi had what he thought at the time was a bad cold, but it transpired that he had contracted TB. He was supposed to inform everyone with whom he'd spent enough time to potentially infect them, but he had been too embarrassed to tell the Liberal Party leader that he might have a communicable disease just before going out on the election trail. Then, when Howard came down with a bad cough, Bernardi was terrified that he'd 'done John Howard in'. Thankfully Bernardi was not to go down in history as the Typhoid Mary of conservative Australian politics.

In 2007 Brendan Nelson appointed him the Shadow Parliamentary Secretary for Families and Community Services, but he had barely taken this job before he started making it very clear that his definition of 'family' was exclusively where the parents were legally married and resolutely heterosexual. He began publishing articles condemning climate change science, railing against what he saw as a war on Christianity (including, predictably, pieces about the dangers of Islam), declared that same-sex relationships were 'not the same as marital relationships and to treat them the same is to suspend common sense', and began campaigning against the availability of safe medical abortions—positions that were to become especially awkward when Nelson was challenged and defeated as leader of the party in September 2008. The new leader, Malcolm Turnbull, took a less sanguine view of Bernardi's peculiar dismissal of reliable science, his religious bigotry and his obsession with the love lives of other people.

This came to a head when Bernardi openly railed against the Same-Sex Relationships (Equal Treatment in Commonwealth Laws—Superannuation) Bill 2008 in the Senate, despite the shadow cabinet having agreed to support it. Bernardi felt that providing gay couples with access to superannuation was clearly a slippery slope to sexy moral chaos. 'We have expanded the membership of the marriage club to include heterosexual couples who do not, for whatever reason, actually want to get married,' he declared. 'Now we want to throw open the doors and welcome into the fold those whose relationships are uncharacteristic of the most basic elements of a marital union.'

Turnbull upbraided Bernardi for what he accurately saw as open defiance of the leadership, but Cory wasn't about to fall into line. Instead, he decided to up the ante by taking to his blog to rail against Liberal Party members whom he felt had been insufficiently committed to (Bernardi's very particular definition of) the conservative cause, taking aim at one unnamed MP who, Bernardi alleged, had chosen his party not because of a firm commitment to right-wing principles but purely on the grounds that he lived in a safe Liberal seat.

Turnbull was not alone in assuming that this was a thinly veiled libel against Christopher Pyne and removed Cory from the shadow cabinet. But this indignity was short-lived, because in December 2009 Tony Abbott became party leader. Bernardi had been a key warrior against the proposed emissions trading scheme upon which Turnbull had staked his leadership and, once the dust settled, Bernardi was back in the shadow cabinet, this time as Shadow Parliamentary Secretary Assisting the Leader of the Opposition and Shadow Parliamentary Secretary for Infrastructure and Population Policy.

While Bernardi was clearly more closely aligned with Abbott philosophically, there were those within the party who were not exactly enormous fans of the man and his outlook. An unnamed Liberal Party colleague let fly about him to Sally Neighbour for a profile in the December 2011 issue of *The Monthly*, using language that was to become increasingly familiar in descriptions of the senator.

'Cory is deluded,' the anonymous Liberal declared. 'He is one of the least effective or important members of the parliamentary team. Cory is a person without any intellect, without any base, and he should really never have risen above the position of branch president. His right-wing macho-man act is just his way of looking as though he stands for something.'

Another (similarly nameless) colleague interviewed for the article went further. 'He wants to be some sort of conservative warrior but he's not up to it intellectually. In reality he's like the kid in the playground who pulls his pants down so everyone will look at him, but he has no idea how he's embarrassing himself in the process. He's basically kryptonite for any serious person in the party because he's a complete embarrassment.'

Even so, his star rose further yet in August 2012, when he was appointed the Deputy Manager of Opposition Business in the Senate. But then came the fall: the following month he was forced to step down after declaring in parliament that ratifying same-sex marriage would possibly lead to the legalisation of polygamy and marriage to animals. The outcry was predictable, but that his leader would fail to support him clearly came as a surprise.

This badly expressed slippery slope argument was beyond the pale even for Abbott's conspiratorial mindset, and he didn't appoint Bernardi to any ministerial or official post in the new government.[9] However, the senator celebrated his recurrent freedom from the strictures of cabinet by calling for an end to

---

9 That being said, Bernardi's claim that changing the definition of marriage to recognise same-sex unions would leave the way open to further changes of definition wasn't wrong, but only in the sense that all federal laws can be changed by parliament provided parliament sees fit to do so and the political support is there to pass such amendments. As a senator you'd think that Cory might have been across what is, after all, a pretty huge part of his job.

the abortion 'death industry'[10] and, for good measure, decided to take aim not just at gay parents but also divorcees, single parents and stepfamilies.

'Given the increasing number of non-traditional families, there is a temptation to equate all family structures as being equal or relative,' he wrote in one of his playfully fact-averse books, *The Conservative Revolution*. 'Why then the levels of criminality among boys and promiscuity among girls who are brought up in single-parent families, more often than not headed by a single mother?'[11]

Again, the data upon which Bernardi was basing his claim seemed to exist only in his fevered imagination, but it was a great way to insult both Turnbull (who was raised by his father after his mother left the marriage) and the relatively new Opposition leader, Bill Shorten, who was a doting stepfather to his second wife's children and who really didn't appreciate being told that their children would be sluts and thugs.

'There are hundreds of thousands of children who thrive in loving stepfamilies, blended families or in families with a single parent,' Shorten fumed. 'On what basis is Senator Bernardi suggesting these children are more likely to be criminal—or is it just his own out-of-date prejudices?'

---

10 He claimed, incorrectly, that '80,000 to 100,000' terminations were carried out per year, a claim which a) didn't correspond with any measure, although that's partially because different states collect their data differently and b) is even more than the Medicare data would suggest, and that included all non-viable births, including tragic accidents and miscarriages.

11 Just to be clear, this is another piece of data published exclusively via the Bernardi Arse Institute, from the unpublished paper 'Because I Thunked It: things I made up when reality failed to comply'.

The PM's office was only slightly more polite, declaring in an official statement that 'Senator Bernardi is a backbencher and his views do not represent the position of the government'.

Bernardi's career had stalled under Abbott, and it was obviously not going to proceed under Turnbull. So Cory went for a different approach: if he couldn't ingratiate himself into the regime, he'd declare war on it.

'We have now probably had so many prime ministers and leaders of oppositions in the last eight years that I think we've set a new record for the entire Pacific,' he announced after Turnbull's ascension. 'Is that really a badge of honour that we want? I'd suggest no, and the people that have been rewarded today have been instrumental in that instability.'

Bernardi's diminished position was made clear when the SA senate ballot was announced for the 2016 election, with Birmingham at the top and Bernardi demoted to the number two spot. He was still safe, of course—in a double dissolution election the top four positions could expect to romp it in—but symbolically it represented Bernardi's waning control over the state arm of the party.

Fortunately he had a contingency plan, in the form of the Australian Conservatives, a party he'd registered in 2014.[12] There was obviously no way that he was going to leave the Liberal Party before the 2016 election—after all, with the party behind him, he'd be guaranteed a senate seat, and not even as avowed a Cory Bernardi fan as Cory Bernardi himself would have believed that he'd be guaranteed a quota on the basis of his personal electoral support. However, as the former

12 At the time there was some suggestion that Bernardi had been in talks with Family First's SA senator Bob Day about jumping ship.

Palmer United senators had made clear, using a party to win a seat and then jumping ship was now a perfectly acceptable political strategy.

After all, it's good to have a fallback position.

———

Despite presenting himself as a warrior for conservative causes in the Liberal Party, Bernardi was not part of the Monkey Pod group, consistent with the aforementioned *Monthly* article's claim that 'even the conservative wing finds him to be a complete screwball'.

However, he did have one confederate who shared his hardline conservative views, inflexible adherence to conservative Christianity and outsider status in the Liberal Party: Tasmanian senator Eric Abetz.

The two men had a lot in common. Like Bernardi, Abetz was a child of immigrants and yet saw no contradiction in taking a hard public line against immigration.[13] Like Bernardi, he was a big fan of dismissing evidence that contradicted his religious convictions, and was perfectly fine with picking and choosing which scientific evidence seemed worth accepting (climate science: no; abortions cause breast cancer: yep!).[14]

---

13 Indeed, since he was born in Germany, Abetz was an immigrant himself. His great-uncle, Otto Abetz, was a German SS officer imprisoned for war crimes, specifically the deportation of French Jews to Nazi death camps.

14 Abetz made a nationally televised fool of himself on *The Project* in 2014, citing long-discredited claims of a link between women getting abortions and having a higher risk of breast cancer. This claim was made in a single piece of heavily flawed research in the 1970s and was rejected as nonsense even then. However, the study was a firm favourite of conservatives trying to pretend that their quest to outlaw safe access to medical terminations was motivated by their concern for women's health—the abortion-themed equivalent of endorsing indefinite mandatory offshore detention in the hopes of 'saving lives at sea'.

Like Bernardi, he'd entered parliament only after a vacancy became available (in Abetz's case, he'd failed to win a seat in his own right in 1993 but was plonked into the Senate following the resignation of nondescript senator Brian Archer in 1994), and was a past state president of the Liberal Party, and therefore in a position to guarantee himself a safe spot at the top of the Senate ballot when he made the leap into parliament.

And, like Bernardi, he wasn't shy about contradicting and criticising Malcolm Turnbull—especially on the subject of whether the new leader was right to dump him from the Employment portfolio and the role of Leader of the Government in the Senate. 'There are Senate colleagues who still call me "leader" in the corridors, which is very nice,' he told Jane Cadzow for *Good Weekend*'s revealing feature in March 2016, 'because they think a great injustice has occurred for no good reason.'

Turnbull and Abetz's relationship had come unstuck over the OzCar affair involving Godwin Grech, as we saw in chapter one. Abetz had been entrusted with convening the Senate inquiry into this matter and, in Cadzow's interview, he modestly described his own questioning of Grech as 'nearly faultless'.

Exceptional though Abetz's questioning might have been, it didn't prevent everyone involved in the inquiry looking like a dupe. Abetz claims that he'd warned Turnbull of the risk ('I was laughed at! Laughed at and ridiculed!') and that his public apology had been issued not because he'd been wrong, but 'to suck up the public odium, to protect the leader'.

He needn't have bothered: Turnbull's days were numbered, and in any case Abetz would find a lot more common ground with Abbott. Abetz was to become part of what was later referred to as Abbott's 'praetorian guard', along with Kevin Andrews and Mathias Cormann; but when Abbott fell as PM in September 2015, Abetz knew that his ministerial future had fallen with him.

The Hobart *Mercury* had some words of warning for Turnbull: 'Even his friends sometimes have a nervous chuckle at the zeal with which he pursues an opponent . . . an exiled Abetz with time on his hands is a dangerous proposition for the more progressive political faction led by the new PM.'

And Abetz had form: his influence in the Tasmanian party was absolute, and he was not afraid to wield it. He ensured that Senator Richard Colbeck, a Turnbull supporter who had been made Minister for Tourism, was given the unwinnable fifth position on the Tasmanian double dissolution Senate ticket. Even while the votes were being counted, following the hapless senator's brave and doomed attempt to convince moderate Liberals to vote below the line and elevate his position up the ticket, Colbeck was quietly and pre-emptively dismissed from the ministry in the July 2016 reshuffle.

Thus Abetz's main gig in the months that followed the leadership change was acting as a human *What Would Abbott Do?* bracelet for the media, taking to the airwaves to advocate the return of the former PM to the front bench—and assiduously ignoring anyone who responded 'coughKEVIN RUDDcough'.

———

And, finally, there was George Christensen.

Before deciding to make the leap to federal politics by standing for the seat of Dawson, this former journalist and regional newspaper publisher had been a prominent figure in Queensland politics, serving on the Mackay City Council and then the Mackay Regional Council. Dawson had been a fairly safe LNP seat for more than a quarter of a century, since the heyday of the Whitlam-era minister Rex Patterson, but it had fallen to Labor in the 2007 Ruddslide before Christensen took it back in the knife-edge election of 2010.

While Mackay is a fairly cosmopolitan city, the rest of Dawson enjoys the sort of hardline conservatism associated with rural Queensland—and that suited Christensen just fine.[15]

During the 2010 campaign the press dug up articles the candidate had published in the *Student Advocate* during his university days, twelve years earlier, including jokes about gay men dying of AIDS, an editorial declaring 'the truth is that women are bloody stupid', and calling John Howard a liar for reneging on farmer protections from Native Title claims.

These revelations didn't damage his standing within the party, though. Abbott declared that too much was being made of undergraduate larks, insisting: 'There's colourful stuff from my uni days, there's colourful stuff from Julia Gillard's uni days.' And thus from the outset there was a unity of outlook between the two men.

Christensen also had a lot in common with Bernardi in religiosity and in their shared attitude towards things like marriage equality and climate change. Both were fans of Dutch right-wing politician and outspoken not-fan of Islam,

---

15 While Christensen, like all Queensland Coalition parliamentarians, is techni-cally of the LNP, for the purposes of party room discussions he is a National. This means he didn't vote in the leadership spill, although there's little doubt where his vote would have gone.

Geert Wilders. When Bernardi was warned off attending Wilders' 2013 speaking tour, he obeyed his leader's instructions—but Christensen popped along in Sydney and found much to inspire him, although he emphasised that he was a believer in freedom of religion and didn't agree with Wilders' demands that the building of mosques be banned. Lest this seem like a dangerously respectful attitude to Muslims, by November 2014 Christensen was raising the important question of whether halal certification was funding terrorism.

This was a provocative question that, fortunately, had a clear answer: no—as confirmed by multiple Australian security agencies, including the Australian Transaction Reports and Analysis Centre (which investigates money laundering and the funding of terrorist groups), the Australian Federal Police and ASIO. But those so-called experts in their ivory towers with their 'resources' and their 'agents' and their 'ability to investigate the matter and actual, genuine responsibility for establishing the truth of possible security threats, no matter how unlikely they might sound' were no match for the peerless authority of George Christensen's vague and unsupported suspicions.

'I don't know whether my grocery spend is going to fund extremist versions of that religion or extremist religious activities that I would rather not see in Australia. While it's not terrorism, there is no doubt halal certification is funding organisations with extremist views and activities in Australia,' he inaccurately wrote on his website. 'It's lovely to know a jar of the salty black stuff [Vegemite, which has no animal products and is therefore halal by definition] is sponsoring the advocacy of robbing women of all of their marital property rights.'[16]

He also shared Bernardi's obsession with the link between same-sex marriage and polygamy, insisting: 'If we would open the door to same-sex marriage, no valid argument remains against polygamy or the multiple other type of unions that could be out there because the term "marriage" becomes meaningless.'

He was also a big fan of telling those at the bottom of the economic pile that they'd never had it so good, most notably as the criticism against the 2014 budget ramped up. All those people complaining about cuts to health and welfare—of the sort explicitly ruled out by Abbott before the elections—should, he tweeted, 'do a tour of Asia & live like locals to put these 1st world complaints re budget in perspective'. This was accompanied by a photo of an unidentified slum. When that got a less-than-entirely-positive response, he scoffed: 'Try getting any serious form of welfare in Thailand or other SE Asian nations,' before telling 'the lefty twitter warriors . . . sometimes the truth hurts'.

He also didn't care for environmental activists concerned about the increasingly parlous health of the Great Barrier Reef running along Dawson's coastal border, describing them as 'gutless green grubs' for campaigning against the expansion of the Abbot Point Coal Terminal and declaring that 'the

16 Just as an aside: one of the oddest things about the fashion for anti-Islam rhetoric is watching outspokenly sexist and homophobic individuals—the very same people happy to insist that the feminazis are part of the homosexual agenda—suddenly get terribly, terribly worried about the ghastly treatment of women and gay folks under Islam. Bless.

eco-terrorists butchered the international tourism market for our greatest tourism attraction, not for the reef but for political ideology'.

Yet, despite his friendship with Abbott and their many shared perspectives, there was never any suggestion that Christensen was going to be given a position of any responsibility.[17] That didn't change with Turnbull's ascension—and Christensen gave the new leader a rousing message of support a fortnight after the challenge, telling the ABC: 'Look, it doesn't matter whether I am gritting my teeth or not. Malcolm is the leader: what can we do?'

It turned out that question was absolutely not rhetorical.

———

Bernardi, Abetz, Andrews and Christensen might have been the ghosts of conservatism past in the new thoroughly modern Turnbullscape, but they still had some chains to rattle. And they were about to get the perfect opportunity to do some serious poltergeistin'.

---

17 As a nominal National MP, that wouldn't have been the PM's decision anyway: National leader Warren Truss would have made that call.

6
ONCE, TWICE, THREE TIMES AN EX-MINISTER

In which the PM hits his peak . . . but the pebbles start tumbling down

With his popularity at record levels, Turnbull had had an opportunity at the start of his PMship to make some serious changes. But since he'd pretty much ruled out doing anything with regards to actual policy, this meant unveiling a new-look ministry that showed off a lot of fresh faces and illustrated the sheer breadth of talent that the government possessed in its ranks.

By reshuffling his front bench so comprehensively, Turnbull had made clear that he was all about dynamic renewal; every decision to retain or replace a minister meant that the new PM was taking direct ownership of everything that was to happen from then on in. And strategically, it meant that the previous prime minister would be unable to take credit for any successes that were to flow from such wise choices.

On the minus side, it meant that any future ministerial embarrassment would call Turnbull's judgement into serious question, since the perception would be that competent ministers had been turfed out to be replaced by geese. But what were the chances of that happening any time soon?

By mid February 2016, Turnbull had an answer.

———

One of Turnbull's biggest supporters during the leadership battle had been Queensland MP Mal Brough. He'd been gathering the numbers for Turnbull from the coup's very earliest days—and he was the perfect man for the job, since he had direct experience of carrying out clandestine operations. However, to explain this, we must drift back to the simpler times of 2010.

Labor's Julia Gillard had maintained government in the federal election in August that year, despite both Labor and the Coalition stalling on seventy-two seats apiece, but only by gaining the support of four independents in the lower house: the Greens Member for Melbourne Adam Bandt, Tasmanian independent Andrew Wilkie, and NSW ex-Nationals Tony Windsor and Rob Oakeshott.

Still, this put the lower house on a knife edge, with Labor only having a one-member parliamentary majority. Except then Gillard executed a strategic masterstroke.

Labor's Harry Jenkins was Speaker of the House, meaning that he couldn't vote with the party on legislation. So in November he was encouraged to stand down and was replaced by a new speaker: Peter Slipper.

Slipper had entered parliament in 1993 as the LNP's member for the Queensland seat of Fisher and had not served without controversy. He was difficult, eccentric and—it was alleged—extremely fond of a drink, notoriously falling asleep in parliament in June 2010 during an after-lunch speech by Indonesian president Susilo Bambang Yudhoyono (leading one anonymous Liberal source to tell the *Sunshine Coast Daily* that this was hardly an isolated incident: 'If he turns up at a branch function or parliament with alcohol on his breath he's gone . . . How can a mature man get thrown out of a Canberra nightclub at 4 am in the morning and off a plane in the Northern Territory for being drunk?').

More importantly, there had also long been accusations that Slipper was rorting his expenses, especially when it was reported that he'd claimed $640,562 in travel and other expenses for the last six months of 2009, making the size of his claims second only to the prime minister, Kevin Rudd, and significantly greater than those of the treasurer, Wayne Swan, who'd been racing all over the world consulting as the sheer size of the Global Financial Crisis became horrifyingly clear. Pointed questions were asked about how a backbencher—in opposition, no less!—could possibly run up such exorbitant bills. While Opposition leader Tony Abbott defended him and the matter eventually died down, it was clear that Slipper and the LNP were starting to get heartily sick of one another.

Slipper finally ripped the Band-Aid off by quitting the party in November 2010, and thus was technically independent when Gillard appointed him, defying the convention which typically has the party in power appoint a speaker from its own side.[1] This gave Gillard a two-MP buffer on any vote, which provided her government with a little bit of breathing room.

And as it happened, Slipper turned out to be an impartial and impressively assiduous speaker of the house. But this wasn't to last.

———

Mal Brough had been a minister in the Howard government and had weathered a number of scandals as employment minister and Minister for Aboriginal Affairs (under which he imposed the Northern Territory Emergency Response, aka the NT Intervention, on largely dubious evidence); he was unceremoniously turfed out of his Queensland seat of Longman in the Labor landslide election of 2007.

He was placated by being made president of the Queensland Liberal Party, but stood down in 2008 in protest at the merging of the Liberal and National parties that created the LNP, and didn't seek preselection for the 2010 election because he refused to kowtow to the new LNP executive—led by Brough's despised rival, former National and then Queensland Opposition leader Lawrence Springborg.[2]

That resolve didn't last too long, though. By June 2010 he was publicly agitating for the LNP to drop Slipper, and

---

1 This typically works to the government's advantage, since speakers are a wee bit more forgiving about breaching standing orders in Question Time when the person involved is from their party. For example: Bronwyn Bishop expelled 400 MPs between November 2013 and June 2015, of whom 393 were Labor. Take a guess which party she represented.

2 Fun fact: it was Springborg who quashed Ian Macfarlane's ill-starred attempt to jump into the Nationals' camp after he was dumped from the front bench. See how it all fits together like a horrific ghastly puzzle?

in this he was supported by John Howard; he also made a tilt at getting Alex Somlyay to give up the seat of Fairfax in return for a juicy diplomatic posting—an offer supposedly made directly by Brough's then-pal Tony Abbott. The venerable Somlyay refused the overture, serving one last term before retiring at the 2013 election—at which point an upstart ex-LNP member named Clive Palmer ran for and won Fairfax by a margin of a few dozen votes.

By 2012 Brough's resolve had softened even further, and he accepted LNP preselection to run as their candidate in Slipper's seat of Fisher. It was at this point that he reached out to a couple of Slipper's staffers, James Ashby and Karen Doane, seeking to substantiate rumours of sexual harassment from their boss.

It transpired that Slipper had been chuffed to bits when he first discovered that Ashby was gay and proceeded to text him about sex in language that a twelve-year-old would have found immature—notoriously comparing the vagina to a 'shell-less mussel' and giggling about naughty swears. 'Funny how we say a person is a cunt when many guys like cunts' read one text message, to which Ashby replied, 'Not I.' While another read, 'I'm going to smack u. Arhhhhhhhh.' To which Ashby replied, 'Ah I might like it. Tho I'm not into pain.'

Ashby had quit the LNP at the same time as Slipper so he could continue working in his office, which turned the situation into organisational espionage—especially as reports were to emerge that Ashby had met with Brough three times in March 2011. Brough also may or may not have had a meeting at this time with well-known LNP member and party donor Clive Palmer about whether he'd stump up $200,000 in a fighting fund to 'destroy' Slipper. Palmer demurred, since he had his own agenda taking shape at the time and, as it turned out, was not going to stay within the LNP fold much longer himself.

Ashby had also met with Wyatt Roy, the young MP from Longman, who either told Ashby to diarise what was going on in order to better bring charges of sexual harassment (according to Roy) or asked him to copy Slipper's parliamentary diary and forward it on (according to Ashby). Indeed, according to Ashby, Roy went so far as to give him a sheet of paper with detailed instructions on what to do. This was to become significant down the track.

Ashby had also met with Christopher Pyne, at Roy's instigation, and Pyne allegedly confirmed that, if he moved against Slipper, he'd be looked after both in terms of legal representation and a job—probably in the Queensland government of Campbell Newman, who everyone correctly assumed was about to win a landslide victory against then-premier Anna Bligh in the upcoming state election. Again, the details of this meeting were to be hotly disputed down the track.

Subsequently, in April 2012, Ashby made explosive allegations against Slipper, presenting evidence of 'sexually explicit' text messages and claiming that the speaker had been in the process of 'forming a sexual relationship'. Over two hundred pages of correspondence between the pair would be made public in the eventual sexual harassment case. The case completely blindsided Slipper, who had no idea that Ashby was plotting against him, and the calls for his resignation became harder for the government to ignore.

If the harassment allegations against Slipper weren't enough, he also faced a new slew of apparent travel rorts, suggesting that he'd charged the taxpayer $954 to be shuttled between some nice wineries around Canberra. He'd been able to dodge accusations around his use of travel allowances before, but this time there'd be more than the predictable 'Our Greedy Pollies' headlines: coming as they did on the back of the existing scandals, his position as speaker was becoming increasingly untenable.

The question of the exact source of the information about his travel arrangements was hinted at when Brough was subpoenaed by the Australian Federal Police on 24 July, five days before he was preselected as the LNP's candidate for Fisher. Sure, that suggested behind-the-scenes manoeu-vring; but when Ashby accepted a settlement of $50,000 over the failure of the government to provide him with a safe workplace, it seemed clear that things were moving in the Opposition's direction.

In October Abbott and the Coalition (and Wilkie, and the newly independent ex-Nationals Western Australian MP Tony Crook) moved for the removal of Slipper as speaker, without success. By this point Gillard was losing the war, but she did at least win one battle: Abbott's crocodile tears about Slipper's sexist text messages and his declaration that Gillard was leading 'a government that should have already died of shame'[3] prompted what was arguably her finest moment in

3 The 'shame' dig was a deliberate echo of Alan Jones' much-circulated statement at a Sydney University Young Liberals function, when he claimed that Gillard's father had 'died of shame'.

parliament, when she tore strips off the Opposition leader with what became known as 'the misogyny speech':

'I say to the leader of the Opposition I will not be lectured about sexism and misogyny by this man. I will not. And the government will not be lectured about sexism and misogyny by this man. Not now, not ever. The leader of the Opposition says that people who hold sexist views and who are misogynists are not appropriate for high office. Well, I hope the leader of the Opposition has got a piece of paper and he is writing out his resignation. Because if he wants to know what misogyny looks like in modern Australia, he doesn't need a motion in the House of Representatives, he needs a mirror.'

Unfortunately for Gillard, events were shortly to overtake her: Slipper resigned, tearfully, on that same day.

In February 2013 it was announced that the Australian Federal Police had suspended their investigation into Brough and Ashby, and Brough handily won the seat of Fisher that September, with Slipper, who stood as an independent, garnering a pitiful total of 1207 votes in his former seat.

The sexual harassment case against Slipper fizzled early; there was a costs ruling against Slipper in August 2012, but then the case against him was thrown out of court in December 2012. Ashby lodged a motion to appeal against this decision in 2013 and this was granted in February 2014, but his appeal was finally dropped by his lawyers in June 2014, when they decided they'd had about enough. Ashby attempted to have Slipper pick up the costs of the legal battle (although Slipper's were covered by the Commonwealth, thanks to an 'act of grace' passed by Special Minister of State Gary Gray in 2012) and lost, meaning he was left on the hook for around $3 million in legal fees.

By July 2015 Ashby was working as an adviser for One Nation and personal pilot for Pauline Hanson, and Slipper's political career was well and truly over. Mal Brough, on the other hand, was in government and about to be elevated to the high-trust role of Special Minister of State, responsible for ensuring that all ministers and departments behaved to the high standard expected of them.

And that's where things would have rested, had Brough been a little bit less smug about what a very clever boy he'd been.

———

While the AFP had suspended its investigation, that didn't mean the matter was closed. This little distinction didn't appear to occur to Brough though, so when *60 Minutes* interviewed him on camera about the whole matter, he wasn't perhaps as circumspect as might have been wise.

'Did you ask James Ashby to produce copies of Peter Slipper's diary for you?' asked Liz Hayes in the episode which aired on 27 September 2015, to which Brough, on camera, replied, 'Yes, I did.'

'Why did you do that?'

'Because I believed Peter Slipper had committed a crime.'

The problem with this statement was that it contradicted what Brough and Ashby had both been insisting all along. Ashby, for example, had assured Alan Jones on air that Brough had 'never, never, ever, ever' asked that the diary be copied.

And just to be clear: copying and distributing information from the diary was a serious crime. Technically, it was several crimes. Specifically, the warrants that had allowed searches in

18 November 2015 of the premises of Brough, Ashby, Karen Doane and then-News journalist Steve Lewis made clear that the AFP was investigating breaches of the Crimes Act and of the Criminal Code. So this was no small thing.

Shadow attorney-general Mark Dreyfus asked Brough in parliament on 30 November: 'Isn't it true that the Federal Court judgment was handed down before the minister admitted on national television to procuring copies of the former speaker's official diary?' But Brough insisted that the *60 Minutes* footage had been edited and he had in fact made no such admission.

On 2 December *60 Minutes* helpfully released the unedited footage of the interview, which showed that Hayes had stopped the question midway through—as a plane flew overhead—and then repeated it. Brough's answer had been exactly what went to air and had not been edited.

So now there were three exciting problems for the Special Minister of State. One, that he had implicated himself in a criminal conspiracy (and also revealed that Ashby had lied about Brough's involvement); two, that he had misled parliament, which was a serious offence that would require resignation at the very least, made all the more embarrassing since ... three, he was the Special Minister of State, with oversight of parliamentary behaviour and conduct, and therefore couldn't exactly claim that he didn't realise what he was doing.

Ashby was interviewed on *60 Minutes*, where he said that he'd been offered a job and legal protection by Christopher Pyne, who supposedly also warned that he'd denounce Ashby as a liar if this got out. The AFP's investigation now snapped back into life, as did Roy and Pyne.

The former suffered from a tragic sudden onset of meeting-specific amnesia, becoming regretfully unable to confirm in mid-December whether he'd said anything to anyone about copying and/or distributing diaries, or giving documents with specific instructions thereon.

Pyne had far better recall, specifically that he had idly mused that if Ashby wished to leave Slipper's employ then there might be some sort of employment opportunity for him at a state level after the LNP won the 2012 Queensland election, in theory. However, he made very clear to media and subsequent investigators that his statements to Ashby were merely speculative in nature, definitely in no way constituting either the inducement of a job or legal protection.

Despite the gathering vultures, Brough was prepared to brazen it out as late as 2 December, when he made a qualified apology to parliament, explaining that he wished to clarify his earlier statement regarding what he'd said to *60 Minutes*. His claim that the question had been edited was because his recollection of the interview was that 'the question was put to me in a somewhat disjointed manner. I answered the question without clarifying what part of the question I was responding to.'

It was not clear which part of the question could have been answered with a 'yes' or 'no', aside from the bit about whether Brough had told Ashby to copy the diaries. So Dreyfus decided to clarify things further: 'I ask the same question that was asked by Channel Nine's Liz Hayes on *60 Minutes*.

Did you ask James Ashby to procure copies of Peter Slipper's diary for you?'

'No,' Brough replied.

So, to recap, to this question Brough had answered 'yes' on TV and 'no' in parliament. This was going to be tricky for Brough to spin. However, it was all made a good deal easier when the Queensland LNP executive failed to endorse him for preselection for the next election, at which point he didn't have much choice about whether or not his political career had come to a sudden halt. On 29 December he made a voluntary(ish) statement that he'd decided to stand down from his ministerial position for the good of the party, and in February he confirmed that he would not be contesting the next election.

The matter was still open, of course. The AFP interviewed both Pyne and Roy about it again in January; in February it successfully applied to access federal government computers to search for evidence; and in May it successfully accessed details and papers relating to the unsuccessful sexual harassment case in the Federal Court.[4]

And with that, Mal took the fall. But at least he had some company on the way down.

———

In November 2015 South Australian MP Jamie Briggs was feeling on top of the world. He was cities minister—a junior ministry, sure, but at least he wasn't a backbencher. And that

---

4 AFP commissioner Andrew Colvin was very coy when speaking to the Senate Estimates committee in early May 2016. 'What I will say is that the majority of the investigation has been completed. However, there are still a couple of significant avenues of inquiry that we are following.'

could easily have happened: his two years in the gig hadn't exactly been a series of high-profile triumphs, and he was a known Abbott loyalist. Indeed, he'd drunkenly partied down with the deposed leader following the leadership coup and turned up the following day in a wheelchair, insisting that he'd torn his anterior cruciate ligament during his morning jog rather than, as was actually the case, while drunkenly trying to crash-tackle the shirtless ex-PM for some reason.

That might have been the first public hint that maybe this Briggs chap wasn't quite as agile as one would expect for a Turnbull minister, or even that maybe he was a bit of a boozily loose cannon and potential liability.

But there he was, in a bar in Hong Kong, having a whale of a time. He and some staffers from the Department of Foreign Affairs and Trade had been swanning about on a fact-finding trip to 'inform the Australian government's agenda for the future of Australia's urban areas, including discussions around innovative finance, long-term strategic planning and accessible housing', and ended up finding some lovely refreshing Friday night facts at Stormies, a popular bar in Lan Kwai Fong, with his chief of staff, Stuart Eaton, and a young vice-consul working with the Australian consulate-general in Hong Kong.

Briggs had been entranced by the 'piercing eyes' of said staffer and complimented her thereon, in the sort of casual, perfectly normal eye-piercingness assessment that all diplomats recognise is part and parcel of any professional relationship. And while both Briggs and the woman in question agree that this exchange took place, their stories differ wildly from this point on.

According to Briggs, he and this woman had a few drinks, parted with a touch on the shoulder and a peck on the cheek, and then he and Eaton went back to their respective hotel rooms, where the minister would have a well-earned rest before heading off in the morning to carry on doing his very tippity-toppity best at finding exciting new facts on behalf of the people of Australia.

According to the woman in question, Briggs was 'intoxicated'—a suggestion not contradicted by the news that Briggs had left his phone somewhere during the evening—and had been 'overly affectionate'. On the following Monday she contacted Eaton to advise that while she didn't want to make a formal complaint about Briggs' behaviour, he should warn the minister that he had not acted appropriately and that he needed to watch himself.

Things escalated, however. An internal memo was filed in DFAT and a senior officer decided a review was warranted, guaranteeing that this would come to the attention of foreign minister Julie Bishop. A meeting of senior cabinet members was convened.

As the story got more traction, rumours of other less-than-ministerial behaviour emerged as former staffer Rebekha Sharkie—who was, admittedly, gearing up to run against Briggs in Mayo as candidate for the Nick Xenophon Team and therefore had a decent impetus to paint him in a less-than-flattering hue—made the comment that she'd left his employ because of difficulties in his office, including that females were treated as 'either beauty queens or ironing ladies'.

With the writing now covering pretty much every inch of available wall, Briggs announced his resignation on 29 December. His statement was unambiguous: his crime, for which he was willing to resign his ministry, was that he had a drink while on an official trip—and he knew that going to a bar was the sort of breach of public trust up with which the Australian people would not put.

'At the conclusion of the dinner (which I paid for personally) we went to a popular and as it transpired very crowded bar for drinks during which we interacted between the three of us and with others in what I believed, at the time, was an informal manner,' he wrote. 'At no point was it my intention to act inappropriately and I'm obliged to note for the record that nothing illegal has been alleged or in fact did occur. However, in the days following the evening, the public servant concerned raised concerns about the appropriateness of my behaviour towards her at the venue.'

Despite his paying for dinner and not intending to act inappropriately, for some reason she'd grasped the wrong end of his intention-stick. But that's not the reason he was quitting, mind.

'I've apologised directly to her but after careful reflection about the concerns she raised and the fact that I was at a bar late at night while on an overseas visit I have concluded this behaviour has not met the particularly high standards for ministers.'

Noble words indeed, somewhat undercut by certain revelations percolating through the media, such as that a photo of the woman—which mysteriously turned up on the front page of the *Weekend Australian*—had been taken by Briggs, was on his phone and had been sent to colleagues, presumably to clarify that her eyes were indeed noticeably piercing. This little detail did not enhance the prevailing opinion of Briggs' professionalism and reliability.

The story was making its way elsewhere, too, with *The Australian*'s Samantha Maiden writing a particularly scathing column about Briggs' being 'dumb as all get out' to behave thusly while on an official trip.

Given the oft-convivial relationship between the government and *The Australian*, this criticism burned. Fortunately Briggs had the unwavering support of well-wishers like immigration minister Peter Dutton, who texted commiserations, including his assessment of Maiden as a 'mad fucking witch'.

Unfortunately, in Dutton's passion, he didn't send the text to Briggs so much as to Maiden, who openly mocked him on the matter on morning television. 'I think some of these MPs, they're having a bit of a problem with their phones,' she said on *Today*. 'They might just want to put them down.'[5]

Labor called for a formal investigation by the government, on the grounds that the leaking of the photo would appear to constitute victimisation of someone who had made an allegation of sexual harassment. Turnbull declined to do so, arguing that official probes 'tend to come up with very little'—and in February the Public Service Commissioner shrugged and said it was really an issue for DFAT, where the matter died.

---

5 One assumes she meant that the phones should be put down, rather than the ministers. Impressively, as of June 2016 Maiden's own Twitter bio included the description 'totally mad witch'.

Even so, that was two ministers down. And there was already another drama brewing.

———

Few folks outside of Queensland's Gold Coast had heard the name Stuart Robert before. The member for the safe LNP seat of Fadden had not exactly distinguished himself since being elected in 2007 following the retirement of long-time Liberal MP David Jull. Since then he'd pretty much been seen, if anything, to be an unmemorable part of the bloc of members affiliated with Scott Morrison, who were notable only for being mainly NSW-based and mainly Pentacostalist.

He'd been Abbott's assistant defence minister but, that aside, this former soldier had not captured the nation's attention until he was promoted, somewhat surprisingly, to the ministries of both Human Services and Veteran's Affairs.

This was interpreted as being in recognition of Robert's successful wrangling during the leadership challenge of a bloc of votes for Turnbull. Those votes had been decisive in his taking the prime ministership and, because Morrison himself had voted for Abbott, it ensured that Turnbull had the numbers without Morrison being directly implicated in the betrayal of his leader—at least, not initially.

Robert's time in his new gigs was, however, to be short-lived.

It soon came to light that in August 2014 he'd popped over to Beijing, where his old pal (and large-scale Liberal Party donor) Paul Marks was signing a deal between Nimrod Resources, of which Marks was the chair, and the Chinese government-owned China Minmetals.

This didn't at first appear to be anything particularly noteworthy, until reports started to surface that Robert had given a little speech at the ceremony, which seemed a bit official-ish. It certainly appeared that way to the Chinese government; in the press release announcing the deal, Robert's involvement was portrayed as having been an official duty by an Australian government minister.

At this point Robert would probably have weathered the scandal if he'd argued that there must have been a misunderstanding and that the Minmetals executives had misinterpreted his support for an old friend as being the Australian government giving its imprimatur to a business deal. Instead, he went for a blanket denial, insisting that he went to China 'in a personal capacity' and that he'd paid for the trip himself.[6]

However, a few things then came to light. One was that Robert was an investor in Metallum Holdings Pty Ltd, which in turn had an interest in Nimrod—meaning that Robert stood to materially benefit from the Chinese deal.

Second, it was confirmed by Minmetals' own website that Robert had attended 'on behalf of the Australian Department of Defence' and had even given a speech about how 'the good relationship between Nimrod and the Australian Government will effectively promote the success of the operation'—which rather undercut the notion that he was just there as his pal's plus one. He also reportedly presented a medal to Chairman Zhou, one of the senior Communist Party officials, supposedly on behalf of the prime minister. This was all accompanied by pictures of the ceremony, including shots of Robert presenting officials with things.

---

6   Although he did feel cool about charging taxpayers $900 in flights and transfers from the Gold Coast to Sydney to catch the flight.

When this started to blow up, Labor demanded answers as to whether the Turnbull government was doing favours for big donors to get their resources deals over the line.

Perhaps sensing that this was a lost cause, not even a week elapsed between Robert being lambasted in parliament (on 7 February) and stepping down from the ministry (on 12 February). Perhaps the PM's patience had worn out after the Brough and Briggs brouhahas. Whatever, Stuart Robert was clearly hung out to dry—and the person who seemed the most furious about the entire thing was Scott Morrison, who fumed that the punishment of his friend was unwarranted; he declared it 'a massive overreach and . . . a shocking beat-up'.

There were some rumblings about whether the sacrifice of one of the treasurer's cadre would damage the relationship between Morrison and Turnbull, but by this stage they both had bigger things to disagree over.

In any case, by May Robert was defending his use of office money to run two of his staffers as candidates in the Gold Coast local council elections—one, Kristyn Boulton, as an independent, without any disclosure that she worked in his office—with the explicit intention of stacking the council against Labor. And that might have been terribly embarrassing, but Robert was a backbencher by that point and therefore no-one really cared, so the matter barely caused a ripple.

Sure, this all looked bad—but the Turnbull ministry still had some secret plans and clever tricks . . .

7

LOVE AND (EXCLUSIVELY STRAIGHT) MARRIAGE, AKA THE RIGHT TO BE A BIGOT, REDUX

In which the government creates—and the Cat maintains—a completely unnecessary problem for itself

As far as symbolic issues inexplicably beloved by the conservative end of politics go, there have been few as passionately fought as their resolute objection to same-sex marriage.

Which is weird, since marriage is about as conservative an institution as one can get. It is championed by hardline right-wingers, who—as we were reminded only a chapter or so ago—are typically enthusiastic about explaining exactly why single parents, unmarried couples and those who indulge in pre-marital sex deserve every terrible consequence that said hardline right-wingers could contrive to throw at them.

Yet the second that gay couples started making noises about possibly tying themselves into exclusive, stable relationships of the sort expected of straight ones—indeed, for a long time all but demanded of them—marriage was apparently under threat. And thus it was no surprise that the Abbott government fought hard to ensure that marriage equality was kept off the agenda for as long as possible, despite entirely understandable pressure from within and without the party. The issue was clearly destined to be a source of contention that would not go away.

On the one hand, Prime Minister Abbott, the Nationals and the religious conservatives in the Liberal Party had zero intention of letting them gay folks use up the nation's precious and apparently finite stores of marriage, lest they tarnish its sanctity in some irreversible and yet-to-be-determined manner.

On the other hand, the majority of western democracies were unambiguously moving in the direction of marriage equality and there was growing public pressure for progress in Australia. Polling consistently estimated support for same-sex marriage at somewhere between two-thirds and three-quarters of the Australian population, while actual opposition to it hovered at less than 10 per cent.

Even the Victorian Country Women's Association—not an organisation generally regarded as being at the forefront of progressive issues—was to make the surprising announcement in May 2016 that it was in favour of marriage equality, indicating that this was no longer some sort of a fringe matter exclusive to inner-city lefties.[1]

---

1   You know that this book was written by a bearded, bespectacled man frantically typing in a caffeine-fuelled haze in cafés in Sydney's inner west, right? Good.

Ahead of the 2013 election Abbott had avoided being locked into any clear position on same-sex marriage by insisting that it was a matter for the party room to debate once in government—and then he spent his first eighteen months in government assiduously ensuring that it didn't get debated in the party room.

This was a bold move. After all, with the UK, New Zealand, Canada and other countries with similar cultures (and, in many cases, reciprocal visa arrangements) embracing marriage equality, it seemed inevitable that Australia would eventually be forced to recognise foreign same-sex marriages from its allies and trading partners. The issue was made more urgent in 2015 as a referendum allowing same-sex marriage was passed by the religiously conservative Catholic Republic of Ireland, followed by the US Supreme Court ruling that state bans were unconstitutional and that same-sex marriage was therefore legal across all fifty states.

The local outcry against this was predictable, with Abbott insisting that just because all Australia's friends were choosing to jump off their universal civil rights bridge, it didn't mean that they had to do it.

'What happens in the United States is obviously a matter for the United States, just as what happened in Ireland a few weeks ago is a matter for the Irish,' he pontificated, while then-employment minister Eric Abetz penned a Fairfax op ed piece in which he lamented: 'The US Supreme Court majority has set a dangerous precedent for the US by asserting that the American people have, since inception, somehow misunderstood their own constitution.'

There was some public discussion that Australia might follow Ireland's lead and hold a referendum, but the PM explained to the ABC on 25 May that 'questions of marriage are the preserve of the Commonwealth parliament'. And that was entirely true, having been demonstrated in 2004 when the definition of marriage was changed to specify that only opposite-sex couples could marry, and again in 2010 when a bill introduced by Greens senator Sarah Hanson-Young legislating same-sex marriage was voted down by both the Coalition and Labor.

Despite this, when the 44th Parliament started considering the matter, which was indisputably within its preserve, Tony was somewhat less than supportive. He reacted angrily when Liberal Democrat senator David Leyonhjelm, the Greens and Labor each announced their own plans to introduce marriage equality legislation, arguing that it was not because he opposed the issue in question, you understand—why, perish the very thought!—but purely because he didn't care for their divisive and partisan tone for, as he piously explained, 'If our parliament were to make a big decision on a matter such as this, it ought to be owned by the parliament and not by any particular party.'

And yet, given Abbott's evident zeal for multi-party ownership of the issue within the exclusive preserve of the Commonwealth parliament, he was less than entirely delighted with the announcement in July that a marriage equality bill was being co-sponsored by Liberal backbencher Warren Entsch and Labor MP Terri Butler, seconded by a multi-party coalition of Liberal MP Teresa Gambaro,

Labor MP Laurie Ferguson, independents Cathy McGowan and Andrew Wilkie, and the Greens' Adam Bandt.[2]

With the announcement of the bill it appeared for a brief, shining moment as though the government was preparing to make a strategic retreat and was about to embrace what is, after all, a stone-cold historical certainty. By allowing his backbenchers to introduce the legislation, the PM could have enjoyed multiple victories: he could have still personally opposed the very notion of The Gays getting married, thereby placating the party's conservative supporters; he could have appeared to be a pragmatic leader, not wedded to any rigid ideology and with respect for the rule of law; and, most importantly, this would have removed marriage equality as a dangerous wedge issue well ahead of the election.

Furthermore, by showing flexibility and clear support for his backbench, he'd have slowed the momentum of the leadership challenge that was to come. And finally, given that support for expanding the definition of marriage was one of the big symbolic issues making Turnbull more appealing as leader, for Abbott to have stolen the potential challenger's thunder would have been an impressive tactic. It's not even all that likely that the legislation would have passed, given that many Coalition MPs were weighing up whether voting on a matter of principle was worth having their card marked by the prime minister.

---

2 In other words, literally every party and independent in the lower house with the exception of the outspokenly anti-gay Queensland independent Bob Katter, who had memorably insisted in 1989 that he would 'walk to Bourke backwards if the poof population of North Queensland is any more than 0.001 per cent' (a few years before his younger brother and future Labor candidate Carl rather inconveniently came out as gay) and PUP's Clive Palmer—who, to be fair, would have had to actually turn up in parliament to sponsor it.

In short, a free vote on marriage equality could have given Abbott a desperately needed opportunity to defuse the ticking time bomb that was his leadership.

However, he chose to speed up the timer instead, and so he called for the matter to be decided by the worst of all options: a national plebiscite.

Abbott had learned his lessons well when prosecuting the pro-monarchy case during the ill-fated push for an Australian republic—another historical inevitability over which he fought with Malcolm Turnbull.

Getting that issue to the point of a referendum, as the pro-republic side of the debate soon discovered, was less than half the battle. Australians don't like voting and resent being forced to do so, and just about every Australian referendum has failed (a total of eight of the forty-four referenda since federation have resulted in a 'yes' vote).

What was even better about the same-sex marriage vote was that it wouldn't even be a referendum, which is both compulsory and legally binding. No, this would be a plebiscite: a voluntary national vote with similar legal standing to public voting in the Logies.

The three plebiscites held in Australia have enjoyed results as stellar as the referenda. The first two failed in their attempts to enshrine military conscription and to increase military commitment to overseas battlefronts during World War I.[3]

---

3   These public votes were called referenda at the time, but have been retroactively defined as plebiscites because the results were non-binding and because the government already had the unambiguous legislative power to rule on the matter, so it was effectively an opinion poll to defuse a controversial issue.

However, the most recent one, in 1977, succeeded in replacing 'God Save the Queen' with 'Advance Australia Fair' as the national song (although, since it was a multiple-choice plebiscite, it was destined to produce some sort of a result.)[4]

The reason the same-sex marriage vote would be a plebiscite was due to the happy situation that marriage was not a topic covered by the Australian Constitution. Until 1961 it wasn't even a federal concern: the states had their own individual marriage laws, containing varying degrees of racism,[5] until the federal government decided that having marriages appear and disappear at state borders didn't make a lick of sense. Thus the feds took the matter under their legislative wing and created a uniform definition that was entrenched in the *Marriage Act 1961*—where it remained essentially unchanged until 2004, when John Howard saw the need to legislate that only straight folk could marry.

The government had already done its homework on this matter. Abbott had looked into the plebiscite strategy in 2011 when those from the opposition side of the house had briefly attempted to force a plebiscite on the Gillard government's ill-fated Carbon Pollution Reduction Scheme. So he presumably already had a folder in his desk drawer marked 'Po-Faced

---

4   Incidentally, that's 'national song', not 'national anthem': 'God Save the Queen' remained Australia's anthem until 1984, when it was finally officially replaced by 'Advance Australia Fair'. However, in the 1977 plebiscite AAF won 43.29 per cent of the vote, beating out 'God Save the Queen', 'Song of Australia' and 'Waltzing Matilda'. The result might surprise readers, but that's because the release of the nation's true anthem—John Farnham's 'Pressure Down'—was still nine long years away.

5   It's probably not going to surprise anyone to learn that Aboriginal folks had their ability to marry—especially to marry white people—administratively curtailed in Queensland, right?

Delaying Tactics' and he was ready to have the words 'Carbon Tax' scratched out and replaced with the words 'Not-marriage for The Gays'.

Dispatching a spokesperson to release a statement to the press on 12 August, the PM reiterated that he was a supporter of the current definition of marriage and that private members' bills, such as the proposed multi-party legislation, were generally not debated in the party room and therefore would be unlikely to come before parliament—and that there was no guarantee of a free vote on the issue in any case.[6] Thus there would be no movement towards allowing legislation on same-sex marriage to be introduced during the current term of parliament but, after the next election, he would consider 'a people's vote', rather than a mere 'parliament's vote'.

This very much hung Entsch and Gambaro out to dry, offering them the chance either to have their legislation ignored or, were it permitted to go before the lower house, to be forced to vote against it along party lines.

The following week Entsch and Butler's bill was read in parliament, while Abbott was making his aforementioned exciting announcement about the dangers of ice addiction, with only two ministers sitting prominently in the otherwise-empty

---

6   Specifically, the statement read: 'Any member can introduce a private member's bill into the parliament but they do not come before the joint party room for discussion unless they will be voted on in the parliament. It is rare for a private member's bill to be voted on and any bill would be subject to the usual process . . . The prime minister's position remains the same as it has always been and he supports the current policy that marriage is between a man and a woman.' It's worth noting, since this appeared to be lost on the PM, that the proposed law also supported marriage being between a man and a woman: legislating for same-sex marriage didn't immediately invalidate opposite-sex marriages or anything.

front bench: education minister Christopher Pyne and communications minister Malcolm Turnbull.

———

Yet, in spite of his own personal beliefs, Turnbull committed himself to this plebiscite when he renewed his party's marriage vows with the Nationals in September 2015, even though the problems with the plebiscite were immediately obvious.

No-one seemed under any illusions regarding its purpose. Clearly the plan was to offer the glorious illusion of direct democracy in action even as it quietly allowed those tasked with actual representative democracy to sidestep the messy responsibility of doing their jobs.

For before the plebiscite could happen, there would have to be a ruling on what question it would ask—a divisive and combative process that could be drawn out indefinitely. And then, supposedly, it would be followed by an education period to make the public aware of the arguments supporting both the Yes and No cases.

In a telling indication of just how respectful and sensible the No camp was planning to be, in February 2016 the Australian Christian Lobby announced that it would seek a temporary suspension of Australian anti-discrimination and hate speech laws for the duration of the campaign.[7]

Then there was also the small issue that a plebiscite still wasn't going to actually make same-sex marriage legal in

---

7 Incidentally, the popular 'frame the question in such a way that even the advocates of the matter under discussion can't agree to support it' strategy was a roaring success in thwarting moves toward Australia becoming a republic, and is currently working exactly as planned with all discussions about constitutional recognition for Indigenous Australians. It's a versatile trick.

Australia—it would only act as a very arduous national poll on the matter. There would still need to be a parliamentary vote to create any legislative change.

At first the general assumption appeared to be that if the vote came up Yes then the government and opposition would agree to wave the legislation through. Indeed, Turnbull insisted that: 'When the Australian people make their decision, that decision will stick. It will be decisive. It will be respected by this government and by this parliament and this nation ... Let me tell you this. If you imagine that any government ... would spend over $150 million consulting every Australian on an issue of this kind and then ignore their decision, then they really are not living in the real world.'

Unfortunately it was already perfectly clear that some of his party didn't much care for this 'real world' thing and it didn't take long for conservative politicians to walk away from any suggestion that they'd let marriage equality pass just because the people had voted for it. Eric Abetz, for one, promptly announced that he had no intention of being hemmed in by any plebiscite outcome he didn't like, and he and other gay-marriage-averse MPs and senators would vote according to their consciences—almost as though, despite Abbott and Turnbull's protestations to the contrary, it was a matter to be determined in the traditional way within parliament.[8]

'Every member of parliament will make up his or her mind after the plebiscite is held,' Abetz declared to *The Guardian*

8　Which, to be fair, it is.

in January 2016. 'People will take into account the views of the electorate, the views of the nation and their own personal views. It would be up to each member to decide whether the plebiscite accurately reflects the views of the Australian people, whether it reflects the views of their electorates and whether it is good or bad public policy in their view.'

And although Turnbull and other pro-change Liberals still insisted that the parliament would accept the plebiscite result (with Warren Entsch pointedly telling Fairfax: 'It will be a very brave individual . . . who seeks to challenge the views of the Australian people'), they were awkwardly hazy regarding any details as to how that might work legislatively. Constitutionally dubious suggestions were bandied about, such as pre-passing legislation that would be triggered into law by the plebiscite result, but whenever the PM was asked how, exactly, he could prevent his party from blocking the law regardless of a Yes vote, he was reduced to spouting variations of 'because I said so'.

However, on top of all of the excellent go-slow and get-out-of-plebiscite-free cards available to those keen to stop marriage equality, there's another handy thing for conservatives about the plebiscite, which can't have been lost on those of them with a knowledge of the constitution. And it is this: under Section 51 of the Constitution of Australia, only the federal government has the right to create laws and parliament holds the exclusive power to legislate around marriage (Section 51 (xxi)) and 'divorce and matrimonial causes; and in relation thereto, parental rights, and the custody and guardianship of infants' (Section 51 (xxii)).

This means that any law resulting from a piece of tabled legislation and by a method other than by a vote in parliament—by some sort of plebiscite, let's say—would be at best highly unusual and quite possibly constitutionally invalid. So, in the event that the people of Australia voted Yes and the government actually moved to legislate on the matter, and not enough MPs and senators bravely ignored the result, there would still be an opportunity for an appeal to the federal court to argue that the law had been made via a method other than federal parliament, and was therefore invalid under Section 51. It might not work, but at least it would be another time-consuming and expensive delaying tactic—and that, after all, is the strategy to which the government is already committed.

In other words: sacrificing a vote in parliament on existing legislation in favour of months (if not years) of debate, a bitter national culture war, a $160 million public vote, a potential split of the Liberal Party, and a costly and drawn-out High Court challenge could easily result in absolutely nothing at all.

———

While viewed positively by a clear majority of Australians, marriage equality has struggled to achieve the necessary level of urgency in Australia, partially because of social inertia and partially because same-sex partners have the option of officially registering as de facto couples, meaning that most—but by no means all—of the rights of married couples are applicable to them. And this was often cited by anti-marriage-equality adherents as evidence that going to all the trouble of removing the words added to the Marriage Act in 2004 was just unnecessarily onerous busywork for our parliament to waste time over.

So queer folks couldn't have a wedding, or any official recognition of their union. They could apply to access a late partner's superannuation, for heaven's sake! Was that not enough? After all, what difference does a piece of paper make?[9]

In January 2016, even as Eric Abetz was sniffily refusing to respect any theoretical plebiscite result, the legal importance of having one's marriage recognised was made horrifically clear.

British newlyweds David and Marco Bulmer-Rizzi were embarking on their dream holiday—a trip around Australia—when tragedy struck. While staying in a house in Adelaide, David slipped on the stairs and fell, smashing his head open at the bottom of the stairwell. He was put in a medically induced coma, but his injuries were too severe. He never regained consciousness.

And then things got even worse for the heartbroken Marco, who discovered that he had no rights regarding his late husband. The death certificate stated that David was 'never married'. Marco couldn't arrange a funeral or have the body returned to the UK since, as far as Australian authorities were concerned, he was basically a stranger. David's father, Nigel Bulmer, had to authorise everything as the recognised next of kin. South Australian premier Jay Weatherill apologised

---

9   Some readers might reflect on the logical consistency shown by those arguing that marriage was so gosh-darn important that its 'sanctity' couldn't be sullied by gay couples while also lambasting said gay couples over making such a fuss over so unimportant a thing as marriage. One might even conclude that the anti-equality side was basically a bunch of bigots and hypocrites—but that, obviously, would be incredibly unkind and accurate.

personally to Marco and to David's family, declaring that he was 'deeply ashamed', making the entirely reasonable point that 'a man's just lost his husband, someone he deeply loves, someone he's legally married to, and he's been treated with disrespect in my state'. But Australian law was clear: Marco was not David's husband.[10]

This despicable mess was followed by a memorable on-screen interview with the head of the Australian Christian Lobby, Lyle Shelton, who revealed that he'd already been sounded out by the government to take a leadership role in the No case for the plebiscite. In order to show why he'd been proposed for such an honour, he put forward the only cogent anti-same-sex-marriage argument hitherto expressed. Appearing on Sky News, Shelton was asked by host Patricia Karvelas to explain how other people being able to marry would affect him in any way whatsoever. And my, he was ready! In a moment of breathtaking idiocy he explained proudly: 'If the definition of marriage is changed, it's no longer assumed . . . that I'm married to a woman. So that affects me straight away.'

Karvelas, to her considerable credit, didn't immediately burst into uncontrollable laughter but instead asked the question to which she and everyone else watching already knew the answer: 'So you're worried that people may think you're gay if the law changes?'

---

10 Just to add further insult to an already horrendous situation, Hong Kong airport authorities confiscated David's ashes from Marco on the grounds that since same-sex marriages are not recognised there either, Marco couldn't possibly be David's next of kin. It was eventually sorted out and Marco was able to finally bring David home, but . . . seriously?

'They may or may not,' Shelton replied, 'but certainly the terms of my marriage have changed, and of the millions of other marriages in Australia.'

And at that moment, the country discovered just how pathetically flimsy a case the anti-equality side possessed, and the pro-change side figured they'd be looking at a victory by default.

But then a new front opened up in the DelCon's strange, sad culture war. And this time, the victims were children.

————

The Safe Schools Coalition began life as an independent organisation created by the Foundation for Young Australia, supported by a coalition of non-government organisations, including the WA AIDS Council, SHine SA, Family Planning NSW and other state-based organisations dealing with sexuality and sexual health issues. As elucidated at the Safe Schools website, 'Safe Schools Coalition Australia is a national network of organisations working with schools to create safer and more inclusive environments for same sex attracted, intersex and gender diverse students, staff and families.'

And to that end the coalition created resources and support for any school that chooses to get involved in tailoring anti-bullying programs to meet the needs of its students, whether in the public, independent or faith-based sectors. The system is opt-in, and the resources can be used as much or as little as the school deems appropriate.

At first glance—and at second, third and all subsequent glances—this would appear to be spectacularly smart and highly necessary, given the high rate of youth suicide in Australia (for those aged 15–19, the rate is 5.6 per 100,000 for females and 14.3 per 100,000 for males; for those 20–24, it's 6.5 for females and 17.7 for males).[11]

There is a strong link between suicide and issues around sexuality and sexual identity. The highest correlation is among young transsexuals, where 84 per cent have reportedly considered ending their lives and, shockingly, half have actually attempted it, while gay, lesbian and bisexual young people have fourteen times the rate of suicide attempts as their straight peers.

The greatest reason given for wanting out is bullying, sometimes by family or strangers but most often—80 per cent of the time, in fact—by peers at school. Apart from suicide and self-harm, bullying of non-straight kids has plenty of other negative outcomes: it worsens school performance, and creates higher rates of youth homelessness and survival prostitution, as well as higher rates of addiction and resultant poor health. In short, doing something about addressing bullying at a school level could have a wide-ranging beneficial effect on preventable ill health, misery and death.

The Safe Schools program was initially rolled out in Victoria in 2011 and proved enormously popular—so much so that in 2013 the Rudd government announced a funding commitment of $8 million to take it nationally. The Abbott government honoured that commitment, with the parliamentary secretary for Education, Scott Ryan, launching the

---

11 The gender difference in statistics is slightly misleading, by the way, since it would seem to indicate that males attempt suicide more often than females. Horribly, that's not really the case. Males tend to choose violent methods that bring quick results, like hanging and gunshot, while females skew more toward poisoning and cutting, which have a higher chance of failure and also of discovery before death. Sorry, this is genuinely heartbreaking stuff.

program nationally in June 2014, noting that: 'What we seek to teach is empathy, to better understand the perspective and experience of another.'

So, naturally, that was the DelCons' new target.

———

Before going on, it's worth pointing out that there were a few legitimate criticisms of Safe Schools floating around. There was a need to bring in external educators, rather than training teachers at a school level, and for proper program evaluation beyond school-based audits, because the lack of hard evidence would make it harder to guarantee ongoing funding. (Anecdotal reports were glowing, but it's important to remember that anecdotes ain't data.) In other words, these were the sorts of things you'd expect to be raised as Safe Schools made the transition from local pilot to a national program.

In January the Australian Christian Lobby began its campaign, joined by other conservative voices, including the News Corp papers (most notably *The Australian* and the regular screed-writers at the *Daily Telegraph* and *Herald Sun*), who misrepresented the scheme, and the curriculum, by railing against what they declared was a 'radical program . . . being used to introduce children from primary school age up to sexual concepts that are not age appropriate'. The claims made by these critics ranged from the seriously misleading to the downright false, including that the program sought to 'teach girls to bind their chests so their breasts won't develop', 'encourage students cross-dressing' and 'teach kids gay and lesbian sexual techniques'.

The Safe Schools material was all freely available online and therefore presumably accessible by politicians curious about what the program actually involved. But that wasn't nearly as much fun as angrily decrying the imaginary version invented by the ACL, and that non-existent version was the one the DelCons set to work opposing.

Tony Abbott, conveniently forgetting that he had been the prime minister who had originally implemented the program nationally, now insisted that 'It's not an anti-bullying program, it's a social engineering program [and] its funding should be terminated', while Eric Abetz claimed it was a 'gateway drug' for children to experiment with sex. Most baffling was the complaint of Cory Bernardi, who insisted that Safe Schools sought to 'indoctrinate children into a Marxist agenda of cultural relativism'—a phrase that distinguishes itself most by its failure to contain any discernible meaning—and who told one constituent via email that 'Bullying isn't something confined to homosexuals yet you are encouraging a program that actually bullies heterosexual children into submission for the gay agenda'.

George Christensen went further, dredging up a contro-versial article called 'Boiled lollies and Band-Aids', written in 1982 for *Gay Information* by Gary Dowsett—the La Trobe University academic who in 2003 had co-authored the ground- and heartbreaking report *Don't Ask, Don't Tell: Hidden in the crowd* that identified the need for research into suicide and self-harm among LGBTI youth and who had worked on research that led to the Safe School program, despite having no actual involvement in the program itself.

Christensen somehow deduced that Professor Dowsett's piece written thirty-four years earlier meant that Safe Schools was overseen by 'a paedophilia advocate'[12] and that, 'Given the shocking information, it's imperative all federal funding for Safe Schools be suspended immediately, pending a full Parliament inquiry.'

Bernardi, Christensen and other furious backbenchers demanded that the PM investigate the insidious cultural Marxism of this anti-bullying program—and, somewhat surprisingly, he did. Education minister Simon Birmingham was given the task—even though, as he pointed out, high schools were state concerns and therefore not under his actual purview—and the conclusion was that the program was, well, fine. A couple of things were tweaked as being not age-appropriate, but for the most part it was concluded that Safe Schools was a worthwhile and valuable addition to the existing programs.

However, this had now become a cultural battleground, inextricably tied to same-sex marriage and, worse yet, Labor values. The Victorian government of Daniel Andrews announced that, regardless of the federal government's opinion, he'd be making Safe Schools part of the state school system. And thems, clearly, were fighting words.

Another concerted barrage of angry public statements later, and Turnbull backed down. Safe Schools would be altered, he made clear: it would be put on a federal government website,

---

12 Just for context, the article—its full title is 'Boiled lollies and Band-Aids: Gay men and kids'—in no way suggests support for, much less advocacy of, paedophilia. Dowsett, a gay man, wrote about how gay parenting was looked at with suspicion from both inside and outside the gay male community. It's not a great piece, to be honest, but it was written at a time when certain schools of thought equated gay liberation with a rejection of the hetero-normative mainstream. Fittingly, the article was published in a journal subtitled, *Information and Ideas as a Stimulus for Thought and a Catalyst for Action.*

where it would have control over content; it would be limited to secondary schools, and only accessible with parental consent. The changes were largely cosmetic, but the DelCons correctly interpreted this as the PM capitulating to their demands.

'It's all going,' a delighted Christensen incorrectly crowed. 'Boys in girls' school uniforms, girls and boys using the same toilets, classroom role plays where kids imagine they have no genitalia or they're gay ... I doubt the Safe Schools Coalition—who came up with the weird and wonderful elements of this, attempting to instil queer theory, sexual liberation and Marxism into classrooms—will accept this. And if they don't, the funding will be cut.'

That wasn't entirely true: the funding, as Birmingham pointed out, had been a one-off and there was no suggestion of ongoing funding that could be cut. But hopes of ensuring the future of the program were clearly now on the back burner, and its very name was now synonymous with the insidious influence of the shadowy, imaginary leftist gay cabal.

Indeed in May, Lyle Shelton went even further on his blog, making the entirely predictable connection between acknowledging human sexual identity and, y'know, Nazis: 'The cowardice and weakness of Australia's "gatekeepers" is causing unthinkable things to happen, just as unthinkable things happened in Germany in the 1930s.'

And with this victory, the DelCons learned the same valuable lesson that all indulged infants learn: if you scream and cry and wet your pants, Mumsie will give you want you want in the hopes that it'll briefly shut you up.

But Mumsie was about to have his patience sorely tested.

8
BOUNCEBACK BILL

*In which the man dismissed as alternative prime minister
starts to look like a viable alternative again*

While grey clouds were starting to gather in the sunny skies of the new Turnbull government, something very odd happened to the Leader of the Opposition during the 2015–16 Christmas break. Somehow, despite his recent poor form and two years of snide jokes, Bill Shorten suddenly—and unexpectedly—started looking like a potentially electable leader.

During the first year of his leadership, Shorten had been the leader that Labor had to have: a tolerable figurehead to keep the party in line while it licked its wounds from the comprehensive shellacking of the 2013 election, mending the factional rifts torn wide open by the Rudd–Gillard–Rudd wars, and rebuilding that party—a process that it could safely assume would take at least two parliamentary terms. After all, the only government that was chucked out after a single term was the cursed Labor government of James Scullin, who had the exquisite poor fortune to be sworn into office in 1929, two days before the great stock market crash that precipitated the Great Depression. So it was generally assumed that there would be no pressure on Shorten to rush things.

Bill Shorten was not particularly well regarded out in the community, simply because he wasn't particularly regarded at all. The first most people knew of the man was when he won the party leadership following Rudd's resignation, narrowly beating left faction rival Anthony Albanese; but before that he'd been one of the 'faceless men' who installed Julia Gillard and then reinstated Kevin Rudd. Sure, maybe a few people remembered him as the articulate union boss liaising with the media during the Beaconsfield mine collapse in 2006, in which one man was killed and two others trapped for over a fortnight, but that was a distant memory at best.

He'd been a competent member of the government since being elected in 2007, first as Parliamentary Secretary for Disabilities and Children's Services under Rudd (where he was one of the architects of the National Disability Insurance Scheme), before being bumped up to Minister for Financial Services and Superannuation under Gillard. Later he added Workplace Relations to his portfolio, before Rudd returned and made him his education minister.

This fast rise seemed to be mainly due to the fact that Shorten's trade union-organising past had made him a powerful figure in the Victorian party. His elevation to the leadership seemed more a matter of him being one of the few people left standing and there being an insufficiently large number of the splintered and wounded party who hated him enough to fight it.

One thing Shorten was, however, was a negotiator. He also had form at stitching broken organisations back together, as evidenced in his work as secretary of the Australian Workers Union, which had been riven by leadership battles and was languishing deeply in debt when he took it on in 2001. He genuinely knew how to cut a deal and how to placate a rival (as his on-again-off-again friendship with Victorian Labor powerbroker and future member for Batman David Feeney demonstrated).

But the AWU turnaround had come at a cost to him: in 1999 he'd been preparing to walk into the safe state seat of Melton, where he'd most likely have risen rapidly under Premier Steve Bracks and perhaps even become premier himself. According to Paul Howes, his mate and successor at the AWU, 'He gave that up to turn the union round.' But it was a calculated gamble, and once there was a possibility of becoming federal leader there was no way he was going to let the bigger prize of the prime ministership slip through his fingers.

As the humiliation of the 2013 election sank in for Labor, it was the perfect time for a man whose main selling points were internal rather than public: he knew how to unite Labor, he was factionally acceptable across the board, and he'd seen worse things. Not exactly the most appealing of packages, all things considered, but it was a definite start.

———

Still, even as the party fell in behind him, no-one seemed to accuse Shorten of being an inspiring leader of the Rudd stripe.

He spoke with the strange, halting, slightly hectoring Labor cadence so many of the party's previous leaders had adopted—Gillard and South Australian premier Mike Rann among them—that suggested the listener was both elderly and hard of hearing (which, to be fair, was a decent bet in South Australia).

He also couldn't land a joke. ABC satirical program *Shaun Micallef's Mad as Hell* turned this into a recurring gag, replaying footage of Shorten awkwardly delivering limp semi-jokes—such as marking the Coalition's abolition of the mining tax with the support of Palmer United with: 'Unfortunately now it would appear that we have two prime ministers in Australia: Prime Minister Abbott and Prime Minister Palmer'—accompanied with a flashing 'ZINGER!' graphic and a tiger's roar.

That, probably more than anything else, seemed to discount Shorten as a serious contender for PM. After all, a successful leader can be hated or feared, but few survive being made to look like a clown.

Fortunately for Shorten, his rival was busily convincing the public he was exactly that—threatening to 'shirtfront' Vladimir Putin at the G20, chomping on an unpeeled onion, and awarding a knighthood to the Duke of Edinburgh in the Australia Day honours.

It's impossible to accuse Labor of winning the hearts and minds of the public, but the tanking approval ratings of Abbott personally and growing unhappiness with his government generally meant that Labor was becoming more electable by default, precisely as Abbott had done in 2013. Nobody predicted it when Shorten took over the leadership, but by the

middle of 2015 it looked as though the man with the obsequi-
ous smile and no comic timing was on track to become the
least popular prime minister ever elected, purely by virtue of
not being Tony Abbott.

Then, of course, the picture changed abruptly as the Liberal
Party replaced its leader with someone less loathed by the
public. Shorten's popularity immediately tanked.

———

The Royal Commission into Trade Union Governance and
Corruption (to cite its full, not-entirely unbiased name)
had been announced in February 2014 by Tony Abbott in
response to findings by the Fair Work Commission, as well
as to the enormous public scandal that had torpedoed the
Gillard government when Labor MP Craig Thomson was
discovered to have used the credit card issued for official use
as national secretary of the Health Services Union to, among
other things, hire sex workers.

There were clear public interest justifications for the
commission—and if it also happened to double as a fishing
expedition into the trustworthiness of the Leader of the
Opposition and his seven years as national secretary of
the Australian Workers Union, that was just a magical bonus!

However, the commission failed to destroy Shorten for a
few reasons. First, the only dirt it dug up was that he hadn't
reported labour hire firm Unibuilt's donation in 2007 of a
'research officer' to assume the role of his full-time campaign
director until a few days before the commission began its
hearings. Shorten insisted that his belated correction of the
public record was simply because he'd only just had this
failure to disclose brought to his attention and that he had

immediately sought to amend it, rather than that this was incredibly dodgy-looking and he'd quietly swept it under the carpet until he'd realised there was no way that it would escape the notice of the commission.

And while it was impressive that this was the worst example investigators could find of Shorten's supposed involvement in union corruption, the fact that at the time Unibuilt was negotiating an unusually beneficial deal (to its advantage) with the Australian Workers Union—represented by a team headed by one B. Shorten—didn't look great. In fact, this could quite possibly have proved terminal for Shorten's leadership had it not serendipitously come to light that the commission's chief investigator, Justice Dyson Heydon, had been booked to speak at a Liberal Party fundraising event.

While Heydon did withdraw from the event once it became a public issue—insisting that he'd not been aware that it was a Liberal fundraiser as he'd not seen the emailed invitation personally but had had the details read to him by an assistant—this controversy demolished any semblance of the commission being non-partisan. Heydon did briefly recuse himself to inquire into his own impartiality and reached the conclusion that no, he was totally not being in any way influenced by any connection to the Liberal Party—a farcical process that failed to reassure anybody. So when the final report was handed down, no-one particularly cared.

And by that stage the Coalition had far larger problems to deal with, like the revelation that the Speaker of the House had charged the public over $5000 for a helicopter ride from

Melbourne to a party event in Geelong.[1] Shorten must have been all but picking out new wallpaper for the Lodge when Turnbull made his move.

———

After walking away from the barrage of bullets fired by the Royal Commission barely bloodied and entirely unbowed, it was too much to hope that fortune would favour Shorten again by somehow leaving Abbott in the leadership.

But Labor did have several things going for it. One was that it recognised the need to be united and present itself as a solid team. The rivalries of the previous years were put aside—or, at the very least, kept out of the public eye—while it focused on policy. This was made all the easier by the party's historically strong internal discipline, including the recognition that fundamental disagreement with policy could be expressed only by resignation.

Second, Shorten was not the presidential leader that Rudd, Abbott and Turnbull presented themselves as being. He very wisely didn't attempt to trade on his own personal charisma, instead providing airtime to lieutenants such as deputy leader and shadow foreign minister Tanya Plibersek, shadow treasurer Chris Bowen, shadow finance minister Tony Burke, and Penny Wong, the party's leader in the Senate. This might have been born of necessity, but the effect was to emphasise that Labor was not reliant on a single figurehead but had a strong team ready to take on the challenges of government.

1   Maybe at this point you're thinking, 'Say, wasn't there going to be a government review of politician travel entitlements in the wake of Bronwyn Bishop's Choppergate scandal?' There was, and it was decided that the system was working totally fine and everyone should stop worrying about it. So that's a relief!

He also wisely used some of the more charming and persuasive members of the party—notably Wong, Anthony Albanese and Sam Dastyari—to negotiate with minor parties, independents and crossbenchers while the government was largely relying on the talents of employment minister Eric Abetz and attorney-general George Brandis to either bulldoze or bully them. If minority government needed to be formed in the future, then this relationship-building would be crucial—but it was also just genuinely good, respectful policy.

For whatever it was worth, of course. At this time the polls were clear: Shorten wasn't Abbott, but Turnbull was even more not-Abbott and had the extra advantage of also not being Shorten. Turnbull was the most popular PM in recent memory, and when the election came he would wipe the floor with the unpopular unionist and his band of no-hopers.

Columnists nationwide presented Shorten's resignation for the good of the party as a foregone conclusion. But Bill's luck held out for two reasons. One was that Labor had learned the lessons of reacting too quickly to a dip in the polls and the tenor of the media commentariat generally, helped by the fact that changing leader was now a difficult and complicated process that required a public ballot of the entire membership rather than a swift and brutal late night coup.

The other reason was that Turnbull had conveniently begun to unravel.

———

In the new year, a different Shorten emerged: fitter, sharper, less worried about gag lines and more concerned with substance. He began to take the fight to the government, arguing about matters of substantive policy and presenting himself as the leader of a united, focused party with a plan for Australia's future.

But, as the polls showed, it made no difference. The government maintained a Labor-slaughtering lead, and rumours of a Labor leadership challenge started to circulate in earnest. Plibersek, Bowen and Albanese were all supposed to be considering their options ahead of parliament sitting in February. This didn't eventuate, possibly because of Labor's commitment to its hard-won unity, and possibly because no-one fancied being the person to lead Labor to what looked like an embarrassing defeat.

But then, in keeping with most of Shorten's term in opposition, Labor's fortunes began to rise. It's not as though the public was falling in love with Shorten exactly; but with expectations so low, he could barely help but exceed them. Conversely, Turnbull was suffering the effects of failing to reverse the unpopular and divisive policies of the Abbott epoch, compounded by an apparent inability to show the economic leadership upon which he based his challenge.

Suddenly this was a two-horse race. And as the graph lines of the popularity of the government and Opposition started to move closer to each other, the conclusion started to look a lot less foregone.

The plans for an early election were well underway, of course, but now there was an unexpected problem facing the Turnbull camp: had it left its run too late?

9

SENATE VOTING REFORMAPALOOZA, OR HOW DO YOU SOLVE A PROBLEM LIKE THE CROSSBENCH?

In which the Cat makes a cunning strategic move,
with unexpected results

By March 2016 Turnbull's stratospheric popularity had descended somewhat from its earlier 'honeymoon' readings, but he was still way ahead of Shorten as preferred PM and most polls gave the Coalition a 4 per cent lead on Labor. The obvious thing to do was to get the nation voting as quickly as possible. This would solve a lot of problems swiftly and decisively, while also avoiding the pitfalls of having an election further down the track.

First and foremost, a decisive landslide would eliminate any question regarding the new prime minister's authority. The result would doubtless eclipse Abbott's 2013 win and confirm to the party unambiguously that it had been correct to switch leaders.

A comprehensive win would also give Turnbull an opportunity to kill off that restrictive deal with the Nationals before the voters noticed any suspicious inaction around certain iconic issues like marriage equality or emissions trading. The Coalition agreement would need to be renegotiated after an election win and, if Turnbull had a thumping victory behind him, then the Nationals would be neatly plonked back in their box, where they could once again be safely ignored.

It would also mean a clear three years in which to prosecute the Turnbull political agenda, except . . . well, there were still a few nagging problems.

First up, there was the fact that Turnbull had expressly ruled out an early election; it's hard to argue that one is offering stability in the sea of chaos that one's predecessor had created and then immediately call down the typhoon of a double dissolution election.

Double dissolutions are generally thought of by voters as being equivalent to an early election, and for good reason: that's precisely the purpose for which they're almost exclusively used. Sure, a DD is a massive constitutional event that one imagines is held in a prominent red cabinet on the wall with 'Break Glass In Case of Senate Blockage' emblazoned thereupon, but Australia's history of Double Ds is one of governments using rejected legislation as a flimsy pretext to get the nation to the polls early rather than because the legislation under discussion is genuinely pivotal.[1]

---

1   The big exception to this is the 1975 Dismissal, which came about when the Coalition under Malcolm Fraser started refusing to pass the 'supply' bills that funded the running of the government, thereby creating a crisis which ended with Governor-General John Kerr dismissing Gough Whitlam's Labor government. This neat trick of using a largely forgotten piece of constitutional law to force one's political rival into a humiliating corner clearly stuck in Turnbull's mind.

Technically the government had the necessary trigger to call a double dissolution—a bill for the abolition of the Clean Energy Finance Corporation had twice been rejected by the Senate—but that was perhaps not the greatest grounds on which to fight a campaign. No-one was going to be under any illusions that this election was entirely about getting in while the getting was good, regardless of what the trigger issue supposedly was, but even so it'd be better to have something a little less cartoonishly Abbottian. A similar problem faced the transparently anti-union Fair Work (Registered Organisations) Amendment Bill, which sought to set up an ASIC-style regulatory body to police unions; this too had been knocked down during the Abbott epoch. So, ideally, there'd be a new trigger, one that the PM could more aggressively get behind—and since there was no shortage of legislation that had been rejected by the Senate during Abbott's two years of near stasis, it was just a matter of picking something suitably symbolic, whacking it on the parliamentary schedule, seeing it get shot down again by the upper house, and using it as an excuse to call an early election.

The other problem was the Senate itself.

The eight-person crossbench had been a thorn in Abbott's side since it first sat in July 2014, leading him to describe it at various times as 'feral', 'recalcitrant' and, most oddly, 'populist'.[2] Turnbull had no intention of going to a regular

2   A Fairfax analysis of every government vote from July 2014 to May 2015 found that certain members of the crossbench were actually huge supporters of the government. Family First's Bob Day was practically a Coalition senator, voting with the government 90 per cent of the time, and Liberal Democrat David Leyonhjelm was onside 70 per cent of the time. By comparison, Labor voted with the government 35 per cent of the time, beaten in the feral recalcitrance stakes by Nick Xenophon (30 per cent) and the Greens (2 per cent).

election. After all, a) seven of the senators, including all of the least pliant ones, had been elected in 2013 and were therefore safe until the 2019 election, and b) there was a good chance of another few independents joining them, making for an even more annoyingly complicated Senate in the term to come.

Following the 2013 election the Joint Standing Committee on Electoral Matters had looked into making a change to the Senate ballot, with the explicit goal of preventing minor parties 'gaming' (or, to put it another way, 'successfully using') the system to engineer representation by cutting deals with each other regarding the distribution of preferences. The government argued, not unreasonably, that giving a Senate seat to someone like Ricky Muir of the Motoring Enthusiasts Party, who had won a Victorian Senate spot with a primary vote of 0.51 per cent, wasn't a reflection of the explicit will of the voters.

This stance was strongly opposed by the independents, who rightly saw their main hope of winning seats being taken from them, and by Labor, for reasons that had more to do with the timing of a likely change than the substance of the argument.

This next bit gets into how the Senate vote worked and the thinking behind the change, which is either a bit dull or screamingly obvious, depending on how interested in the mechanics of parliament you are. You might want to skip forward a bit—we won't be offended, honest.

———

For the rest of you ... Man, can you believe those smug jerks who skipped ahead? What's the rush, smug jerks? Got another book to get to? Honestly, the gall of some people. These things don't write themselves, you know.

Anyway, there are two houses of federal parliament: the House of Representatives, also called the lower house, because it's full of the people you most want to bury, and the Senate, or upper house, so-called because it thinks it's better than those lower house plebs.

The House of Reps is where the government is formed via a method of preferential voting—get the necessary majority of seats and congratulations, you're the government!—and it's made up of 150 people representing electorates of roughly equal population, in which every MP serves a three-year term before being forced to stand for election once again.

Because this would skew things dramatically in the favour of the three big east coast states, where around 18 million of the nation's 24 million people live, the Senate was specifically designed to give each of the states an equal representation,[3] whether they had over 7.5 million people (as per New South Wales) or just over 500,000 (in the case of Tasmania). Each of the six states has twelve senators— determined by a proportional voting system—who serve a six-year term and therefore contest one election out of two, while the ACT and Northern Territory each has two senators who only serve three-year terms for reasons that make zero sense and basically guarantee that NT maintains its proud

---

3   Yes, despite the Australian parliament being heavily modelled on the West-minster system of parliament used in Britain, the idea of having a senate that acts as a states' house and can also introduce legislation in its own right is copied from the US congress. In other words, our Federation was basically a weird hybrid of British and American ideas, which neatly sums up the subsequent century-plus of Australian culture.

status as The Bit of Australia That Gets Ignored Outside of Tourism Ads.[4]

A regular Australian election, therefore, decides all of the MPs in the lower house and half of the senators in the upper. This ensures a degree of continuity in parliament since it guarantees that there are at least thirty-six senators who know the Wi-Fi password and where the good biscuits are hidden.

However, a double dissolution election throws all of the Senate seats open, meaning that all seventy-six senators are campaigning for re-election. This also creates a weird situation whereby half of the senators get the usual six-year term and the other half have to make do with three, just to get things back into sync.

It should also be pointed out that it's very rare for a government to have control over both houses. This has only happened a few times since Federation (most recently after the 2004 election that handed John Howard his final term), not least because it turns out that governments with no checks on their power invariably abuse it, which turns the voters violently against the government (most recently in the 2007 election that ended John Howard's final term).

One unique problem with a double dissolution—at least for a government hoping to get control of the Senate as well as the

---

4 It also explains why things like the NT Intervention (aka the Northern Territory National Emergency Response, enacted by the Howard government in 2007, or the functionally identical current Stronger Futures Policy) can be enacted in NT without there being some sort of popular uprising. It's fair to say that the people of, say, Tamworth or Ballarat would not react especially well if the federal government was to arbitrarily announce that it was taking compulsory acquisition of the entire township, much less that alcohol and pornography were now illegal—but announce that about a remote Aboriginal community and evidently everyone seems pretty much down with it. Except those it affects, obviously.

House of Representatives—is that, because all twelve senate spots are being contested per state rather than the typical six, the quota of votes required is effectively halved.[5] This means that a double dissolution makes it much easier for independents and micro parties to get into parliament: partly because of the lowered quota, and partly because the way that preferences work means that it's harder for a major party to win six seats out of twelve than it is to win three out of six. Parties like the Liberal Democrats or the Sex Party might struggle to get 14.3 per cent of the vote, especially in the larger states where that percentage translates into hundreds of thousands of ballots, but could potentially get the 7.7 per cent required in a double dissolution.

And, finally, there are preference deals.

From 1984 until 2016 the Senate ballot paper worked on a group voting ticket basis: either you voted for one party above the line, or you laboriously numbered every single individual candidate in order of preference. Since this typically involved ranking between sixty and a hundred-plus boxes for people of whom even the most ardent upper house enthusiast had never heard, only a tiny fraction of the voting population bothered to do so—less than 3 per cent in the 2013 election—typically because they bore a particular grudge against a specific party or candidate and were willing to sacrifice quarter of an hour of box-numbering simply to experience the righteous thrill of putting their political nemesis last.[6]

---

5 It's slightly over half, technically: the quota of votes required is determined as the total divided by the number of vacancies, plus one. That ghostly extra one represents the fact that one senator per term is haunted.

6 Not that I've done this in literally every election in which I've voted, to be clear.

Historically most of the vote went to Labor or the Liberals/ LNP/Coalition in each state, who would win an easy quota or two, and then everyone else would squabble over the leftovers via preferences.

The upshot of this was only two or three senators in each state were actually voted in by direct vote, and the remaining spots were won not by candidates being rewarded by a grateful electorate, but by getting enough votes via the more popular majors. And that resulted in some very odd folks getting Senate gigs.

The parties would all sign deals with one another to ensure that leftover votes that failed to make the necessary quota would sluice into the vote-bucket of a party with which they at least vaguely agreed—or, at the very least, which they thought would be a strategic buffer against whichever other party they felt was a bigger threat.

In the case of the micro parties, they would often receive in the first instance a tiny dribble of a few dozen or hundred votes apiece but, once the lowest-voted parties were eliminated and their votes assigned to whomever they'd preferenced, this unpromising beginning would gradually accumulate into a quota—which is how Muir's 0.51 per cent eventually swelled to the required amount in 2013.

Anyway, that's how the Senate worked. And now, back to our thrilling tale of upper house legislative intrigue!

———

Had Turnbull called a double dissolution in the early weeks of his government, he'd probably have got rid of some of the pesky crossbenchers, but would also have run the risk of new and potentially even peskier ones getting in—or, worse, of the Greens getting enough votes to increase their bloc, forcing constant negotiation over every little thing.

However, he had another option. And it was already set to go.

The aforementioned Joint Standing Committee on Electoral Matters had handed down a number of recommendations in the interim report delivered in May 2014, one of which was eliminating group voting tickets and adopting a system similar to that used in NSW since 2003, which offered the voter optional above-the-line preferencing. This way voters would be forced to number the boxes of the parties in the order in which they wanted their preferences to go, rather than for their preferences to flow according to the arcane deals hashed out between the parties in each state.

This had a number of advantages in the eyes of the government. One was that it would ensure that each voter had greater control over where their vote went. It would also mean that the upper house vote would look more like that of the lower house, since both were directly determined by voters.

Another was that the NSW system had demonstrably worked to the significant benefit of the major parties and the better-established independents—especially those on the hard right, like Fred Nile and the Shooters and Fishers Party, with whom the NSW Coalition government was comfortable dealing. This came at the expense of the smaller parties and independent individuals, thereby effectively pulling up the ladder to prevent any upstarts lobbing in. Only parties with the resources to manage a state-wide campaign—in other words, Labor, the Liberals, the Nationals, the Greens and well-backed candidates in smaller and therefore cheaper states like South Australia and Tasmania—would have a realistic chance of getting a seat.

The Greens had long advocated for direct democracy as a matter of principle and were also in favour of ending preference harvesting, despite modelling suggesting that, if anything, such a change would be to their disadvantage. Of the ten Greens senators in the 44th Parliament, at least two—SA's Sarah Hanson-Young and WA's Scott Ludlum—had been voted in on preferences and would almost certainly not have made the cut under the system their own party was now advocating.

As mentioned above, most Labor parliamentarians were staunchly opposed to any such change, despite modelling suggesting they'd benefit—for a start, by picking up the Greens spots that had been previously gifted thanks to Labor preferences.

One notable and outspoken exception was Gary Gray, the anagrammatically named WA MP who had been a member of the Joint Standing Committee on Electoral Matters and who argued passionately for the adoption of the proposals in parliament in February 2016, before conceding that the party was not going to support them and that he, therefore, couldn't vote in favour without leaving the party—and he didn't need to worry about his future within the parliament, at least, having indicated that same month that he wouldn't stand for re-election.

There was one other little wrinkle, though: the window for a double dissolution was rapidly closing.

As the parliament's sitting calendar set out, the lower house would sit for a total of four weeks for the autumn session, three days in early February, then back for three straight weeks from 22 February to 17 March. It was during that session that the government would, in theory, have to pass the Senate reform and also present the doomed legislation that would give it a fresh trigger to call a double dissolution. This was because once parliament rose, it wouldn't sit again until 2 May—with the federal budget due to be handed down on 11 May. And this was a huge problem for the government.

Constitutionally, a double dissolution can't be called in the last six months of a parliamentary term. The 44th Parliament first sat on 13 November 2013, meaning that a double dissolution had to be called by 12 May: the day after the budget was handed down. This was impossible for a bunch of reasons: it would deny the Opposition a budget reply and look awfully dodgy to the electorate, but also there'd be no time to pass the necessary supply bills to ensure that the government could continue to function.

There was a solution, though: bringing the budget forward to 3 May would give a clear week before the double dissolution window had closed. And this became the plan—which indicated to the Opposition that its job was to ensure that the Senate ballot legislation debate took the longest possible time to pass. Even if the Senate was forced to sit longer in order to get the legislation through, there wouldn't be enough time to discuss anything else—thereby robbing the government of the opportunity to create that other necessary element: a new and politically palatable double dissolution trigger.

That was the thinking, at least. Reality would prove to be a little different.

———

On 17 March, the last day of the parliamentary session, there was an epic twenty-eight-hour debate as Labor and the independents put up a number of delaying tactics to prevent what was clearly a foregone conclusion with regards to the Senate changes.

Every minute spent discussing the Senate reform bill was one not spent re-examining the reintroduction of the Australian Building and Construction Commission, a body that had been introduced by the Howard government in 2005 to provide oversight of the building industry and clamp down on industrial action—or, as those observers with a more jaundiced eye insisted, to intimidate unions with powers more suited to the secret police than a regulatory body.[7]

In fact, the ABCC had never actually gone away: the Gillard government had put a series of safeguards in place in 2010 in an attempt to moderate its power, but it still existed—kind of—as Fair Work Building and Construction, established in 2012.

However, the fact that the ABCC couldn't act with impunity was a thorn in the side of the Abbott and then Turnbull governments. Employment minister Michaelia Cash insisted that the reinstatement of the ABCC was 'absolutely vital' in order to combat the rampant 'union thuggery' that was apparently rife on Australia's construction sites, and taking the nation to a

7   Among the 'coercive powers' of the ABCC were the authority to compel people to attend interviews with no legal or union representation, with no right to silence, and the ability to determine jail time for those deemed to have acted illegally.

double dissolution on legislation designed to curb union power was on-message with the attempts to smear Bill Shorten as a sinister union factotum in 2015's Royal Commission into Union Corruption.

Why the government felt it especially needed to go to town on the ABCC when it had a perfectly good anti-union trigger in hand with the Fair Work (Registered Organisations) Amendment Bill remained an open question.

The Senate ballot changes passed, and there was time left to debate the ABCC bill. Even with the early budget, there wouldn't be any time left to get the ABCC bill up to a vote in time for it to get knocked back by the upper house and create a double dissolution trigger. But, as Turnbull liked to boast so enthusiastically, he was full of secret plans and clever tricks. And he was about to deploy one that was perhaps his cleverest.

10
THE MORRISON GAMBIT

*In which the new treasurer come galumphing into
the portfolio, and it doesn't go entirely to plan*

Of all of the great What Ifs connected with the short and excruciatingly embarrassing reign of Tony Abbott, the greatest is this: what would have happened if Abbott had replaced stumbling treasurer Joe Hockey with Malcolm Turnbull?

It was never going to happen, not least because Abbott's loyalty to his team was absolute; even, as was the case with Hockey and Abbott's chief of staff Peta Credlin, when the team was clearly creating more problems than it was solving and a halfway objective leader would have realised the urgent need to cauterise those gaping, spurting wounds.

And while Abbott spun his loyalty to lost causes as a virtue, it suggested a deeper cowardice at work. Leaving Turnbull in a low-rent portfolio like Communications merely gave him the time and resources with which to strategise, while the promotion of Abbott-allied duffers like Kevin Andrews,

Eric Abetz and Peter Dutton to important portfolios allowed
new problems to arise while giving Turnbull cover to continue
with his secret plans and clever tricks.

Of course, the history of ambitious treasurers ready to
strike for the leadership is almost a cliché in Australian
politics: unsuccessfully (Peter Costello), successfully (Paul
Keating), and first-one-then-the-other (John Howard). And
the treasurership would have undoubtedly given Turnbull a
national platform even greater than the one he already had—
but, as happened with Abbott and Hockey, it would also have
tied Turnbull's fortunes to that of the PM. Any successes
Turnbull enjoyed in the job would have reflected well on the
leader wise enough to have appointed him, while any failures
would have damaged the aspirant leader's own future hopes.

In other words: a bold PM might be wise to appoint their
greatest rival to the position of treasurer, where their vaunting
ambition is likely to be more readily neutered.

Which brings us neatly to Turnbull's appointee, Scott
Morrison.

———

If there's one thing upon which both Tony Abbott and Malcolm
Turnbull apparently agreed, it was that Scott Morrison was
the perfect candidate to take the reins of Australia's mighty
economic chariot. Both men had reportedly approached him
about the gig in September 2015 (although, as covered in
previous chapters, Abbott later categorically denied doing so);
but the oddest thing about these approaches was that they
didn't seem all that odd.

Morrison was one of the stars of the Abbott Cabinet:
first he bravely and boldly Stopped The Boats as Minister

for Immigration and Border Protection; then he took over the Human Services portfolio in the ministerial reshuffle of December 2014 and showed his caring, sharing side as the nation's firm-but-fair Papa Bear. So the idea that he would be promoted to the treasury had been flagged by observers as being a knock-down inevitability, as was his likely future leadership of the party and, as seers including Pauline Hanson and Sophie Mirabella had publicly declared, his ascension to Prime Minister of Australia.

And this neatly illustrated the way that being treasurer had become a political appointment, effectively vice prime minister,[1] rather than necessarily being the job to which someone was elevated because they knew a lot about, say, economics.[2]

Indeed, as University of Tasmania economist Saul Eslake pointed out in the *Saturday Paper*, 'Morrison is the first person to be treasurer who hasn't ever been a shadow treasurer, finance minister or assistant treasurer since [brief Hawke-era appointee] John Kerin. He has come into the portfolio without any familiarity that those three portfolios would bring.'

---

1   The treasurer certainly seemed to have more clout than did largely ceremonial roles like deputy leader (Julie Bishop) or, thankfully, deputy prime minister, a position always held by the leader of the Nationals (under Abbott the deputy PM was first Warren Truss and then Barnaby Joyce), which carries with it around about the same power as Vice Principal of Narnia.

2   Actually, this is not uncommon, as surprisingly few recent treasurers have had economic qualifications: Morrison's predecessor Joe Hockey was a lawyer, as was Howard-era treasurer Peter Costello and John Howard himself. Labor treasurers have generally been more credentialled: while Rudd/Gillard-era treasurer Wayne Swan had Bachelor of Arts (Hons), majoring in political science, both Chris Bowen and John Dawkins had degrees in economics while Ralph Willis held a Bachelor of Commerce. Then again, Paul Keating never even finished high school.

Scott Morrison was a different chap from many in the
upper echelons of the NSW Liberal Party. He belonged to
a church that wasn't Catholic (the Pentecostalist Shirelife
church in Sutherland), went to a Sydney university that wasn't
the University of Sydney (University of NSW) and studied
a degree that wasn't law (honours in applied economic geog-
raphy). Nevertheless, he overcame his tragic failure to be
part of the Sydney Uni Young Liberals boys club and rose to
prominence in the NSW party—to the point of having that
clash with Turnbull over Malcolm's preselection advertising
mentioned earlier. In the Abbott government he occupied a
unique position as a staunch conservative with his own bloc
of supporters, loyal to Abbott but not beholden to him, and
acceptable to all factions of the party.

Assumption of this role—that of the trusted outsider
brought in to get the job done—had also been his method of
leaping from the wilderness to become director of the NSW
Liberal Party in 2000, a time when the factions were tearing
the organisation asunder. And even then he showed the sort
of brutal pragmatism that was to become his trademark as
immigration minister.

One of his more interesting schemes as director was a plan
to end the destabilising internecine leadership battles in the
NSW Liberals following Kerry Chikarovski's comprehensive
loss to Labor, led by Bob Carr, in the 1999 election.

Chikarovski's leadership was clearly terminal following
the defeat, and Morrison had a strategy in place whereby the
federal party would offer a nice diplomatic position to some
member of the NSW Legislative Assembly and then parachute

an acceptable alternative leadership contender into the seat.[3] And he had just the person in mind: one Malcolm Bligh Turnbull.[4]

However, in March 2002, before Morrison could execute this cunning plan, Chikarovski was successfully challenged for the leadership by John Brogden, who won by a single vote. Morrison very much did not care for Brogden; the two clashed 'like two bulls in a paddock', according to an anonymous party source. But Brogden's leadership ended in August 2005, when reports emerged of drunken lechery and unwanted advances to female journalists at an event for the Australian Hotels Association in late July, at which he also reportedly declared that the then-former premier Bob Carr could 'ship his mail order bride back to where she came from for all I care'.

Brodgen apologised publicly for the slur on Carr's Malaysian-born wife Helena, but the damage was done. He was happy to name names on the way out, though— specifically accusing evangelical religious conservative and then-NSW Young Liberals president Alex Hawke of having leaked the stories to the media in a deliberate attempt to force a leadership change in protest at what he saw as Brogden's dangerously progressive views.

'Alex Hawke has been named as pushing it,' Brogden told the *Sydney Morning Herald*. 'He needs to take a long hard

---

3 Their first call would presumably have been to Peter Debnam, member for Vaucluse, thus saving Turnbull the inconvenience of having to leave his swanky Point Piper digs. Of course, that would have deprived the NSW Liberals of another future state party leader who was to launch the party to electoral defeat and slink away following a humiliating leadership challenge.

4 This was before the Wentworth preselection stoush of 2003, at a time when state politics might still have been worth Turnbull's while.

look at himself. It is pretty obvious that everybody in politics has people out to get them.' Hawke, for his part, rejected the accusations and insisted he had nothing whatsoever to do with the stories coming to light.

Brogden stepped down as leader on 29 August, and was found the following night in the back room of his electorate office having attempted suicide by cutting his wrists. He was rushed to hospital and survived his injuries, but his political career was clearly over; in late September he left politics for good.

Conversely, Hawke was to do rather well for himself, becoming the federal MP for the NSW seat of Mitchell and a key member of the bloc of Morrison supporters in the 44th Parliament, eventually becoming assistant treasurer on Turnbull's front bench.

Morrison, evidently, had an eye for talent.

———

The downfall of John Brogden solidified the suspicion that Morrison's great strength was deploying other people to fight his battles, thereby giving him a degree of insulation from any blowback. His pre-political life had included a controversial stint working for New Zealand's then-new Office of Tourism and Sport in 1998, which immediately descended into a bitter power battle with the NZ Tourism Board. The matter was eventually the subject of an investigation by the Auditor-General, whose final report singled out Morrison for particular approbation in sowing internal discord. Speaking years later, former NZ Tourism Board member Dr Gerry McSweeney told Fairfax that Morrison 'was the strength behind the minister's throne . . .

Morrison was making the bullets and other people were firing them'.[5]

He faced similar accusations from the pro-Abbott faction after Turnbull's successful leadership challenge; his subsequent elevation to the treasury amplified the charges of disloyalty. His insistence that he'd voted for the then-PM was rejected amid accusations that he hadn't instructed his bloc of supporters to follow his lead, and that they had subsequently voted for Turnbull. He dismissed this as mean-spirited conspiracy-mongering, but the suggestion that he'd made a point of being seen to feint while instructing his troops to move in another direction did seem . . . well, downright Morrisonian.

That's not least because one thing that Morrison and Abbott shared was a deep passion for the military—a zeal that manifested itself in their transformation of the once largely bureaucratic Department of Immigration into the quasi-military Border Force, a name better suited to a 1980s straight-to-video action flick than a government department.

In fact, as Morrison made clear to Fairfax's Deborah Snow in a very revealing *Good Weekend* feature that was presumably designed to humanise the treasurer ahead of the May 2016 budget, he had long yearned for the Defence portfolio: 'If Tony had asked me to serve in that role, I would have loved it.' And, as the feature made clear, his office decor backed up the claim: his shelves were festooned with military memorabilia,

5 It wasn't the last time that Morrison was to receive condemnation for a tourism-related mess: after leaving the NSW Liberal Party gig to head up Tourism Australia, Morrison oversaw the 'Where the bloody hell are you?' international tourism campaign—a notorious flop that bought him into conflict with federal tourism minister Fran Bailey and eventually ended in him being sacked in 2006.

including various caps from different army and police units, and photographs of his grandfather serving in World War II.

Tony did not give him the Defence portfolio. Neither did Malcolm. Instead, he was heading the treasury—and it was, according to the same article, 'not a place where I anticipated ending up. No one believes me when I say that, but it's true.'

By then it probably wasn't that great a shock, but it seems the treasury hadn't anticipated him ending up there either.

———

Morrison's reputation had been based on his success in the Immigration and Border Control portfolio, in which he became known for his uncompromising position with regards to the treatment of people seeking asylum—that they should be turned back, towed back, or incarcerated in offshore detention—which Abbott heralded as one of the great resounding successes of his government.

While there was a lot of discussion about the moral implications of these policies, it was generally assumed that they worked. Not actually in the camps, obviously, given the ongoing reports of rapes, suicides, self-harm, riots, beat downs and murders that were occurring on Christmas Island, Nauru and Manus Island,[6] but in terms of 'stopping the boats'.

An unkind observer might point out that the difference in reports of the number of boats attempting to reach Australia

6 There's a chapter coming that goes into this at downright unpleasant length— get excited!—but it's important to remember that Christmas Island is owned by Australia and is technically subject to Australian law; Nauru is theoretically a sovereign nation, although one that is funded almost entirely by the Australian government; and Manus Island is part of Papua New Guinea. This gives the people on them different legal standings as far as Australia is concerned, although the actual treatment seems hellishly standardised across centres.

between the Rudd/Gillard era and the Abbott epoch might have had less to do with people smugglers being impressed by the government's resolute policies and more to do with the fact that the Department of Immigration reported arrivals under Labor and didn't under the Coalition; they were now classified as 'on-water' matters and were not to be reported to the public lest people smugglers drew inspiration and intelligence from Australian media reports. When that proved insufficient, the government passed laws making it illegal for whistleblowers to disclose any information about offshore detention or boat arrivals and for the media to report on such information.

Praise for Morrison's resolve also increased dramatically in the wake of the badly misjudged 2014 budget, when the government was scrambling to contain the fallout from the sudden realisation by the electorate that pre-election promises were no longer operational and that maybe, just maybe, this Joe Hockey character wasn't quite the economic savant we'd been promised. However, when Abbott reshuffled the cabinet that December he switched Morrison to the portfolio of Human Services.

Morrison had just successfully got the Migration and Maritime Powers Legislation Amendment (Resolving the Asylum Legacy Caseload) Bill 2014 through the Senate, giving the immigration minister unprecedented powers over asylum seekers—including the right to detain people indefinitely without charge and to return them to their country of origin, despite that being illegal under the international human rights agreements to which the government was a signatory.[7] It was

---

7 Refoulement—the return of victims of persecution to their persecutors—is forbidden under the terms of the United Nations Human Rights Commissioner's 1951 Refugee Convention. So not exactly a new law, in other words.

achieved by promising the Senate crossbench that if, and only if, it passed the law, Morrison would release the children still held in detention on Christmas Island.

There was some confusion as to why Abbott would suddenly remove Morrison at this exciting and triumphant moment and replace him with Peter Dutton, who had made a comprehensive hash of the Health portfolio over the previous year. Officially it was to give Morrison a chance to apply his eye for detail to Human Services, one of the largest ministerial budgets in the government; more suspicious observers speculated that perhaps it was a way of clipping the wings of a minister who was starting to fly a little too high for comfort—especially as the change coincided with Abbott's popularity entering what looked awfully like a death spiral.

Indeed, as backbenchers started agitating for a leadership spill in January 2015, following Abbott's baffling and internationally mocked decision to give a knighthood to Prince Philip, Morrison was one of those being spoken of as a potential challenger, along with Julie Bishop and, naturally, Malcolm Turnbull.

The idea that Morrison was perhaps in cahoots with the presumptive challenger was strengthened by reports that Morrison and Turnbull had been seen dining together in Canberra. It wasn't known at the time, but during this period Morrison, Bishop and Turnbull were in fact actively strategising around the need to replace the party leadership before the next election.

Morrison was not destined to shine in Human Services, but he was credited with having softened some of the more damaging blows from the 2014 budget—to the degree that the 2015 budget was described as having been more Morrison's work than Joe Hockey's, which softened the ground nicely for his future ministerial harvest.

When the eventual challenge came in September there was a sense that now, finally, there would be a can-do treasurer ready to back up the new PM's agenda of bold and exciting economic reforms—the likes of which Abbott had promised, then threatened, then failed to come close to delivering. However, there was a bit of organisational shuffling going on, suggesting that maybe the new PM didn't have complete and unqualified respect for his new treasurer's economic nous.

One of Turnbull's earliest appointments was to (re)hire Martin Parkinson as head of the Department of Prime Minister and Cabinet, where he was reunited with his former deputy, David Gruen, who had been moved sideways from Treasury to Prime Minister and Cabinet under Abbott. As one of the first acts of his prime ministership, Abbott had sacked Parkinson as treasury secretary and replaced him with the more pliant John Fraser.

The appointment of Parkinson was in keeping with Turnbull's policy of surrounding himself with well-qualified experts in a variety of fields, but it also meant that he had someone with voluminous knowledge of the inner workings of Treasury right there in his office. He also didn't have to rely on his actual, less-equipped treasurer, who in his first few months failed to make much of a go of it, let alone display the sort of immediate grasp of his portfolio that Turnbull clearly expected.

Parkinson and Gruen were to be tasked with developing the government's policy on tax reform going forward, meaning that after a few short months Morrison was looking distinctly junior in his own department; a situation that might explain a few of the somewhat embarrassing situations in which he was about to find himself.

———

In the bullish first few weeks of the Turnbull government, both the newly minted prime minister and his shiny new treasurer were keen to emphasise that all economic options were on the table.

This was exciting news, not least because one of the recommendations most often suggested to Joe Hockey—and, for that matter, one of the most assiduously dismissed—was that Australia should take immediate advantage of the record low global interest rates and borrow up big while money was insanely cheap. Given Australia's triple-A credit rating, earned by Wayne Swan in 2011, it would be possible to borrow at close to zero interest and use the money on large-scale infrastructure projects that a) the nation very much required, b) were big employers of the exact same workers who were losing their jobs in the mining industry, and c) would act as a significant stimulus for the economy as a whole.

That was the suggestion of Glenn Stevens, Governor of the Reserve Bank, who thought that Turnbull and Morrison would be more receptive to the idea; but, while the plan had the pleasing benefit of being a legitimately good one, there were a couple of problems with it. First up, it sounded like the sort of leftie, big-spending socialist, government 'n' unions notion that would give the free market economic dries in the party head-exploding conniptions. Second, massive and welcome cheap debt was still debt, and debt—as both sides of politics had made clear over the past five years—was terrible and stupid, even when it was obviously useful and wise.

So while all ideas were supposedly on the table, some ideas were less idea-ish than others and seemed to mysteriously evaporate of their own accord—such as, for example, borrowing free money for the nation's benefit—to be replaced with schemes that were more ideologically appropriate as the government instead pursued the vague but apparently vital goal of tax reform.

Barely had Morrison assumed the new mantle than he was following in the footsteps of his esteemed predecessor by saying things that were to rapidly create new and avoidable problems. In this case, it was the pronouncement that, despite the evident funding shortfalls that were crippling government at all levels and helping to inflate government debt to record amounts, 'Australia doesn't have a revenue problem; it has a spending problem.'

This claim didn't even begin to make sense as a description of the situation—compared with the Howard era, spending was up by 1 per cent of GDP while revenue had dropped by 1.5 per cent. So economists argued that there was a problem with spending *and* revenue, and that they had to be tackled in concert, with revenue the more urgent issue. This was largely dismissed amid talk of the need to cut taxes—i.e. revenue—as a matter of urgency.

That the Turnbull government would maintain this line, when it was widely recognised that the brutal (and still largely unpassed through parliament) all-cuts budget of 2014 had mortally wounded the Abbott government, was remarkable— not least because the Australia Institute had set out a case for raising $20 billion a year simply by removing distortions in the existing tax system.[8]

And Morrison stuck to the it's-a-spending-problem line in all his pronouncements on the matter of the economy. This was interpreted, correctly, as being both a message to the nation that it should expect some more austerity-style cuts to services and a signal to conservatives that any talk of tax reform was not going to lead to anything radical, like increased taxes. Indeed, it was clear that part of the goal was to reduce personal income tax and, especially, company tax, and replace them with taxation that took non-income-based forms.

Raising the GST had for some time been a beloved policy of the federal Coalition. The introduction of a goods and services tax had been one of John Howard's great triumphs, and was therefore imbued with the mystical power the Liberals ascribed to everything done by their greatest living prime minister, even though the GST had actually almost cost Howard the 1998 election. He'd lost eighteen seats to Labor and garnered less than half of the national vote on a two-party-preferred basis at that poll, where the main issue was his stated intention to introduce the GST—yet for some reason the result has been remembered as a mighty pro-GST

8   To be fair, the 'progressive' Australia Institute presumably knew how enthusi-astically the government was going to dismiss its suggestions when it titled its May 2015 paper 'It's the Revenue Stupid: Ideas for a brighter budget'. The gist of their plan was to modify the benefits of the negative gearing of investment properties, which was about to become an even less popular idea.

mandate bestowed by the grateful people of Australia for the Coalition's brave economic reform.

The GST was a flat tax that didn't affect the wealthy—sorry, the *job creators*—nearly as much as it did the poor peop—sorry, the *leaners*. And, most wonderful of all, it was a way to throw responsibility for unpopular spending cuts to things the public tended to like, such as schools and hospitals and police and so forth, back on the states.

Abbott had been a fan of the idea just before his removal, insisting, 'There is an efficiency argument for taxing earnings less and taxing spending more.'

As reports started to emerge that the government was looking at a GST hike, Morrison didn't shy away from suggesting that it was a serious plan. 'That's what the Commonwealth has done, there's no secret about that. That's been hiding in plain sight,' he mocked reporters. 'News flash: the Commonwealth is having a discussion with the states and territories about how we make our tax system better. That's what's happening.'

It was also popular with a surprising number of state premiers: specifically, two of them. NSW Coalition premier Mike Baird and SA Labor premier Jay Weatherill had expressed guarded support for the idea, but since any GST rise requires the unanimous assent of all premiers, the idea was still falling significantly short of the necessary numbers.[9]

The model beloved of Abbott, Turnbull and Morrison alike involved raising the GST to 15 per cent and removing all exemptions, including the exemption on fresh food. This,

9   There was plenty of support from the business community, however, who declared that a GST rise was the 'magic bullet' to pay for the corporate tax cuts it would very much like.

it was claimed, would raise over $45 billion a year that would principally go to the states. This, in turn, would obviate the need for the states to ask for grants for hospitals and schools from the federal government, and the extra cost to voters of the GST increase would be offset by income tax cuts. It was win-win-win!

The idea might have been a (win-win-) winner in the party room, but out in the real world it was political poison. As mentioned above, the GST had not been a winner with the electorate back in 1998 and the public recoiled at the mere mention of the exact sort of tax hike the government kept emphasising was unnecessary—since, after all, there was no revenue problem.

As enthusiastic as Turnbull and Morrison were about the plan, in January 2016 the government backbench made it very, very clear to Cabinet that there was no way in hell it was going to support a GST rise. The ABC reported that twenty MPs had banded together in opposition to the plan. Unsurprisingly, Cory Bernardi was right in the middle of it.

'There is nothing that I have seen or heard that convinces me that a rise in the GST is in the long-term interest of taxpayers,' he thundered righteously to Sky News. 'It's the all-consuming desire of governments to take more money from taxpayers. We don't want to see that in this country.'

Russell Broadbent, the member for McMillan, had served under Howard and was one of the MPs who had lost his seat in 1998; having returned to parliament in 2007 after almost a decade in the wilderness, he was less than enthusiastic about the possibility of history repeating itself. He also went on Sky

to point out that many of the state budgets that would supposedly be buoyed by the GST increase were actually already in
surplus, unlike the federal government budget, adding that
increasing a tax paid by everyone, rich and poor alike, 'doesn't
go down very well . . . I don't think it raises that much money
anyway and the compensation you would have to pay sort of
ameliorates all the benefits you would gain.'

On 28 January Treasury gave Morrison new modelling
at his request, factoring in the highest possible GST rise
along with a raft of income tax cuts (almost) equalling the
increased revenue. If he was hoping that the result would
be proof that the tax burden wouldn't fall disproportionately on the poorest segments of society, then he was to be
disappointed.

The result was horrific: while the wealthy would be over-
whelmingly better off under the changes, things for those at
the bottom would get significantly worse. In particular, those
who didn't earn enough to pay income tax and were therefore
unable to benefit from Morrison's cuts would have their cost
of living dramatically increased with zero offsets. This didn't
immediately kill the plan off, however—although with the
prospect of an early election already in play, it was clear that it
would be a challenge to sell it to the electorate.

In early February a less ebullient Morrison was telling the
nation that there would be no income tax cuts for anyone
if everyone was going to be so sulky about the GST rise—
especially those greedy state governments.

'The only reason we were looking at issues, and continue
to investigate those, is because it gives the only opportunity

there really is for big income tax cuts,' Morrison told the
Daily Telegraph, adding that it would have raised $40 billion
a year—a little less than had been suggested a few months
earlier, but more than the $35 billion modelled in January
(without mentioning the $30 billion refunded in income
tax cuts), assuming that everyone kept their expectations
adequately low. 'Now if for the reason that other issues prevent
that [increase in revenue], i.e. the compensation bill is too big,
if the states only want an increase in the GST so they can
spend more money—then they are big problems and those
problems do work against the objective.'

By 8 February the anticipated rise in revenue had dropped
back to $36 billion a year, with $8 billion going on compensation to people with low incomes for their higher cost of
living. The PM now started to walk back his claims about the
massive benefits of the GST rise, although that message was
not being picked up by all of his front bench. On 15 February
Michaelia Cash emphatically denied that the GST increase
was dead, telling Helen Dalley on Sky News: 'We haven't
taken it off the table completely, not at all . . . We are still
looking at everything.'

And that was the position to which the government was
committed for literally hours, until Turnbull cheerfully contradicted her the following morning. 'The work we have done
demonstrates that the so-called GST tax mix switch does
not give you the economic dividend, the growth dividend,
that would justify doing it,' he said with a shrug to the press
in Rockhampton. 'There will be no GST increase taken to
the election.'

This was a bit of a problem, because Morrison was all prepped to do an address to the National Press Club the following day at which—as he had already backgrounded a number of journalists—he was going to announce the Coalition's case for a GST increase. And thus on 17 February the treasurer got up in front of the clubbed-up national press and gave a speech in which he announced . . . um, nothing.

It made for less than exciting listening, as Morrison regaled the gathering with riveting snippets like: he knew some American folks when he lived in New Zealand; there were more optimists than pessimists out there; China was looking nice; and his forecasting couldn't be trusted as 'an economist's prediction is a mistake between two facts'. Finally, he confirmed that they were leaving the GST as is—the benefits of which had mysteriously shrunk from $45 billion, back when the government liked the idea, to not enough to make it worthwhile now that they didn't.

'The results were released last week,' Morrison said to the press with a straight face. 'On the best possible scenario in terms of maximising the increase in the cuts in personal income tax that would come from a tax mix switch of a rise in the GST at 15 per cent, the best with a compensation bill of just $6 billion, which only dealt with the indexation of transfer payments . . . So, this government will not be taking a GST increase to the next election. The times are not right for that, and this government would never seek to change the GST unless we put it to the Australian people first.'

The whole debacle was the first indication that Turnbull was, like his predecessor, not above abandoning a supposedly strong piece of policy because of unwanted political fallout. Nor would it be the last.

The damage it did to Morrison, however, was brutal. Not only did he look similarly unprincipled, he also looked incompetent. Worse, it looked like he had no back-up plan, suggesting that he was as inept a politician as he was an economic steward.

It also gave observers a heads-up that, if the government was chickening out of a GST hike, then the remaining options for dealing with the nation's bottom line were far less appealing. Turnbull had made it clear that he agreed with a cut to company tax, but that left only a few areas in which the government could pursue its reform agenda.

Unfortunately those were areas the right wing of the party had a keen, personal interest in not changing, such as limiting the tax advantages of negative gearing property investments and/or the benefits of stashing otherwise taxable income in superannuation funds. Thus, with myriad philosophical and personal reasons to oppose movement in these directions, the party's conservatives started to agitate accordingly.[10] This was to become the battleground over which the government would fight their election campaign—but we shan't pre-empt all that fun just yet!

———

It became increasingly apparent that the government was going to move to an early double dissolution election, which had to be called before 12 May. This was a problem because

———

10 We'll plunge into the election-platform battle that was superannuation and negative gearing reform in another chapter, because, dammit, you've endured enough pointless bickering over incremental changes thus far.

the budget was due to be brought down on 10 May, offering nowhere near enough time to pass the necessary supply bills before asking the governor-general to dissolve parliament.

Thus it was assumed that the budget would be moved to 3 May, but this in itself created a bunch of problems, not least in the entire mechanics of the treasury. Of course, the quality of the budget document would be especially important since it would effectively be the first shot in the government's campaign for re-election.

Questions about the date for the budget were asked by journalists of every Coalition MP and senator, all of whom either fobbed off the question to the relevant departments or made gnomic statements about 'the plan' being to bring the budget down as usual. Amid the controversy, the treasurer decided that now was the time to definitively state that the budget would definitely, absolutely, be handed down as scheduled.

Morrison regularly had a catch-up with his old mate, Sydney radio's Ray Hadley, on his morning show. During their chat on 21 March, Hadley insisted that he'd heard rumours that the budget would be handed down on 3 May, but Morrison decried this as ridiculous. 'May 10, May 10! We're preparing for May 10, Ray.'

While this was going on at about 9.30 am, some important paperwork was being signed by the governor-general. Barely two hours after Morrison's appearance on Hadley's program, the PM announced that actually the budget would be brought forward to 3 May, with parliament prorogued to return early and sit from 18 April in order to debate legislation to restore the Australian Building and Construction Commission. If that bill was not passed, it would be used as the trigger for a double dissolution.

'The time for playing games is over,' the PM declared.[11] 'Today, I called upon His Excellency the governor-general to advise him to recall both houses of parliament on April 18, to consider and pass the Australian Building and Construction Commission Bill and the Registered Organisations Bill, and he has made a proclamation to that effect.'

As time went on it became clear that Morrison hadn't lied to Hadley: he genuinely hadn't known that the budget was going to be moved forward. This meant something significantly worse than lying: it indicated that Turnbull and the PMO had deliberately kept him out of the loop. What's more, at least three cabinet members—Attorney-General George Brandis, who had to prepare the document for the governor-general; Arthur Sinodinos, who'd had to arrange a cabinet meeting so the plan could be executed; and Michaelia Cash, whose ABCC legislation was the reason for proroguing parliament—all knew what was happening with the budget before its supposed author did.

Morrison tried to shrug it off with explanations like, 'It's my job to deliver the Budget, it's [Turnbull's] job to decide on what day it's delivered,' and he insisted that he'd been part of the broader plan: 'In terms of the overall scheme of what we were attempting to do, obviously I had been part of that planning for some months; but the final decision, going to see the governor-general and being across the constitutional issues, they're things for the attorney-general.'

---

11 When the proper time for playing games had begun remained tantalisingly opaque.

Shadow treasurer Chris Bowen released a press release crowing that the treasurer 'has been completely emasculated and has no influence over tax policy or even the timing of his own budget', and rumours of Turnbull and Morrison's increasingly frosty relationship began to circulate in earnest.

———

In March one last big pre-budget idea was splashed around for literally days, before being withdrawn in what seemed like a desperate attempt to propose some kind—any kind!—of bold reform, regardless of whether it was practical or not. And it was this: to give the states the power to levy their own income taxes, on the condition that they no longer asked for money from the federal government.

Such a fundamental change to the way taxation was levied in Australia would typically be considered and discussed at great length, since it would require very delicate legislation and education at all levels of government. It would be a complex operation to unpick a system that had remained essentially unchanged since the Income Tax Act was passed in 1942, decreeing that only the federal government could levy taxes on income.[12] However, it was instead presented to the media in late March, ahead of the Commonwealth Heads of Government meeting on 1 April, at which Turnbull and Morrison were, very reasonably, anticipating a hostile reception from the state premiers and treasurers, who were all set to ask questions about what the federal government was planning to do

---

12 The law, designed to raise money to fund Australia's involvement in World War II, was bitterly fought by the states—especially South Australia, Queensland, Victoria and Western Australia, who challenged it in the High Court as being unconstitutional.

about the $80 billion in state funding (mainly for schools and hospitals) that Abbott and Hockey had slashed in the 2014 budget.

Reinstating the money seemed like an unviable response, and the idea of state-levied taxes was exactly the kind of agile, outside-the-box thinking that the PM was all about encouraging. It wasn't entirely unprecedented either. South Australia's Jay Weatherill had floated a similar sort of idea in 2015, and the WA and ACT leaders had expressed cautious in-principle support for being able to raise their own taxes.

The idea was Martin Parkinson's, and Turnbull was an enormous fan of it: so much so that he began spruiking it, apparently without first briefing his surprised-looking treasurer, who made vague noises about it being one of the options still 'on the table', even as the PM was presenting it to the press as a fully formed proposal.

'In the longer term, a state should be free to lower that amount or indeed raise it, and then they are accountable to their own voters,' Turnbull explained enthusiastically the day before the COAG meeting. 'If we need more money, the state would go to their parliament, raise the money, go to the people and persuade them of the merits of it. This is a real opportunity to make the federation work. It will reduce an enormous amount of duplication and it will promote greater efficiency . . . You get this debilitating debate where the state says: "We don't have any money; Canberra, you have to raise the tax to give it to us." . . . The states came together and formed the Commonwealth. They should have access to the source of funds to be able to fund their services.'

The problems with the scheme weren't hard to parse. For a start, the public is, for the most part, not especially aware of which tranche of government is responsible for which specific area of service provision, so wasn't especially up for a long debate about the merits of increasing the burden on the states in order to make life easier for the federal government. Second, as with the proposed GST rise, it looked like the Coalition was adding a fresh new tax, which seemed rather at odds with the whole not-a-revenue-problem rhetoric.

That might have been explainable with some sort of campaign outlining the trade-offs for federal income tax, but a stickier problem was how a government ostensibly determined to minimise red tape was going to persuade voters that creating eight separate-but-overlapping tax jurisdictions was going to do anything but transform an already complex taxation system into a baffling nightmare of constantly shifting regulations.

There was also the issue that smaller states like Tasmania and South Australia would be forced to have higher tax rates than larger states like Queensland and New South Wales, which would put the already marginalised states at a disadvantage while also appearing to contravene Section 51 (ii) of the constitution, which gave the federated government the power to level taxes 'but so as not to discriminate between States or parts of States'.

The vague idea that this 'competitive federalism' would encourage economic competition between the states, and therefore efficiency with regard to the services they could provide, was also laughable—not least because someone in Mount Isa was hardly going to be in any position to rationally and painstakingly assess if the hospital system in Fremantle, Launceston or Port Adelaide might be better able to fix their broken leg or gaping head wound.

In any case, resistance to state-based income tax had already fomented by the time the COAG meeting began. Both SA's Labor premier, Jay Weatherill, and Tasmania's Liberal premier, Will Hodgman, pre-emptively rejected the notion, while Victoria's Labor premier, Daniel Andrews, was similarly scathing: 'In a conversation with the prime minister he indicated to me this would be revenue neutral. Well, if it's revenue neutral, how's it dealing with funding gaps in hospitals and schools?' NSW's Liberal premier, the generally supportive Mike Baird, hedged his bets, suggesting: 'These matters can be considered in the longer term. What is required right now is a partnership between the Commonwealth and the states for the health and education services we need.'

When the proposition didn't survive the first hours of the meeting, the PM confirmed that it was dead and not even up for future debate, the latest tax reform to be taken out of the hands of the treasurer without any sign of his involvement. The stories of increasingly snippy meetings between the men intensified, with one anonymous treasury source telling Fairfax: 'It is as bad as it looks and, if anything, internally it's a little bit worse.'

Clearly realising the need for a public show of unity, a press call was put out for the media to cover the thrilling sight of the PM and treasurer leaving the COAG meeting in the same car en route to the airport. The idea was to show they were great pals, but the uncomfortable photographs of the two added

to the impression that they could barely stand each o
company. Even Morrison's pal Ray Hadley made reference
it during their weekly on-air catch up. 'If the aim was to show
you were a united team, I think it looked a little forced,' he
suggested with uncharacteristic understatement on 2GB. 'And
so did other people who saw the photo.'

Sounding a little put upon, Morrison prissily countered,
'Well you're entitled to your view.'

And with that, Scott Morrison prepared for his big
moment—his first budget, his chance to finally put his mark
on the role he never especially wanted in the first place—
secure in the knowledge that the rushed final document would
be based on unpassed spending puts created by Hockey, its
policy hemmed in by the designs of Parkinson and Gruen,
and its timing determined by Turnbull, with most of the
available sweeteners ruled out for political reasons. Meanwhile, the national deficit—which the Coalition had rather
inconveniently spent the last five years fetishising as the sole
indicator of economic competency—had ballooned from the
$18 billion that Abbott and Hockey had declared a 'debt and
deficit disaster' when taking power in 2013 to $38.6 billion by
the time Morrison stepped up to deliver his budget.

Truly, it had never been a more exciting time to be responsible for the nation's economy. And Morrison, rightly, looked
scared as hell.

11
THE ROAD TO DOUBLE DISSOLUTION

In which the government finally gets its trigger, and fires

Depending on which side of politics you lean towards, or which Facebook groups most frequently post to your feed, the shadowy organisation known as the Australian Building and Construction Commission (ABCC) was in its heyday either the sole arbiter of justice in the otherwise lawless post-apocalyptic dystopia that is the construction biz, or a sinister secret police with extra-judiciary powers tasked with the near-religious mission to bust unions on an official party-political basis.[1]

And that's because on both sides of Australian politics the ABCC was a totemic organisation. Which was entirely appropriate, given that the legislation intended to restore it to its former glory existed less as a matter of practical necessity than as a trigger for a double dissolution election.

---

1 Or perhaps you don't care one way or the other, which is also fine.

As mentioned earlier, the government already had in hand
a number of bills that had been blocked twice in the Senate
and therefore could technically trigger such an election, but
these bills were either not sexy enough to justify using such
a sledgehammer or they related to environmental matters to
which the government didn't want to draw attention. And thus
was the ABCC elevated by the government's rhetoric from
'bureaucratic organisation that still largely exists' to 'cruelly
thwarted *21 Jump Street*-style construction-biz police force-
cum-superhero productivity team, doling out rough justice to
the villainous union thugs while keeping the world safe for
improvements in investment outcomes'.

At this point Labor's leaders were still congratulating
themselves on how very cleverly they'd postponed debate on
the ABCC legislation by making the Senate reformapalooza
debate drag on for a comically unnecessary amount of time.
When they rose for what they assumed was the end of the
parliamentary session on 18 March, the ABCC bill was still
safely untabled.

However, it turned out that Labor wasn't the only party
ready to waste time and public money on denying the other
side a win, and thus it was laughing less heartily three days
later when it was informed that the governor-general had
prorogued parliament, wiping the slate clean and bringing
parliament back early to sit on 18 April, at which point it
would debate and vote on the ABCC bills.

Proroguing parliament was an impressively obscure trick
to pull, since many parliamentarians had no idea it was even
a thing that could be done. Historically it has most often

occurred as a photo-opportunity-enhancing process to ensure that parliament coincides with a royal visit, which was the case the last time it was implemented, in 1977. In fact, the most recent non-regal reason that the governor-general had felt it necessary to call parliament was in 1968, after the disappearance and (presumed) death of Harold Holt in the waters off Cheviot Beach in Victoria.[2]

In his letter to Governor-General Peter Cosgrove, asking him to exercise his power to prorogue parliament in order that parliament could debate the ABCC legislation, Turnbull said: 'The Government regards this legislation as of great importance for promoting jobs and growth, improving productivity and also promoting workplace safety through taking strong measures to deal with widespread and systematic criminality in the building and construction industry.' And Cosgrove assented.

The problem, however, was this: the ABCC had never actually dealt with criminal activity. Like, at all. This was not even slightly within its remit.

As established by the Howard government in 2005, the commission's role was to oversee workplace relations—and it had had remarkable, some might say 'brutal', powers to fulfil that role. This was what the unions and Labor objected to: the existence of what was referred to as 'coercive powers', such as compelling people to appear before the commission using only ABCC-approved legal counsel (at the witness's expense);

---

2 Seeing as though he'd be 108 years old in 2016, at this point we can probably conclude that he's not still out there. Perhaps we need to consider turning off the Holt signal a hopeful nation still shines into the clouds over Point Nepean, in the increasingly forlorn hope that the Wet Knight Rises.

reopening settled issues; making all deliberations and rulings confidential; and undertaking compulsory interrogation of witnesses, regardless of whether they were actually workers or, as happened in one notorious 2007 example, simply passers-by.

Those were the elements the Gillard government had rolled back when it transformed the ABCC into Fair Work Australia, bringing it in line with the legal standards expected of other commissions and tribunals. Criminal activity on building sites remained, as most seven-year-olds would correctly assume, the exclusive preserve of the police and law enforcement agencies.

The unions particularly objected to the ABCC because they claimed it had a negative impact on worker safety, and the numbers bore this out: before the ABCC, deaths on construction sites sat around three per 100,000 workers, then abruptly rose to just under five per 100,000. When its powers were reduced under Gillard, workplace deaths dropped sharply to just over two.

The other big issue, though, was productivity. The only report suggesting that the ABCC had a positive effect on productivity in the construction sector was one by Econotech, commissioned by the government, and it misrepresented much of the publicly available data upon which it was ostensibly based. Indeed, the Econotech report had been publicly discredited in 2009 by Justice Murray Wilcox of the Industrial Relations Court; he described it in a ruling as 'deeply flawed' and added that it 'ought to be totally disregarded'.

Yet Turnbull's version of events was that the ABCC had 'improved productivity by 20 per cent', which was repeated often in the media until Leigh Sales pointed out during an interview on *7.30* that a) the aforementioned Econotech report, upon which the government was making its case, didn't even make that claim (it actually claimed productivity rose by a similarly implausible 9.4 per cent, before quietly removing that section altogether in its updated report the following year), and b) the Productivity Commission, a commission that one might think knew a thing or two about productivity, claimed that productivity actually rose 1.3 per cent during the lifetime of the ABCC and only jumped in 2011–12, which was when the Gillard government removed many of the coercive powers of the ABCC.

'I think you'll find that's not right,' Turnbull incorrectly replied.

When Sales pointed out that she had the Productivity Commission's report right there, the PM waxed condescending: 'Well I'm sure you do,' he said, before repeating his claim that 'there was an increase in productivity following the introduction of the ABCC'.

The fact that the ABCC didn't have the powers the government claimed it had, and that the data didn't say what the government claimed it did, were but two of the grounds under which Labor, the Greens and many of the Senate crossbench had rejected the ABCC legislation in the first place. Since those concerns had been in no way addressed in the interim, there was little sign that they wouldn't straight up reject the legislation when it was reintroduced. And, from the government's perspective, that was completely fine. Indeed, some might argue that that was the deliberate intent.

But proroguing wiped the slate clean of any still-to-be-discussed legislation or other matters, meaning that the government could get straight into reintroducing the ABCC bill. Recalling parliament reportedly cost over a million dollars for the three weeks allocated to allow debate of the legislation. However, as it turned out the Senate only needed a couple of hours: on 18 April the bill was rejected for a second time by the upper house, and the government had its trigger.

And thus the campaigning began, starting with the 2016 Budget.

———

On 3 May Scott Morrison presented his first-ever budget to the nation, and he looked far from confident up at the dispatch box as he ran through a series of policy plans that, accurately, were interpreted less as an economic plan and more as campaign speech setting the terms of the forthcoming election campaign.

His department had avoided the typical briefing documents circulated to journalists outlining the budget 'winners' and 'losers' for reasons that were to become clear: essentially Morrison was proposing a version of 'trickle down' economics, the economic philosophy most often associated with Margaret Thatcher's government in the UK and the Ronald Reagan presidency in the US and characterised by a) the notion that cutting taxes to the wealthy would encourage them to spend that extra money, thereby enabling the money to 'trickle down' to those at the bottom of the economic pile, and b) the fact that it demonstrably doesn't work.[3]

---

3 That's perhaps unfair: it worked great, if you were a wealthy person who hated paying tax. It just didn't work for literally everyone else. There's a reason that the model sounded like something that worked more successfully for urine than economics.

The deficit was not predicted to change in any meaningful way, although there would be massive cuts across education, health, aged care, child care and expenditure on public servant salaries. Necessary spending had been pushed out beyond the budget's scope—most notably for the National Disability Insurance Scheme and for the infrastructure funding to the states and territories that had been negotiated at the recent COAG meeting—in order to make the bottom line look a bit less spendy. And in terms of savings, it did not escape notice that many of the amounts being banked by Morrison were from cuts that had been rejected by parliament, such as the $2 billion cut to university funding that the Treasurer mysteriously included as having taken effect in January 2016, despite the fact it very obviously had not.

There were many such 'zombie savings', which meant that the already not-great economic situation Morrison outlined was actually a good deal more not-great. And then there were the tax cuts. Most significant was a company tax cut for small business, and relief for the top 25 per cent of income earners, who found their tax bracket moved a convenient $7000 further up the scale.

Morrison was also basing his projections for economic growth on a couple of numbers that were at best optimistic and at worst entirely imaginary: that the Australian economy would experience 3 per cent growth (at a time when economists claimed that anything above 2 per cent was ambitious) and a rise in exports based on economic figures from the Chinese government that no-one considered remotely reliable.

But the most controversial element involved changes to superannuation, which were already setting the backbench a-tremble. These included a $1.6 million transfer balance cap on the total amount of accumulated superannuation an individual could transfer into the retirement phase, and—here was the kicker—there was to be no grandfathering clause for those who'd already done so. In other words, this would affect those who had been deliberately stashing their money in their super account as a (perfectly legal) way to avoid paying tax—people who were, one would assume, disproportionately Liberal voters.

It's worth adding that this was actually a genuinely decent policy, addressing a structural distortion in the system that had been intended to incentivise increasing superannuation but which had effectively turned into an onshore tax haven, allowing the wealthy to significantly reduce their taxable income. But given the government had rejected Labor's proposed negative gearing reform, with which it was addressing a similar distortion, this seemed oddly off-message for the Coalition—a point the DelCons were to emphasise with increasing vigour in the months to follow.

In summary, Morrison proposed a budget that rewarded wealthy business; cut services to everyone else; hurt people saving for retirement; pretended unpassed savings existed and that necessary spending was a future problem; didn't address the underlying deficit in any meaningful way, and was predicated on Australia enjoying positive future global circumstances that showed no sign of actually manifesting. It was as though Morrison had read *The Secret* and figured that positive visualisation was a pretty cool way to run an economy.[4]

And the response was ... muted. The public didn't get on board; the usual cheerleaders in the conservative press were critical; and the business community didn't care for the suggestion of greater examination of corporate tax avoidance. Even the concessions to the banking sector, which were estimated at around a billion dollars, didn't win back their love.

The following days were not among the government's best. Scott Morrison fronted up to an interview with Leigh Sales on *7.30* right after launching the budget, and she didn't pull any punches, asking, 'What was the point of your three years in government and why should voters re-elect you?'

Morrison didn't exactly cover himself in glory, saying that the government had suffered with 'a lot of commitments' in a 'difficult environment', before insisting the budget would be in surplus by 2021—adding the rider: 'If estimates and parameters change, we are obviously hostage to those events.'

Sales, for her part, appreciated that get-out clause, asking why the treasury had made what appeared to be wildly optimistic projections for growth and future commodity prices.

'I'd say we're being *realistically* optimistic, like the Australian people,' Morrison replied with patriotic chutzpah, celebrating

---

4   To be fair, as *The Monthly* pointed out in a February 2012 profile, Morrison's Shirelive church advocates the prosperity gospel developed in the US and beloved by many Pentecostal churches—effectively espousing the idea that being personally successful is a sign that God reckons you're a good egg (and, in its most extreme form, that poverty is personal moral failing rather than, say, a result of structural inequality within society). So assuming that happy thoughts and good intentions will have a better outcome than actual policy wouldn't be that huge a leap.

'300,000 jobs and 3 per cent real growth last year, which means we're growing faster than the UK and the US'.

To which Sales pointed out that the Reserve Bank had cut interest rates to a record low of 1.75 per cent on the day of the budget, which didn't seem to bode well for the economy's growth.

This, Morrison insisted, was because of inflation—or, more specifically, the deflation that was affecting the Australian economy. And this was incontrovertibly true; but declining demand was still hardly a seal of approval for the government that had overseen the collapse of consumer and business confidence, thus leading to this decline.

Morrison might have done a poor job of explaining his plan but, having weathered that embarrassment, the prime minister went off to Sky News to chat with David Speers. This was not expected to be a controversial interview: after all, it was the financially savvy PM talking turkey with one of the nation's most experienced financial journalists, on a channel whose audience was almost entirely made up of people in politics or finance, or those sitting in airports waiting to be called to board when it happened to be on.[5]

And, again, this was hardly likely to be a 'gotcha!' moment: the topic under discussion was the budget and the planned tranche of cuts to company tax, which would reduce the rate to 25 per cent over a decade. This had been a centrepiece

---

5   Turnbull would have done well to remember that it was Speers who hosted the excruciatingly painful interview with George Brandis in April 2014, during which the attorney-general argued the importance of the government's metadata retention policies and proved that he genuinely had no idea what metadata actually was. There's a whole section about it in *The Short and Excruciatingly Embarrassing Reign of Captain Abbott*, because it really was god-awful.

of Morrison's plan for jobs and growth, a phrase he used a total of thirteen times in his speech, an average of once every 2.3 minutes, in what was a transparent foreshadowing of the election campaign to come.

However, despite Turnbull's ostensible enthusiasm for the idea, he proved remarkably coy when it came to answering Speers's not-especially-complex question: 'What's it going to cost taxpayers to cut the company tax rate to 25 per cent?'

The assumption was that the government had done modelling, since it claimed it would be part of the plan to get to a surplus by the 2026/27 budget. But Turnbull responded: 'The cost of the plan is set out in the medium-term outlook and shows the budget returning to balance.'

Spears, however, was pretty keen to get an answer that was in the form of a dollar amount, so he asked again. And that's when things got weird.

'What it ensures is that we'll have stronger jobs and growth,' Turnbull responded—a response which, you might notice, isn't a dollar amount or, for that matter, a sentence that means very much at all.

So Speers asked again. And the prime minister *still* didn't answer.

'David, what you are asking is for me to unpick every single line item of those assumptions going out to 2026/27,' he admonished. 'I am not going to add to the detail that is in the budget papers.'

And then Speers picked up the budget papers and asked the PM to explain which bit of detail he was referring to.

The reply was: 'Treasury has modelled [the cuts] and . . . all of those costs are taken into account in the medium-term outlook. It is set out here on page 311 of Budget Paper 1.'

Another attempt to elicit a straight answer resulted in Turnbull choosing to keep things tantalisingly opaque, even as Speers sighed, 'This is not a difficult question.'

The answer Turnbull was ineptly attempting to avoid, incidentally, was '$48.2 billion'—a number the government only authorised Treasury to reveal at 6 pm on the night of Bill Shorten's budget reply, which suggested that either the government wanted the result buried, or it wanted to wrong-foot the Opposition.

As it turned out, neither happened.

———

On 5 May Shorten made his budget reply, and he pulled few punches. There was a predictable attack on cuts to income tax for high earners. 'Now is not the time to reduce the marginal rate for individuals who earn greater than $180,000,' he said and claimed that, according to the independent Parliamentary Budget Office, a Labor move to block such a change was 'estimated to improve the budget by $16 billion over the decade'. He criticised the government's somewhat whimsical definition of 'small businesses' that would be eligible for the company tax cuts. 'Coles is not a small business. The Commonwealth Bank is not a small business. Goldman Sachs is not a small business.'

He also railed against the superannuation plans, conveniently overlooking the fact that all the arguments he was using could be just as readily applied to the negative gearing policy his party was proposing. They were, he insisted, 'chaotic and unprecedented . . . The treasurer claims only a small number of superannuation account holders will be affected. When the system is undermined, everyone is affected, everyone is at risk. Every single superannuation holder can now only guess what Malcolm Turnbull and Scott Morrison will do next.'

Labor made much of the almost $50 billion sacrificed in revenue. But the debate over the budget was always going to be short-lived and would soon be overwhelmed by the demands of the election campaign.

On Monday, 8 May, Turnbull did exactly what everyone knew he'd do: he announced that the governor-general had accepted his advice to dissolve both houses of parliament, 'effective tomorrow', and so Australia was on its way to its seventh-ever double dissolution election, in which the Turnbull government would be 'seeking the mandate of the Australian people to continue and complete that national economic plan, because that is the key to us achieving and realising the great opportunities of these exciting times'.

The times might have been exciting, but the next eight weeks were already looking set to be downright excruciating.

12
PUTTING THE TENSION IN OFFSHORE DETENTION

Or, 'Stand by Your Manus'

It is a truth universally acknowledged that Australia's tough border protection policies are: a) a roaring, unambiguous success, and b) dependent on offshore detention as a vital deterrent to would-be asylum seekers coming by boat. Unfortunately, those truths appear to be a little light on, well, truth.

The thinking appears to be that people would look at the war and persecution going on in their homeland and think, 'Well, I *could* flee the gangs coming to burn my village and rape my children, and attempt to build a new life in a peaceful democracy, but that seems unfair: after all, Australia really should determine who can and cannot come to its country.'

And thus, in increments starting under the Howard government in 2001 and ramping up under succeeding Labor and Coalition governments up to and including Turnbull, the fate for anyone attempting to claim asylum in Australia by coming across the seas to our boundless plains was indefinite offshore detention with no possibility of settlement here.

One problem—which wasn't to get much play during the actual election campaign, for reasons that will become obvious—was that the future of offshore detention was looking incredibly shaky, if not entirely doomed. But not for stupid, selfish reasons, like 'the spirit and letter of the international law' or 'the realisation that populist appeals to nonsensical concepts of sovereignty had been directly responsible for the deaths of people under Australia's protection', but for the most noble reason of all: entrenched political corruption and corporate fear of legal reprisals.

But this will take a bit of explaining. First, some context may be illuminating.

———

North of Papua New Guinea, among the Admiralty Islands, is a lump of land about one hundred kilometres across and thirty wide.[1] It is the main island of Manus Province, the local name for the Admiralties. The whole province only has a population of around 50,000 people (the largest town on Manus Island, Lorengau, has barely 5000), not least because it's a fairly isolated sort of a place.

The isolation has been both a benefit and a curse for this tropical paradise. It's led to some unique and beautiful fauna— the Admiralty Islands have several endemic species of frogs, bats and birds, and Manus itself boasts the unique emerald green snail, whose beautiful bright green shell made it such a

---

1 Just for comparison, Kangaroo Island is 150 kilometres across and 35 kilometres wide. Manus, in other words, isn't a huge place.

sought-after prize that it's now officially endangered, in part as a result of the island's lush rainforests being hacked out for more lucrative coconut plantations.

The province's strategic value made it a major air and naval base in World War II; during the final push against the Japanese, the Allied forces stationed over 600,000 service people on Manus and its close neighbour, Los Negros Island, with which it is linked by a bridge (confusingly, the two islands seem like one and are together often referred to as Manus Island). The cost of developing Manus at the time was estimated at a staggering US$116 million, but was credited with having hastened the end of the war, thanks to its role as the US's staging post for bombing raids on Japanese installations in the Pacific. And after the war it moved into a new phase, one which would neatly mirror its future: as a dumping ground for stuff Australia couldn't be arsed dealing with.

In the 29 July 1951 issue of the *Toledo Blade* a story described the island as 'a rusting junkyard and a monument to official bungling. With no planes, ships or defences and a population of 350, this strategic Admiralty Group island . . . is a victim of post-war neglect by Australia.'[2]

After railing against the pittance for which the installations had been sold to Australia, and how 'Nationalist China' also just lobbed in and took as much stuff as it could carry, the article went on to explain:

Millions of dollars worth of equipment was left behind on Manus, however, and eventually became Australia's property by default

---

2 The *Toledo Blade* is still published, by the way. Since 1960 it's been known simply as *The Blade*, but it's one of the longest-running newspapers in the United States, printed daily since 19 December 1835.

when the United States took no further interest in it. Theoretically this should have enabled Australia to maintain a bang-up base on Manus with the equipment the United States abandoned. Unfortunately this has not been the case ... A qualified observer who recently visited the once powerful base has brought back some startling and discouraging facts. Jungle and rust, he says, have ruined millions of dollars of unused or once-salvageable jeeps, bulldozers, mobile cranes, tractors, trucks, generating units and valuable equipment of all descriptions. The coral roads of Manus are crumbling and many have disappeared altogether. Docks and waterfront installations are rotting and falling into Seedler [sic] Harbour.

Seeadler Harbour is a bay that sweeps around the north-eastern coast of the island, bounded by Los Negros to the east and dotted with a series of smaller islands to the north. That's where Lorengau is located, and a winding forty-minute drive later you get to the detention centre on Los Negros Island's north-east coast, where Australia's proud legacy of leaving things to rot has continued.

The detention centre is on the former site of the US staging base, which became the Australian naval base HMAS Seeadler in 1950 before being renamed PNG Defence Force Base Lombrum in 1974 ahead of PNG's independence from Australia in 1975. The centre—whose official name is the Manus Regional Processing Centre—operates within Lombrum itself. It was first built in 2001, with sister facilities in the tiny banana republic of Nauru and the Australian-owned Christmas Island; in its first life it only held asylum seekers up until June 2004, when Aladdin Sisalem, the sole remaining detainee, was permitted to settle in Australia and it then closed. Nauru's camp closed in 2008 after new

PM Kevin Rudd followed through on his promise to end offshore processing and mandatory detention, although Christmas Island's relatively new facilities were still being assessed for potential expansion.

And that should have been the end of it. But after the number of asylum seeker boats increased dramatically during the era of the Rudd government, in August 2012 Julia Gillard announced that her government was reopening Nauru and Manus. The motivation seems to have been split between reacting out of genuine humanitarian concern for the increase in asylum seekers dying at sea and political fear that the Coalition was successfully painting the government as weak on border security.[3]

In December 2012 the first new wave of detainees was flown in, despite the Nauru and Manus facilities having been determined to be 'inadequate' by the United Nation's High Commissioner for Refugees, who added that putting human lives therein would put Australia in breach of its human rights obligations.

When Scott Morrison became Minister for Immigration and Border Protection nine months later he was determined that Australia's offshore detention become part of a military operation, Operation Sovereign Borders, which meant that it

---

3 It's worth defining a few terms here: an 'asylum seeker' is someone fleeing persecution and asking for Australia's protection; a 'refugee' is someone found to have a legitimate case to seek asylum, as defined by the United Nations. In a nutshell: asylum seekers are asking for help, and refugees have a legal claim of said help. A good way to avoid determining that someone is a refugee, and therefore Australia's obligation, is not to process their claim for asylum and just leave them in a 'processing centre', which is like a waiting room—but with fewer magazines and a lot more typhoid and sexual assault. And that's effectively been Australia's strategy of choice for the last decade or so.

was therefore subject to restrictions on information. This very conveniently allowed the government to develop the impression that it was Stopping The Boats, when a more accurate description was that they were Stopping The Information About What Happened To The Boats And Also To The People On The Boats, Since It Was Genuinely Pretty Horrific.

While there were three offshore detention centres, two were increasingly preferred by the Abbott government. Christmas Island had the most modern facilities; however, because it was technically part of Australia, it was not only subject to Australian law but was also able to be inspected by organisations like the Australian Human Rights Commission. And there was a lot to check up there too: reports of outbreaks of third world diseases, including typhoid and tuberculosis, did little to assure the public that the government was offering the very best of care to those kept on Christmas Island. There were heartbreaking reports of attempted suicide and self-harm, including a protest in December 2013 during which detainees sewed their lips shut.

These unflattering portrayals of Australia's responsibilities were angrily denied by the Department for Immigration, despite multiple independent reports—including the Australian Human Rights Commission's *The Forgotten Children* (which focused on children in detention in Australia and on Christmas Island; the government accused the commission of being deeply partisan in a largely successful attempt to deflect attention from the actual findings of the report), and the subsequent Moss Review (commissioned by the government to prove the AHRC's report incorrect, it inconveniently confirmed the original report's findings and conclusions while including Manus and Nauru in its tales of excruciating waste and torment).

So Christmas Island could be an embarrassment, but Manus Island was part of Papua New Guinea and Nauru an independent sovereign nation. And while the camps were built, funded, legislated, staffed and subject to the direct control of Australia, they were (the government argued) actually the responsibility of the foreign countries in which they were located. This provided something of a tasteful fig leaf for the hideous dangling scrotum of Australia's offshore detention policy, filled as it was with increasingly horrific testimonies of trauma, sexual violence, assault, mental illness, self-harm, suicide, vermin, entirely preventable illnesses and lives spent in endless terror.

It also meant that Australia could shrug and say, 'Nothing to do with us, it's a matter for Nauru,' when, for example, Nauru's government decided to jack up the application fee for a journalist visa from $200 to a non-refundable $8000 in January 2014, with no guarantee that the visa would actually be granted. After all, the Australian government had been fine with the Nauru government deciding to charge it—or, more accurately, Australian taxpayers—$1000 per month per detainee in completely-reasonable-and-definitely-not-extortionate fees.

This insistence that whatever happened at Manus detention centre was totally up to the PNG government was going to come back and bite the government, but let's not get ahead of ourselves; instead, let's recap what was going on there after the Abbott government came to power in September 2013.

Manus had really been thrust into the spotlight in February 2014, when a series of escalating protests—inflamed by a visit from Scott Morrison, who told the detainees they essentially had the choice of either returning to the place from which they had fled or dying in the camp—turned into a full-scale riot. In the course of the hellish scenes that followed, one man—twenty-three-year-old Reza Berati, who had escaped from Iran—was murdered by having his skull smashed in and another sixty-two people were injured, many seriously, when the camp security and local Incident Response Teams (a more official-sounding term than the accurate alternative descriptor: 'untrained tooled-up locals') took matters into their own hands.

In September that year there was another death: that of young Iranian detainee Hamid Kehazaei. He had cut his foot on the rocky ground of the camp because shoes for detainees were in short supply. The cut had become infected, but medical care in the centre was limited and calls for Kehazaei to be moved to somewhere with proper facilities—such as PNG's capital, Port Moresby, or Australia—were ignored until he developed septicaemia. He was finally flown to Brisbane, but by then it was far too late: he slipped into a coma and his heart gave out while in hospital.

The very establishment of the centre had been legally controversial—or, to put it another way, illegal. The problem with Australia managing an offshore detention camp on Manus was laid out in Section 42 of the PNG Constitution, which guaranteed personal liberties to all people in the country, including foreigners—and, problematically, emphasised that the personal liberties of said foreigners could only be restricted if they entered the country illegally. Asylum seekers detained at Manus had a) not broken any PNG law, only Australian ones, and therefore could not legally have their liberty restricted, and b) not consented to enter the country in the first place and therefore could in no way be said to have entered illegally.

The decision to make the camps at both Manus and Nauru 'open'—meaning the detainees could, in theory, come and go as they pleased—was a desperate attempt to get around the question of whether these people had restrictions on their liberty. In Nauru it was somewhat easier to maintain the fiction that detainees had complete freedom of movement, since they were still trapped on a tiny rock in the middle of the Pacific Ocean. However, because Manus Island was part of PNG, it was impossible to argue, as the Australian government nonetheless attempted to do, that the detainees were 'at liberty' to go where they liked, while also being forbidden from leaving the island.

However, this had been largely overlooked for a couple of reasons. One was that the PNG government had attempted to alter Section 42 in 2014 to create a legal loophole that would permit the camp to function. That new amendment—creating an exception in the event of 'holding a foreign national under arrangements made by Papua New Guinea with another country'—immediately drew criticism and the Supreme Court began proceedings to have the amendment deemed unconstitutional and the centre itself declared illegal.

But there was a great reason to overcome these legal difficulties, since the government didn't want to interrupt the

flow of lovely extra foreign bri—sorry, completely reasonable
extra foreign aid it was getting from Australia as a result
of reopening Manus. As the *Canberra Times* elucidated, 'In
exchange for PNG agreeing to host the centre, Australia agreed
to provide an extra $420 million on top of the $507 million in
aid budgeted for PNG in 2013–14.'

This money was desperately needed by the impoverished
country but was spent in PNG generally rather than on
Manus Island specifically. The locals were not treated well, for
the most part: submissions to the Australian Senate inquiry
into the riots revealed that the Manus community had been
growing increasingly furious about the failure of the promised
economic benefits to materialise. In the meantime, waste was
being dumped into food gardens; roads were being damaged
and not repaired; the price of essentials had risen sharply,
while those locals who did get jobs at the centre earned wages
far, far below those of the Australian staff.

The islanders had also been blessed with arrival of the
notoriously violent Royal PNG Constabulary mobile squad.[4]
The squad had been based on Manus at Australia's expense
after the re-establishment of the camp and in 2013 had been
implicated in two deaths of local men. Twenty-one-year-old
Raymond Sipaun was savagely beaten by squad members after
being found drunk in public, then dumped in a jail cell; he
never regained consciousness. Seventeen-year-old Kisawen

---

4 That's not a judgement call: that's the considered opinion of Human Rights
Watch. Australian director Elaine Pearson told Radio Australia: 'The paramilitary mobile squad is particularly notorious for human rights abuses . . . in some
cases, they have beaten and tortured some people who have been detained in their
custody. We are very concerned if the paramilitary mobile squad is actually being
used as security for the detention centre.'

Pokas was on his way home from school when he was hit and killed by a drunk-driving squad officer in his official vehicle.

However, Manus was also politically irrelevant, with only two MPs representing the province in PNG's parliament. The locals could complain all they liked about the damage the centre was inflicting on the island, with the thuggish mobile squad and Australian security forces throwing their weight around, and with a marked increase in crime (particularly assaults and prostitution), but the rest of the nation would look at the money pouring in from Australia and figure it was a bargain in anyone's language. After all, according to reliable internal reports, Prime Minister Peter O'Neill had personally proposed that the camp be reopened when it became clear that the Rudd government's plan to dump its asylum seekers in Malaysia wasn't going to fly.

As long as PNG's prime minister was in favour of the camp, it was probably safe. So it was kind of a problem that O'Neill's grip on power was becoming increasingly tenuous.

———

O'Neill was no stranger to political controversy, in a country where political corruption was very much the norm.[5] He'd become PM under dubious circumstances in 2011, when he'd teamed up with his party's opponents to remove acting PM Sam Abal and assume the prime ministership himself. The legality of this was challenged, but by February 2012 everything had settled down and the new PM was insisting

5   Again, that's not a subjective judgement: Transparency International ranked PNG 139th out of 168 countries in terms of the level of corruption in its government in the 2015 Corruption Perceptions Index. By comparison, Australia ranks 13th.

that he would rid PNG of corruption, thanks to Taskforce Sweep, a crime-fighting unit he had set up, which cut a swathe through the country's government, law enforcement and bureaucracy. But suddenly this taskforce had its funding cut, ahead of being disbanded permanently, when it attempted to issue an arrest warrant against O'Neill over his involvement in a $30 million fraud that laundered public money through Australian banks.

This should have been a quick fix but the scandal refused to die, despite O'Neill replacing his justice minister and altering laws to prevent his being arrested. The opposition also asked pointed questions about a US$1.2 billion loan he had pushed through parliament in order to buy the nation a stake in the company Oil Search Limited.

This all came at a particularly bad time for him, as the Chinese construction slump that had ended Australia's mining boom had done a particularly brutal number on the heavily commodity-dependent PNG economy. His government had imposed swingeing cuts to education, health and welfare, and this had angered much of the community—particularly students, who began a series of demonstrations which resulted in four people being shot dead in June 2016 after police opened fire on a protest march in Port Moresby.

With public support waning and an election due in early 2017, the prime minister had plenty of battles to fight if he wanted to maintain his position. The last thing he needed was a messy and probably doomed constitutional battle just to keep Australia happy.

So, he decided, fuck 'em.

On 3 March 2016 O'Neill gave a speech to Australia's National Press Club in which he described the Manus Island processing centre as 'a problem'; he indicated he was going to solve it. 'We have issues about cost of the resettlement, who is going to pay for it,' he explained, adding that the PNG Supreme Court would be challenging the constitutionality of the camp—almost as though the problem with the amendment hadn't been his own doing. 'Certainly [the] Papua New Guinea government does not have the resources to resettle the refugees as required but we will play our role in making sure [that] those who've got the skills and are able to work can be allowed to work in our communities.'

The response at the time was remarkably sanguine, with Peter Dutton implying that O'Neill was merely feeling political pressure from those pesky do-gooders in the media and that the whole thing would blow over. 'PNG and Nauru have been unfairly vilified by advocates, including by some parts of the media, because of their opposition to our secure borders policy,' he complained. 'It is unfair and the targeting of our regional partners should stop.'

So he was probably very surprised in April when the PNG Supreme Court found the detention centre to be unconstitutional and the government announced that it was shutting the camp completely.

'The detention of the asylum seekers on Manus Island in Papua New Guinea . . . is unconstitutional and illegal,' the court ruled. 'Both the Australian and Papua New Guinea governments shall forthwith take all steps necessary to cease and prevent the continued unconstitutional and illegal detention of the asylum seekers or transferees at the relocation centre on Manus Island and the continued breach of the asylum seekers' or transferees' constitutional and human rights.'

This hadn't come as a complete surprise to the Department of Immigration and Border Protection, which had been frantically looking for staff qualified to process all of the Manus Island detainees post-haste. Even so, it appeared that the Australian government had assumed it would either be able to strong-arm or bribe the PNG government to keep the camp open. Perhaps the government hoped that shunting people off to Cambodia would be an option by then.

Back in September 2014, with a great champagne-popping fanfare, Scott Morrison had signed a deal with the Cambodian government to resettle willing refugees in that country. But by May 2015 this deal had completely collapsed, with new immigration minister Peter Dutton desperately attempting to spin it as a triumph, despite there having been a grand total of five people resettled, at a cost to Australia of $55 million. By the time the Manus problem reared its head in April 2016, all bar one of the refugees who had been resettled in Cambodia had agreed to be sent back to the country from which they'd fled, preferring to take their chances with the authorities they'd escaped from than to endure the homelessness that had awaited them in Phnom Penh.[6]

---

6   The deal had specified that the refugees would be put up in specially purchased villas, and would receive training and language lessons with a view to getting jobs in Cambodia and access to social services. When they arrived, however, it transpired that none of those things had been arranged (two refugees were reduced to sleeping on the floor of the upstairs office of the organisation tasked with looking after them), and when questions were asked of the Cambodian government by Peter Dutton, he was told that Cambodia very much appreciated the $55 million but wouldn't be taking any further refugees, thanks.

In any case, the Australian government didn't appear to have any sort of plan B in place when the court decision was announced. Initially Dutton tried to shrug it off, insisting on ABC radio: 'The findings of the Supreme Court in PNG aren't binding on the Australian government. Our policy is not going to change. We are absolutely adamant that people won't be settling in this country.' This suggested that the PNG government would resettle those found to be refugees—although PNG's high commissioner to Australia, Charles Lepani, made it clear this was not going to happen, since permanent resettlement was 'never Papua New Guinea's understanding'.

However, within days Dutton was attempting to make it look like the government had it totally under control after all, going on *Today* to tell a very sceptical-looking Karl Stefanovic that the decision 'hasn't taken us by surprise . . . We've been anticipating the Supreme Court decision in PNG and we've been planning for this since late last year.'

But if Dutton and his busy planning bees had indeed spent months crafting their response, they'd apparently overlooked the question, 'So, what do you reckon we should do about those detainees, huh?', because the minister seemed downright confused when asked and gave no meaningful response. 'You've been told that this facility's closing and you can't answer the question for what happens to those 850 asylum seekers?' an exasperated Stefanovic probed after Dutton stumbled through a non-answer.

This was remarkable, because the only possible answer was pretty straightforward. There were exactly three options: Nauru, Christmas Island or the Australian mainland. By Friday the government confirmed that Christmas Island was off the list, which limited the options to two. And if Christmas Island wasn't a possibility, there was no way that mainland Australia was going to be an option, since it was forever off the itinerary for any unauthorised maritime arrival.

So that left Nauru. Of course, there were a few teeny-tiny problems with that.

———

Manus Island at least has the decency to be a proper-looking island. Nauru isn't even as large as Melbourne's airport,[7] and it is created almost entirely of shit.

That's not a euphemism. Generations of birds over the millennia had crapped on what was otherwise a lump of rock in the middle of the sea, which meant that it was abundant in phosphate-rich guano. This lucrative resource was exploited from the second it was discovered—first in the 1890s by the British and German governments and their commercial partners in the Pacific Islands Company, which began mining operations there; then by the Australian, New Zealand and British governments that administered the island under the League of Nations; then (briefly) the Japanese forces that claimed the island during World War II. The UN oversaw the nation after that, and Nauru eventually became independent in 1968 and bought its phosphate licences back from Australia in 1970, at which point it began seriously exploiting itself.

For a while Nauru was insanely wealthy—in 1980 it was the wealthiest nation per capita on the planet—from strip mining 80 per cent of the island for its money-making fertiliser. A royalties trust bought up properties around the world as insurance

———

7   Fun fact! Nauru is 21 square kilometres, while Tullamarine Airport is 23.69.

against the island's phosphate-free future, but millions went missing: either into the pockets of less-than-assiduous officials, blown on expensive international investment jaunts, or— according to the single most ridiculous story of all—in backing a failed West End musical about Leonardo Da Vinci.

Amazingly, the Nauru government was convinced to sink £2 million into the development of *Leonardo the Musical: A Portrait of Love*, a musical written by the former singer of pop band Unit 4 + 2 (remembered for its 1965 hit 'Concrete and Clay', and literally nothing else), on the advice of the band's former road manager. The Liverpool-born Duke Minks had come a long way since driving one-hit wonders around: he'd been living in Australia for two decades by this time and had had a colourful career. He'd become a merchant banker with Citibank and had started doing deals for the Nauruan government in the eighties, including buying out the Tamworth-based East-West Airlines for around $8.5 million and on-selling it a year later for over $20 million.

However, he never lost his love for music, and maintained his friendship with Unit 4 + 2's singer, Greg Moeller. The pair came up with the idea of an entirely fictitious love story between Leonardo and the model who sat for the *Mona Lisa*. So Greg knocked up some songs with his brother Tommy and Australian producer Russell Dunlop[8] while Minks gave

---

8 Dunlop was a member of the Australian progressive jazz fusion band Ayers Rock in the seventies, and my father had a copy of its self-titled album when I was growing up. Thus I knew the band from my early childhood as a) having the world's least necessary die-cut cover, where removing the inner sleeve of the record revealed that what *looked* like a picture of Uluru on the front cover was . . . um, actually another picture of Uluru, and b) god-awful noodly rubbish. Fuck you, progressive jazz fusion.

some notes to playwright John Kane to bash out the words. A tape containing just a few songs was enough to seduce Kelly Emu, special adviser to the president of Nauru, to recommend backing the eye-watering investment. The musical made its debut on the London stage at the Strand Theatre on 21 May 1993, and limped to a close five painful weeks later, never to be performed again and reportedly costing the Nauru Government tens of millions of dollars in losses.[9]

It's a shame that it didn't become a timeless theatrical classic, because by 2000 pretty much all the accessible phosphate reserves had been sold, the resource royalties had dried up and most of the island was uninhabitable, thanks to the mines. The soil—ironically, given the guano was being used as fertiliser—was basically useless for growing anything. Unemployment hit a staggering 90 per cent, with almost all of those people who had jobs—95 per cent of them—employed by the government.

Fortunately, the Nauru government had some other creative ideas. One was becoming a tax haven and money-laundering centre, which was briefly very lucrative in the late nineties. Another strong income stream was its indiscriminate sale of Nauruan passports, which proved extremely profitable and allowed people to travel with false identities. This ended when six terrorists were arrested with Nauruan passports in South-East Asia in 2003 and the government was politely warned

---

9   The reviews were less than kind, complaining mainly that the play was dull, not even having the good grace to be terrible enough to be entertaining. The key song, 'She Lives With Me', exists at the Lost West End archive at SoundCloud and is a marvellous example of the sub-Lloyd Webber muse at work, including such lyrics as 'Like a clock, an endless song / Never right and never wrong'. *Enchanting.*

that it might want to crack down on such things if it wished to receive any future foreign aid from the likes of Australia and the US.[10]

Selling off assets—like its airport (which is still for sale at the time of writing)—was another potential earner, as was getting a little something-something from countries in the UN pushing unpopular votes and needing some bolstering support.[11]

Yet another was to appeal to rich countries for foreign aid. That was more successful, because in 2001 Australia had people who needed to be locked up.

———

Nauru's government gets very, very angry when people suggest that the second smallest independent nation on the planet (beaten only by Vatican City) might be, say, a hotbed of corruption. However, the stories about the government— particularly those of President Baron Waqa and his Minister for Justice, David Adeang, are excitingly colourful.

The nation's coroner and magistrate, Peter Law, found himself expelled and returned to his former homeland of Australia in January 2014, just as he was about to open a coronial quest into the not-at-all-suspicious death of Adeang's wife Marilyn in April 2013, when she was carrying a can of petrol through their backyard, as one so often does, and then mysteriously splashed it all over herself, ignited it somehow

———

10 Two of the group had ties with al-Qaeda.

11 For example, Nauru, Palau, the Marshall Islands and Micronesia were four of the nine countries that voted against recognising Palestinian statehood in November 2012—and all, purely coincidentally, happened to be enjoying a hefty amount of 'development funding' from Israel.

and burned to death. At the same time another Australian, Nauru's chief justice Geoffrey Eames, had his visa revoked the night before he was due to return to Nauru. The Australian government felt terrible about the whole business, but pointed out that, really, this was a Nauru thing and it didn't want to get involved.

That the Waqa government might not want the judiciary poking around can also be understood in the context of how the government got into power. Getax, an Australian company that bought phosphate from the nation, had allegedly been more than a little involved in Nauruan politics. Specifically, in 2009 it offered the government of then-president Marcus Stephen a $25 million loan to help pay off the country's debt, but there were a few riders attached—such as an eye-watering 15 per cent interest rate and an agreement to use the country's phosphate industry as collateral, just in case it happened to default on the loan. The Stephen government rejected this offer, and so Getax allegedly went for plan B: funding the campaign of the opposition, led by Baron Waqa, who neither confirmed nor denied the arrangement, telling *The Australian*: 'Getax has always helped Nauru . . . Getax is disappointed with the way the country is running.'

Opposition politicians and three government MPs enjoyed a Getax-funded trip to Singapore, and questions were asked about how politicians on salaries of A$150 a week were suddenly 'spending significant sums of cash on boats, cars, voters and trips'. Leaked emails indicated that Adeang had asked Getax for $665,000 for himself and other Nauruan politicians, which sparked an investigation by the Australian Federal Police.

The election, however, returned the Stephen government—but an argument about who would be Speaker triggered another election, until finally the sides agreed on Godfrey Thoma . . . who moved to dissolve parliament and hold another election. When that failed, he resigned. After more dramas, including the resignation of a second speaker the following month, another election was called. Stephen won again but then resigned, handing the presidency to Freddie Pitcher, who lasted six days before being removed in a no-confidence vote, to be replaced by Sprent Dabwido (who was to reopen the shuttered detention centre in 2011). In 2013 he stood down, and Waqa won the subsequent election.

Waqa suspended most of the Opposition MPs from parliament in May 2014, and in June 2015 he cancelled the passport of Opposition leader Roland Kun, who eventually fled to New Zealand and was granted citizenship there. The NZ government announced the suspension of its aid to the Nauru justice system in September 2015.

Amid this political turmoil and intrigue, in October 2015 it was announced that the Nauru detention centre would become 'open'. There were also reports that Nauru would immediately process all six-hundred-odd claims for asylum within the next week. This new openness came, purely by coincidence, two days before an Australian High Court decision on the lawfulness of offshore detention, and rendered the decision moot since the detainees were now no longer technically incarcerated. So that was lucky!

And then everything improved dramatically for the people who'd been detained on Nauru, because now they . . . Just kidding—nothing really changed at all.

The new openness didn't make a lot of difference, since those detainees determined to be refugees still couldn't leave Nauru or ever come to Australia. Also, the detainees have continued to live for the most part within the camp since there are few employers on Nauru beyond the government and the detention centre itself.

Reports of rapes, assaults and beatings continued. The horror stories included gay detainees being beaten by police and threatened with arrest when they attempted to report the assault, because homosexuality was illegal on the island. People who self-harmed were being charged with attempted suicide, which was also illegal. Both of the oppressive laws involved in these matters were rapidly changed in May 2016 as the stories became more widely disseminated in the international media, but matters were still impossibly grave.

In April a woman referred to only as S99 came to the Australian public's attention when it was reported that she'd fallen pregnant when raped in the throes of an epileptic seizure. With abortion illegal on Nauru, and the medical facilities inadequate to the task in any case, she had appealed to the Australian government to have the procedure done elsewhere—which had ended in her being locked in a Port Moresby hotel room for a week before being returned to Nauru, with no procedure having taken place. The Australian government again argued that it had nothing to do with the detainee and that this was a matter for the Nauru government, but the public outcry was loud and persistent. And then the Federal Court ruled that Australia owed the woman a duty of care, and that she should be treated in Australia. This set a dangerous legal precedent, but things were only getting more complicated for the future of offshore detention.

A twenty-three-year-old asylum seeker known only as 'Omid' had set himself on fire on 27 April in protest at his treatment at the hands of Nauruan authorities. He suffered horrific burns to his upper body, but he was not immediately transferred to Brisbane for emergency treatment; instead, he was left in the woefully inadequate facilities on Nauru for a day while the government assessed whether his injuries justified action.

Malcolm Turnbull made explicitly clear that Australia needed to avoid getting 'misty-eyed' about the treatment of asylum seekers in detention, confirming that Australia's hard line would continue. But hours later, on 29 April, reports came through that Omid had died from his injuries. Dutton released a typically moving statement: 'The man passed away this afternoon in a Brisbane hospital. The department expresses its sympathies to his wife, family and friends.'

Less than an hour later the ABC was reporting that detainees on Manus Island had been put in lockdown and had their mobile phones confiscated. A second detainee—twenty-one-year-old Somali refugee Hodan Yasin—set herself on fire less than a week later, but survived after an emergency airlift to Brisbane.

Throughout all this, things on Christmas Island were going from bad to worse.

———

While the stories of protests and self-harm in detention centres continued, Border Force had decided that it was time to impose an unprecedented crackdown on those who breached Section 501 of the Migration Act, a piece of legislation that gave the government the power to deport anyone who'd committed a crime that resulted in a sentence of more than twelve months in prison. This had recently been amended to include those who'd committed over their lifetime a series of smaller crimes that added up to twelve months, and that turned out to be the real kicker. It resulted in the arrest and deportation of around forty-odd New Zealanders to Christmas Island, in many cases for surprisingly minor property crimes, often committed years earlier. Some of these people had lived, worked and raised a family in Australia over a period of decades.

Dutton was unmoved by this rapid and sudden movement of the goalposts and had no sympathy for those who claimed that deportation was a disproportionate punishment: 'There is no need for any New Zealander, or for that matter anyone from any nation, who has had their visa cancelled under Section 501 of the Migration Act to be in immigration detention in Australia,' he explained. 'These people can choose to depart Australia at any time from the moment their visa is cancelled.'

This didn't really apply to people who were fleeing oppression and were considered stateless and therefore couldn't legally return to their country of origin—for example, the Rohingya people of Myanmar, or the Faili Kurds of Iran.

Those people—unable to stay in Australia, unable to go anywhere else—had the choice of living in detention or dying in detention. And as the former became more horrifically unappealing, the latter started to look better and better.

A massive riot broke out on Christmas Island in November 2015 after the death of Iranian Kurdish refugee Fazel Chegeni, who had broken out of the centre and was discovered dead in mysterious circumstances. The centre was put on lockdown, but things soon spiralled out of control.

The fires and violence caused $10 million worth of damage to the facility, with one anonymous source telling the ABC that 'Christmas Island [detention centre] is actually pretty much destroyed. All the security cameras outside the blocks haven't been replaced, which makes everyone on edge because anything can happen. The other thing is the hygiene . . . we're not allowed to have cleaning products to clean our rooms and we're not allowed toilet brushes. There's a build-up of excrement, if you can imagine on a hot day the smell of excrement and that sort of stuff is pretty intense.' These claims were denied by the immigration department: 'Detainees continue to receive services at least equal to, and often above, those available to many Australians.'

Chegeni's story is impossibly tragic and deserves to be remembered. As a Faili Kurd, he was considered stateless due to the systematic discrimination he faced in Iran (including, but not limited to, being denied education and healthcare), and he had been beaten, degraded and sexually assaulted by the nation's paramilitary force, Sepah, which imprisoned him without charge for forty days before releasing him into the desert. He determined he had no choice but to flee: now that he was known to Sepah officers, he was certain he would be taken into custody if they spotted him again—and that this time it would definitely not end as well.

He bought passage to Australia after borrowing around $11,000 and was held in detention in Western Australia's Curtin Detention Centre, where he was involved in a scuffle with another detainee. In 2013 he was adjudged to be a bona fide refugee and released into the community after multiple assessments showed he was suffering serious psychological trauma from his many, many ordeals.

He then started to make a new life in Melbourne; however, less than a year later he was charged over the earlier incident at Curtin and, as a result, taken back into custody. Scott Morrison revoked his right to live in the community under Section 501. Poorly advised, Chegeni pleaded guilty in the belief that he would be dealt with leniently, but Perth magistrate Barbara Lane sentenced him to six months' jail (she later resigned from the bench under controversial circumstances after her mishandling of another case). While the WA Supreme Court found this sentence excessive, it did not quash the conviction, which meant that Chegeni was put back into detention and shipped off to Christmas Island, where his condition rapidly deteriorated. At the same time Morrison rejected internal submissions from his own department arguing that the indefinite detention of Chegeni and eight other detainees was unambiguously unlawful under international law, according to rulings by the Australian Human Rights Commission.

Following Chegeni's death there were scathing assessments of the management of the facility by contractors Serco;

Chegeni had been fleeing two of the company's officers when his body was found at the bottom of a cliff. Also, it was hard to see the handling of the riot as being anything other than a complete breakdown in management.

——

Just to add further confusion to matters, the company running the Nauru and Manus detention centres—Broadspectrum, formerly known as Transfield—underwent a hostile takeover by Spanish-based infrastructure giant Ferrovial in May 2016 after Broadspectrum's share price dropped following the PNG government's announcement of plans to close the Manus detention centre.[12]

And, as a bonus, Ferrovial announced that it wasn't keen on staying in the offshore detention game. The new owners were well aware of the controversy that had been heaped on Transfield/Broadspectrum because of their involvement, and it didn't need the bad press or any more ethical de-investment, thanks.

'In relation to the provision of services at the regional processing centres in Nauru and Manus province, these services were not a core part of the valuation and the acquisition rationale of the offer, and it is not a strategic activity in Ferrovial's portfolio,' the company said in a statement. 'Ferrovial's view is that this activity will not form part of its services offering in the future.'

---

12 Broadspectrum had knocked back offers of a buyout by Ferrovial at $2 per share in 2014; but, thanks to shrewd negotiation by the board, the directors could finally advise its investors that they would be subjected to a compulsory acquisition at $1.50 per share. Man, it's almost as though people shouldn't have been investing in prison camps in the first place!

And not a moment too soon, since Stanford Law School's Diala Shamas, supervising attorney at the International Human Rights and Conflict Resolution Clinic, had gone public with her concerns, telling *The Guardian*: 'Based on our examination of the facts, it is possible that individual officers at Ferrovial might be exposed to criminal liability for crimes against humanity under the Rome Statute.' She added that she and her colleagues had advised the company of this.

So, to recap: by the time of the 2016 election, the Turnbull government was overseeing a situation where deals with corrupt and arguably criminal regimes were unravelling in the face of blatant human rights abuses; there were mounting legal challenges; and the withdrawal of those commercial partners keeping Nauru and Manus running was imminent. Serco's management on Christmas Island had proved itself dangerously inept—assuming, of course, that it was game to face down a challenge that loomed in the International Court of Justice in The Hague.

And there was an election to win.

13
THE RETURN OF ONE NATION

*In which we chart the rise, fall and unexpected
rise of Australia's most beloved purveyors of
non-fact-based political thought*

Back in 1997 a new political force briefly puffed into being. Its lifespan would initially be short, unimpressive and litigious, but its influence would be felt for the next two decades in myriad ways, mainly to do with its being very uncomfortable about non-Anglo Saxon people. And in 2016 it would flare up once again, like a particularly uncomfortable case of political herpes.[1]

That political force was Pauline Hanson's One Nation.

The hard-right anti-immigration party had been formed in 1997 after Hanson won the Queensland lower house seat of Oxley in 1996, either because she had tapped into the public's growing distrust of multiculturalism or, more accurately, because she'd been the endorsed Liberal candidate in the seat.

---

1 Any suggestion that this comparison might have informed One Nation's choice of branding everything in a bold, angry-looking shade of orange would be incredibly unkind.

Thanks to the national swing against Labor that ended the Keating government and ushered in the storied tenure of John Howard, the previously safe Labor seat would have been a Liberal gain had Hanson not submitted a letter outlining her opinion of Aboriginal folks to the *Queensland Times*. It read in part: 'How can we expect this race to help themselves when governments shower them with money, facilities and opportunities that only these people can obtain no matter how minute the Indigenous blood is that flows through their veins and that is what is causing racism.'

When the letter was printed, there was predictable outrage and the Queensland Liberal Party announced that it was pulling its endorsement of her. However, with less than two weeks until the polls, there was no way to replace its candidate and the ballot papers were already being printed. Hanson was permitted to keep her posters up in the electorate, provided she blocked out the bit saying 'Liberal'; but, as far as most of the public was concerned—and according to the ballot paper being used in Oxley—she was the Liberal candidate for the seat.

Her victory was bittersweet. On the one hand, she won comprehensively;[2] on the other, new PM John Howard had made it clear that she would not be sitting on the Coalition side of the chamber in Canberra—and since the Coalition had a staggering forty-five-seat majority, her opinion was neither sought nor respected.

In her maiden parliamentary speech on 10 September 1996 she delivered the deathless phrase 'I believe we are in danger of

2   The swing was especially brutal in Queensland, with Labor losing all but two seats in the state. In the previously safe Oxley the sitting ALP member, Les Scott, quit politics after being turfed out with an almost 20 per cent swing against him.

being swamped by Asians', a sentiment that was to characterise
the first phase of her political career. However, another passage
from that same speech was to have even more resonance: 'If
I have a right to decide who I invite into my home, then I
should have a right to decide who comes into my country.'

Sure, it was factually incorrect—the right to invite someone
into one's home doesn't in any way confer immigration and/
or border control powers on the heads of Australian house-
holds—but no-one could have predicted that this non sequitur
was to become the basis of Australia's refugee policy for the
subsequent two decades.

Hanson became a figure of fun for the media and political classes. Her past as a fish-and-chip-shop owner and her
childlike 'Please explain?' on *60 Minutes* when asked whether
she was xenophobic seemed to indicate that she had basically
wandered into politics because someone had left the door open.

This supercilious attitude and constant underestimating
of Hanson's intelligence would be to her considerable benefit.
Hanson, after all, was far from stupid: she'd done time in
local government before making the move to the Liberals,
where she'd been given a seat the party assumed she couldn't
win before dumping her off the ticket late, figuring it'd make
no difference. But in December 1997, within her first year
of parliament, she'd registered Pauline Hanson's One Nation
as her own party and was preparing to run candidates in the
upcoming Queensland state election.

Just how shrewd an operator she was became apparent in
June 1998, when One Nation picked up eleven seats in the
Queensland parliament and 22.68 per cent of the primary vote,

a larger percentage than either the suddenly-not-laughing-anymore Liberals or Nationals managed to attract.[3] The Coalition was removed from power, with Labor forming a minority government under Premier Peter Beattie.

This was to be the high-water mark for One Nation, because it had made some powerful enemies during its foundation and things were about to unravel dramatically.

The Liberal and National parties had both preferenced One Nation over Labor under orders from their national head-quarters, due to their bafflingly wrong assumption that One Nation would attract enough Labor votes to prevent the ALP getting a majority. This, as everybody soon discovered, was a huge mistake—polling in the run-up to the state election had accurately shown that most One Nation voters were disgruntled former Liberals and Nationals, who were out for blood.

But this was about more than just parties. For one increasingly important Liberal Party figure—the federal member for Warringah, Tony Abbott—this was deeply personal.

In 1996 Abbott had hired a perky, bespectacled young staffer named David Oldfield, who was to rise to become one of the then-backbencher's most trusted advisers. Oldfield, however, had another agenda: during his tenure he, political strategist David Ettridge and the newly elected independent Pauline Hanson were secretly plotting the founding of One Nation.[4]

3   That's the two individual parties, to be clear: they didn't fuse into the Liberal National Party until 2008.
4   Oldfield and Hanson were also having an untamed and unashamed fortnight-long affair at this point according to Hanson's 2007 autobiography *Untamed and Unashamed*. Oldfield has maintained that the story is false.

Abbott, needless to say, was livid on discovering that Oldfield had used Liberal resources to plot his rival party—and, once the Queensland election result showed how dangerous it had become, he swung into action.

In June 1998 Abbott fired the first shot, challenging the legality of One Nation's registration. 'I am not a lawyer,' he helpfully began, 'but it seems to me that ... One Nation, as registered in Queensland, does not have five hundred members, is not a validly registered political party, and it cannot receive any public funding.'

Abbott's insider was Terry Sharples, who had been disendorsed as a One Nation candidate and was in a vengeancy sort of mood. Abbott funded Sharples' injunction against the party (he initially denied this on the ABC in 1998, but later admitted it to *The Age* in 2003), amid claims that it was fraudulently registered as a party, despite being set up as a business with Hanson and Ettridge as technically the only 'members'.

By August Abbott had established the Australians for Honest Politics Trust, a $100,000 slush fund designed specifically to attack One Nation, a fact he didn't even try to deny. Abbott insisted that the money had been raised entirely separately to the Liberal Party and that he'd simply created it 'as a citizen and a democrat, because One Nation is a fraud on the taxpayers and must be exposed.'[5]

By the time of the next federal election, in 1998, One Nation had become something of a punchline and Hanson's chances of holding on to Oxley seemed remote, thanks to a

---

5   Abbott was as insistent that the AHPT was definitely not connected with the Liberal Party as he was that it definitely didn't have any obligation to reveal who its donors were.

redistribution that turned it into a safe Labor seat. So she jumped across to the seat of Blair, which included a good chunk of her former seat, where she won a respectable 35.97 per cent of the vote, but was defeated by Liberal candidate Cameron Thompson. Even her party's one win—the election of Heather Hill as a One Nation senator—was tainted by the discovery that she hadn't renounced her British citizenship, eventually leading to her being replaced by Len Harris.

In 1999 the Australian Electoral Commission stripped One Nation of its party status because it didn't have the five hundred members required to be a registered party; therefore it had to hand back the $500,000 electoral funding it had previously received, and this paved the way for subsequent charges of fraud. But still it trundled on, with the odd small victory—such as the election of Oldfield to the upper house in NSW in March 1999.

But there were ominous signs. Hanson had launched legal action in 1997 against Simon Hunt—who performed in drag as 'Pauline Pantsdown' and whose dance track 'Backdoor Man' used cut-up samples of Hanson's voice and had been voted number seven in Triple J's 1997 Hottest 100. The controversy made Hanson look like a prissy killjoy rather than a straight-talking battler against political correctness,[6] and also made Pantsdown's follow-up single, 'I Don't Like It', a top-ten hit. The leak of a paranoid video message she'd recorded for supporters in the event of her being assassinated—with the theatrical beginning, 'Fellow

---

6 Which, as many commentators have pointed out, was in constant danger of going mad.

Australians, if you are seeing me now it means that I have been murdered'—didn't contribute to the impression of her as a sane, responsible leader.

Meanwhile, the newly ascendant One Nation in Queensland had barely got into parliament before it started splintering, with six members eventually splitting from the party to form what was subsequently called the City Country Alliance, as in statements like, 'The City Country Alliance failed miserably at the 2001 Queensland election and all its members were kicked out of parliament, and it was stripped of party status by the Australian Electoral Commission in 2003.'

By 2000 Hanson and Oldfield's relationship had become downright poisonous and he was officially expelled from the party in October that year. In response, he cheekily formed a new independent party in 2001 with the name One Nation NSW, exploiting differences in federal and state electoral law. And it remained impressively true to its federal counterpart, in that it almost immediately began to tear itself apart.

Inside of a year ONNSW was embroiled in scandals regarding internal favouritism, including a lawsuit over the upper house ticket for the March 2003 NSW election when Oldfield demoted Brian Burston (a former national director for Pauline Hanson's One Nation[7]) in order to put his wife Lisa first on the ticket. The upshot was that Burston was reinstated, although it made no difference: the party's support collapsed and it didn't make quota, perhaps in some part due to Hanson herself running as an independent candidate. Oldfield quit the

---

7   At the risk of giving away the ending, Burston would rise again, too—as a senator for NSW, no less.

ONNSW in 2004 and served out the rest of his term in the state upper house as an independent, before deciding not to contest the 2007 election following the public revelation of his alleged brief affair with Hanson.

Hanson's political career, too, had rapidly declined. One Nation picked up three seats in the WA state election in 2001, but lost the same number in Queensland the following week. Hanson also faced the Brisbane Magistrates Court in July 2001, pleading not guilty to electoral fraud.

None of this helped her campaigning. At the 2001 federal election she made an unsuccessful tilt at the Senate; she blamed her failure on John Howard having adopted her hardline anti-immigration policies, specifically with regard to asylum seekers. 'It has been widely recognised by all . . . that John Howard sailed home on One Nation's policies,' she told *The Age* in 2003. 'If we were not around, John Howard would not have made the decisions he did.'

And in her defence, there had indeed been definite echoes of Hanson's stilted rhetoric—whether in Howard's introduction of a GST in 2000 (this was the sort of 'flat tax' that One Nation had been rather naively campaigning for in the nineties), or in his 2001 campaign speech launching what would be euphemistically referred to as the Pacific Solution: 'We will decide who comes to this country and the circumstances in which they come.'[8]

---

8   It's been said before in other hilarious and insightful books about Australian politics, but honestly: what sort of political adviser goes: 'Sure, let's add "solution" to the name of our plan to lock up people of different cultural backgrounds in internment camps—we certainly don't see any likeness to certain much-criticised political regimes from 1930s Germany there!'

In 2002 Hanson resigned as the leader of One Nation, and was subsequently expelled from the party altogether. Her electoral fraud case followed, and Hanson and Ettridge each served eleven weeks in prison before successfully appealing the verdict. Their conviction was overturned, but Hanson insisted her political career was over. One Nation sputtered on without her, but eventually deregistered at a federal level.

Hanson found a new career in reality TV, appearing on *Dancing with the Stars* and *The Apprentice*, before forming a new party—Pauline's United Australia Party—and running unsuccessfully for the Senate in 2007. In 2009 she had another state run—this time in the Queensland seat of Beaudesert— and once again failed. This time she was definitely over politics and planned to move to the UK; a move that lasted literally weeks before she returned to Australia, complaining that Britain was 'overrun with immigrants and refugees'.

Predictably, she returned to politics—and to One Nation, which desperately needed someone with a profile—and ran as a Senate candidate for NSW in the 2013 federal election, where she came nowhere near a quota.

———

However, from that time on her prospects started to improve.

To begin with, her once extreme-sounding rhetoric about banning all immigration had crossed over into the mainstream.[9] When Abbott's government started to defend the increasingly horrifying conditions in offshore detention centres, and openly discussed plans to prioritise Christians over Muslims

———

9 Presumably there were all sorts of hipster racists snorting that they were into stripping rights from Muslims before it was cool.

in the humanitarian resettlement plan for Syrian refugees, and criticised Islamic community leaders for failing to adequately condemn the actions of organisations like ISIL and demanded they join 'Team Australia', One Nation's position looked quaintly progressive by comparison.

And while community fear over being 'swamped by Asians' had diminished, fear about Muslims was reaching exciting new highs—and even Hanson, now being advised by James Ashby,[10] knew how to do a search-and-replace on her old policy statements.

There had also been the emergence of a fresh new generation of shrieking right-wing parties, particularly in the states hit hardest by the end of the mining boom and now filled with towns of isolated, angry people who, on seeing their prosperity collapse and looking for something to blame, raced straight past the hard-to-punch scapegoats like 'global neoliberalism' and settled on the far easier target, 'immigrants'. These groups tended to follow the template that One Nation had previously perfected: thinly-if-at-all-veiled bigotry presented as straight-talking common sense patriotism, almost immediately followed by self-destructive internal power struggles involving the invariably paranoid leadership.[11]

---

10 Yes, the same James Ashby from the Peter Slipper/Mal Brough debacle. If you just shook your head and sighed, 'Queensland politics, am I right?' then congratulations: you've immediately qualified as an official Australian political commentator!

11 These groups are largely indistinguishable from one another, partly because they almost always have 'patriot' in their name (Australian Patriots Front, United Patriotic Front, Patriots Defence League etc.) and mainly because they tend to appear in photos with their faces masked by wraparound sunglasses and Australian flags. That might seem off-message, given their collective commitment to 'ban the burqa', but maybe they just all have really bad colds?

The rise of Turnbull in the Liberal Party was another godsend as it allowed One Nation to appeal to those Coalition voters who feared that this socially progressive Sydney millionaire was about to herald a terrifying future of enforced polygamous gay marriages with strictly halal reception catering.

There was also a shift in political thought globally, especially in secular European democracies, where the old parties were increasingly seen as part of the problem rather than the solution. There was the new enthusiasm for the likes of London mayor turned potential PM Boris Johnson, UKIP leader and unrepentant bigot Nigel Farage and, most obviously, the US Republican presidential candidate who was openly opposed to Muslims/Hispanics/women/reality. Donald Trump proved to all aspirant right-wing politicos just how successful one could be while running on a platform that didn't even give the slightest nod to reality, whether it was promoting the non-existent benefits of the UK leaving the European Union or building a technologically impossible wall across the southern US border.

The people who once thought One Nation a serious threat had long ago got used to ignoring the party. They had failed to notice that Hanson's stints on reality TV, in supermarket magazines and on daytime television (including as a paid regular commentator on *Today*) had given her mainstream appeal. No longer was she that red-haired weirdo scared of Asians—now she was the nice lady from on the TV who speaks her mind.

In other words, Pauline Hanson had once again been badly underestimated. And this was to have significant consequences.

14
ARTHUR, HE DOES WHAT HE PLEASES ...

Or, Reflections on the remarkably idiosyncratic memory of Malcolm Turnbull's parliamentary secretary

As the plans for the early election gained momentum the Liberal Party knew it had plenty of challenges ahead: moving the date of the budget speech, changing the Senate voting system, finding a politically acceptable legislative trigger on which to base the double dissolution, selecting just the right three-word slogan to repeat endlessly over and over until it lost what little meaning it might have once contained ... that sort of thing. However, it also found itself in a situation rare in the lead-up to an election campaign: it was dangerously low on cash.

Part of the problem was that donations had dropped off sharply, although that was a bipartisan issue. Both the major parties were facing reduced receipts on previous years, which most likely reflected a lack of confidence in either side comfortably winning another term. Donations typically flow to the likely winner, rather than the plucky underdog, because big corporations and wealthy individuals like to shore up a solid account in the political-favour bank—and unless the favour you're after is something nice from the Parliament House gift shop, you want that favour owed by someone who could actually make some laws.

Donations to the Liberal Party had almost halved between 2013–14 and 2014–15, from $20.2 million to $10.3 million. Those who had given were mainly property developers ($600,000 from Brunswick Property Vic Pty Ltd, $200,000 from Chinese-owned Everbright) and magnates of mining (Tony Abbott's pal Paul Marks kicked in a cool $340,000) and media (Kerry Packer's widow Ros chipped in $100,000). What was missing from the typical list of big Liberal donors was the financial sector, which had been scared by the briefly floated and then hastily forgotten talk of changing negative gearing, less than thrilled by the proposed changes to superannuation, and downright furious about the not-as-definitely-off-the-table-as-they-would-like threat of a royal commission into the banking sector, which Labor was still honking about and which seemed to have a dangerous level of support from the Greens and independents.

The Victorian Liberal Party had also suffered a shocking misfortune when its former state director, Damien Mantach, embezzled $1,558,913 from the party's coffers between May 2010 and January 2015 via falsified invoices. He'd confessed to the crime as soon as suspicious party members asked about some oddly high campaigning expenses and pleaded guilty in court, which was taken into account during his sentencing in May 2016, as was the fact that he'd stolen the money in a desperate attempt to keep his crumbling marriage together by funding his wife's café, but Victorian Liberals were furious— not least because the party could have done with that $1.5 million during their ultimately doomed Victorian state election campaign in November 2014. In July Mantach was sentenced to five years in prison, with a non-parole period of two years and eight months. With less than a third of the money recovered by the time of the sentencing, that was a deep cash-hole to deal with ahead of the federal election—but the real problem was on the other side of the Murray.

As anyone who has ever spent any time observing New South Wales politics would be aware, the state government has historically been occasionally influenced by the construction and property development industry, in the same way that the orbit of the Earth might be said to have been occasionally influenced by the orbit of the Sun.

It was in order to prevent the state from becoming an official developocracy that restrictions were introduced to prevent political parties from accepting donations from the sector following an investigation by the NSW Independent Commission Against Corruption in 2007 which—in a marvellous piece of understatement—made the shocking discovery that letting developers hand over hundreds of thousands of dollars to political parties increased the risk of corruption. And four years later the NSW government leaped into action.

To be fair, though, the response was unexpectedly strong: Premier Barry O'Farrell introduced a law ruling that no corporations, unions or other entities would be permitted to donate to political parties in NSW, with only individuals being permitted to donate—to a ceiling of $1000. When the bill was passed in February 2012, the Coalition government of NSW was confident that this would make matters transparent and unambiguous, and it incorrectly thought that it would damage Labor more than it would damage itself. In any case, it had a back door already set up.

That back door—or, more accurately, one of those back doors—was the seemingly innocuous Free Enterprise Foundation, a little-known charitable organisation and Liberal Party 'associated entity' based in Canberra. Because the FEF was a federal body and not technically based in NSW,[1] there was no problem with it accepting donations from developers—like Westfield, Meriton Apartments, Walker Group, Austral Bricks and other organisations with an evident passion for the very notion of free enterprise. The FEF would then make its own donation to the NSW Liberal Party.

If you find the idea of a charity being shadowy-to-the-point-of-secretive odd—no website, no social media presence, no apparent method of soliciting what amounted to millions of dollars in donations from high-level corporate organisations—then you wouldn't be alone. Especially since this charity didn't appear to do the sort of things that charities typically do with donations, like fund medical research or protect wilderness areas or literally anything else whatsoever. In fact, it looked almost as though the FEF did nothing beyond donate large sums of money to right-leaning political organisations, especially the Liberal Party.

---

1   Though let's be honest, the entire ACT is based in NSW. You're fooling no-one, Canberra.

The Free Enterprise Foundation came to the attention of ICAC in 2014 following revelations about the activities of Australian Water Holdings, a company whose ties to the NSW government and various development projects seemed strangely convivial, for reasons that will shortly become clear. However, the upshot of the FEF's entry into the public consciousness was that on 24 March 2016 the NSW Electoral Commission informed the NSW Liberal Party that it would need to hand over details of the donors that bankrolled the 2011 election campaign, which installed O'Farrell as premier. When it refused, the NSW Electoral Commission withheld $4.4 million in public funding from the party.

'In truth, the [Free Enterprise] foundation had been used by senior officials of the party and an employed party fund-raiser to channel and disguise donations by major political donors, some of whom were prohibited donors,' the ruling read. 'When the foundation purported to pay the money to the Liberal Party . . . it was in truth acting as an agent for the donors. At all times [the donors'] details should have been disclosed by themselves and the party, if the sums involved made them "major political donors".'

This was a major blow for a party that had just started to appreciate it might have more of a fight on its hands at the upcoming federal election than it had assumed. Its lawyers appealed, insisting that the funding was 'of critical impor-tance' and that there would be layoffs if it wasn't reinstated and handed over by the end of April; it threatened to take the Electoral Commission to the Supreme Court. Even NSW premier Mike Baird ended up calling on the party to just release the details of the donors, but he was initially rebuffed. Then, with legal costs mounting and an election around the corner, the party finally coughed up a list in May, revealing a million dollars in illegal donations from developers.

This was a humiliating turn of events for a party about to attempt to convince the nation its people were the only ones to be trusted with the nation's finances, but the ruling also created a very specific problem for Turnbull.

That problem's name was Arthur Sinodinos.

———

Sinodinos had first come to the public's semi-attention when he was plucked from his powerful-but-obscure position as a career public servant within the Department of Treasury to become John Howard's chief of staff, first while Howard was Opposition Leader from 1987 to 1989, and then once again from 1995 until 2006.

In 2003 the *Australian Financial Review* dubbed Sinodinos 'the most covertly powerful person in Australia', and for a long time he appeared happy to exert his influence in the background. He also had an excellent sense of timing: more than a few commentators suggested that his resignation from the PM's office in December 2006 was less because he'd been offered a handsome deal with Goldman Sachs JBWere than because he sensed that Labor's new leader, Kevin Rudd, was going to be too formidable a foe for the flagging Howard government to defeat and he was getting out while the getting was good.

In 2008 he took on another sweet gig, this time as one of the directors of Australian Water Holdings, becoming its chair in 2010. At the same time, he was treasurer of the NSW Liberal

Party, but he gave up both roles in order to follow his true passion and enter conservative politics as a proper participant.

After deciding not to grubby his hands in the competitive preselection battle for the safe Liberal seat of Bradfield following Brendan Nelson's resignation in 2009 (a staggering seventeen candidates duked it out, with the eventual winner being Paul Fletcher), he was instead parachuted into the NSW Senate spot vacated by Helen Coonan, who quit halfway through her final term, perhaps having realised that her centrist politics and concerns about coal seam gas exploration and mining on agricultural land were unlikely to win her friends in the new Abbott-led Coalition. Sinodinos was third on the ticket (under Marise Payne and Nationals senator John Williams) and narrowly won the sixth and final seat. When Abbott rolled to victory, the Howard-approved Sinodinos was given the job of assistant treasurer under Joe Hockey, which he correctly interpreted as an enormous insult. However, he soon had bigger things to worry about: like the fact that his name was coming up with increasing regularity in ICAC's investigations into Australian Water Holdings.

The investigation had begun in 2012, specifically into the conduct of NSW Labor minister Eddie Obeid, who'd been Minister for Mineral Resources, and his predecessor Ian Macdonald.[2] This complex matter initially focused on the granting of mining leases on land owned by Obeid, eventually expanded to the private–public partnership between the government-run Sydney Water and the privately contracted

2 It's important to clarify that this Ian Macdonald is an entirely different person to the Queensland LNP senator who will call for the LNP to have its own party room in a few chapters' time. Um, spoiler alert.

Australian Water Holdings, due to the social and political connections between Obeid and AWH director Nick Di Girolamo. This book hasn't the space to do the story justice, but what began as a sordid business deal turned into a blasted hellscape of political corruption and gross mismanagement on a scale so epic that it begged to be transformed into a Shakespearean tragedy, not least because its final scene would be even bloodier than that of Hamlet.

The revelations of Operation Spicer (regarding the soliciting, receiving and concealment of financial benefit by public officials and politicians) and Operation Credo (specifically into corrupt conduct of Australian Water Holdings) would eventually lead to criminal charges against Obeid and Macdonald, to the dumping of fellow former Labor minister Joe Tripodi from the party, and the resignation from office of a jaw-dropping twelve Liberal Party members, including the then-premier, Barry O'Farrell.

Australian Water Holdings had not been the focus of the initial inquiry, but the investigation of Obeid and Di Girolamo revealed some issues of particular concern to the NSW Liberal Party. Most significantly for former AWH deputy chair Sinodinos, it established that AWH had been one of the major donors to the party. In April 2014 he showed remarkable poise in insisting, on the stand before the ICAC, that he had been unaware that AWH had donated $74,000 to the NSW Liberals in 2010, despite having key roles in the financial oversight of both entities.

ICAC's assisting counsel, Geoffrey Watson SC, pointed out just how ludicrous that sounded, asking, 'You deny knowing the company of which you were deputy chairman was donating to the party of which you were the treasurer?' Sinodinos replied, 'I did not know in precise terms what was being donated to the Liberal Party.' When asked what precise terms meant, he answered, 'I couldn't quote amounts at you, or over what period.' This triumph of barefacedness also included the liberal use of 'I don't recall' in relation to any questions about whether AWH made donations to the party, what donations the party accepted, or what a donation was. When Watson asked whether Sinodinos felt that an annual salary of $200,000 for what he calculated to be 'between twenty-five and a half and forty-five hours of work a year' seemed reasonable, especially given how forgetful Sinodinos evidently was regarding matters to which he might have been expected to be attentive, Arthur replied with a shrug: 'The fact I took the salary indicated it was reasonable from my point of view.'

While 'I have no idea what was going on in the company I chaired' might seem like an excitingly bold defence for a public representative with federal responsibilities—or for someone who didn't want to be taken to court by shareholders waving copies of Sections 180–184 of the Corporations Act, containing highlighted passages regarding duty of care and due diligence—it seemed to do the trick, as did his insistence that being treasurer of the NSW Liberals didn't mean he needed to know anything about the party's financial state. That, he maintained, was the responsibility of finance director Simon McInnes, and Sinodinos utterly refused 'any responsibility for money being raised from prohibited donors', sniffing that it wasn't within his brief to 'micro-manage' others.

It didn't all go Arthur's way, though. He'd stepped aside as assistant treasurer earlier in the year, as mentioned back in chapter two, and certain elements within the Prime Minister's Office had concluded that part of the reason the 2014 budget had gone down so spectacularly badly was that Sinodinos wasn't available to offer guidance on how better to sugarcoat what was largely interpreted by the public as an enormous, steaming turd.[3]

The donations scandal threatened to continue through 2015, thanks to a Federal Court suit filed by angry AWH share-holders against the 'misleading and deceptive conduct' of the company's current and former directors, including Sinodinos. With other matters gathering momentum in Canberra, this was the last thing the senator needed—and thus, on 24 August, he advised Justice Anna Katzmann, the judge presiding over the matter, that he was no longer part of the court case. He had reached a confidential settlement with the plaintiffs under terms that were never made public, and which infuriated his fellow defendants, who were still denying the charges and had no idea what Sinodinos had agreed to as part of this deal.[4]

Even after he had avoided the civil suit, Arthur still had to continue to make ICAC appearances, but by September—by which time he was sitting in his shiny new gig as parliamentary secretary, to which Turnbull had gratefully appointed him after

---

3   Actual technical term.
4   On 8 August Fairfax did report that Sinodinos had updated his pecuniary interests register to note that he had a brand-new personal loan from his former employers, the National Australia Bank, although the report stressed there was no evidence the loan and the settlement were connected.

the coup—he had gone from 'unhelpful' to 'downright snarky'. When asked whether he'd been aware that the Liberals' 2011 NSW state campaign had accepted donations from prohibited groups, specifically property developers, he innocently asked, 'Property developers as defined by *whom*?'

When the NSW Electoral Commission handed down its report, and withheld the $4.4 million in funding, Sinodinos immediately demanded it stop suggesting that he'd had anything to do with it.

'I had no role in the NSW division's decision to decline to update information disclosed in that declaration, as was requested by the commission,' he said in a statement in which he threatened to sue the Electoral Commission. 'For my part, my lawyers have written to the commission to draw its attention to errors of fact in its statement in relation to me. I was not given the opportunity by the commission to comment on its statement before its publication and I was not aware of the publication until shortly prior to its release.'

When federal parliament was prorogued in April 2016, the Senate had a very special surprise: it slipped in a motion to establish a snap inquiry into political donations and for the development of a National Integrity Commission. Moved by Palmer United senator Zhenya 'Dio' Wang in an uncharacteristic display of actually doing something, it was supported enthusiastically by Labor.

'Malcolm Turnbull and [Attorney-General] George Brandis have repeatedly refused to respond to questions on Senator Sinodinos' involvement in the Free Enterprise Foundation,' Labor's Penny Wong said when she spoke in support of the inquiry. 'If Senator Sinodinos has nothing to hide, why have senior ministers used every procedural trick in the book to resist scrutiny of the Senate?' The Greens concurred, as did enough of the rest of the crossbench to get it over the line. But one person who didn't agree was Senator Arthur Sinodinos.

'Given that the calling of a federal election is imminent, the public might be forgiven for concluding that this inquiry is nothing but a political stunt, not a bona fide attempt to inquire into an important question of public policy,' he responded in writing to the chair of the committee, adding defensively: 'I note that Senator Nick Xenophon has described the proceedings as having the appearance of a "witch hunt".'

The threat still hung over him as long as parliament sat, but would evaporate along with any other unpassed legislation as soon as the governor-general dissolved parliament: which, as everyone had accepted by this point, was going to happen well before anyone could implement some sort of silly inquiry into the legality of political donations.

Sure, there was an outside chance that Labor could move for such an inquiry in the new parliament, but that would assume that the new Senate had Labor in a strong enough position to move such a motion. And that would be crazy! After all, any such election would—in theory, obviously— clean out the Senate of those pesky crossbenchers and ensure that the government had a significant enough majority to get on with its mandate unimpeded, right? What sort of government would call an election to make their position even worse?

15

THE GEESE OF THE CAMPAIGN

In which we pay tribute to those who also served when,
realistically, they probably shouldn't have troubled themselves

With parliament dissolved, the parties scrambled to the hustings to begin fifty-six days of what would be the second-longest election campaign in Australian political history.

The longest campaign ever, incidentally, was in 1969 when John Gorton took the Liberal–Country coalition into a sixty-six-day campaign against the Labor Party led by Gough Whitlam. Gorton had never led an election campaign—he'd been sworn in as leader after the disappearance of Harold Holt in 1967—but he'd enjoyed a good deal of support within the party.[1] He was also well respected by the public, but his popularity took a massive beating over the length of the campaign

---

1 When chosen, Gorton was a senator, making him the only PM who wasn't a member of the House of Representatives. That didn't last long, though: he resigned from the Senate to contest (and win) Holt's safe seat of Higgins in a 1968 by-election.

and he only won by four seats, thanks to DLP preferences; the narrow victory only served to inflame tensions within the Coalition, even as it emboldened the Whitlam-led Labor. Rapidly tiring of the internal tensions, and with the polls pointing towards a Labor rout at the next election, Gorton faced a no-confidence motion in his party room and the vote was tied. In theory, Gorton could have soldiered on, but he chose to resign and Labor rode over his successor, William McMahon, in a landslide.

That might have given Turnbull pause, but he didn't let it bother him. After all, as the old saying goes, 'History absolutely never repeats itself.'

———

It seemed like Labor had taken the PM at his word when he'd made his case for replacing Tony Abbott as leader in September 2015. Back then Turnbull assured the public that he was all about eschewing Abbott's much-mocked three-word slogans and embarking on a series of national conversations: 'We need a different style of leadership. We need a style of leadership that explains those challenges and opportunities, explains the challenges and how to seize the opportunities. A style of leadership that respects the people's intelligence, that explains these complex issues and then sets out the course of action we believe we should take and makes a case for it. We need advocacy, not slogans. We need to respect the intelligence of the Australian people.'

Labor, therefore, assuming that the Coalition was going to have a bunch of ideas to unveil to the public, had itself gone big on policy. Perhaps even *too* big, trumpeting 100 Positive

Policies,[2] which it outlined on its website and on the massive Bill Bus, a Shorten-emblazoned presidential-style bus that toured the nation with Shorten and tired-looking members of the press corps inside.

However, Turnbull had wrong-footed the Opposition neatly by not unveiling one hundred policies, positive or otherwise. In fact, there weren't really any policies at all. In their place was a three-word slogan: Jobs and Growth. And this slogan would be deployed with a regularity that bordered on the Abbottian.

As the public would learn, 'jobs and growth' neatly replaced all that annoying 'explaining those challenges and opportunities' nonsense that might be expected of candidates; it provided a nice doorstop-sized response to literally anything. Whenever they were asked why the government was doing or not doing something, all Coalition politicians responded it was 'to encourage jobs and growth', as though the connection was self-evident, or as though they had a daily quota of slogan-regurgitation to achieve. But problems arose when candidates found themselves in situations where they might be expected to provide a more substantive answer.

For example, on 9 May Assistant Treasurer Kelly O'Dwyer was representing the government on *Q&A*, where she was faced with a question about one of the government's few clearly articulated policies—a personal tax cut for those earning over

---

2 Although some of the policies seemed suspiciously similar—'Safeguarding Workers Rights' and 'Protecting Rights at Work', for example—while others seemed they were there to make up the numbers, like 'Reducing Admission Fees to Questacon'. Still, it's fair to say that Labor left all the Questacon-related policies of the other parties in the dust.

$80,000 a year, while personal income tax cuts for lower earners were off the table.

'I've got a disability and a low education, that means I've spent my whole life working for a minimum wage,' audience member Duncan Storrar told the panel, addressing O'Dwyer in particular. 'You're gonna lift the tax-free threshold for rich people. If you lift my tax-free threshold, that changes my life. That means that I get to say to my little girls, "Daddy's not broke this weekend. We can go to the pictures." Rich people don't even notice their tax-free threshold lift. Why don't I get it? Why do they get it? People who make $80,000 a year . . . Well, they don't even notice it, love. We notice that sort of stuff.'

O'Dwyer fumbled through an answer about how this was actually about fairness and 'growing the pie.'[3] But then her co-panellist, Australian Industry Group CEO Innes Willox, helpfully jumped in to make everything worse: 'Duncan, I'll be harsh in my message. If you're on the minimum wage and with a family, you would not pay much tax, if any at all, would you?'

But Storrar wasn't having a bar of it. 'I pay tax every time I go to the supermarket,' he answered, to thunderous applause. 'Every time I hop in my car.'

Storrar looked set to become a working-class folk hero—there was even a Kickstarter fund set up to raise money for his family—but, fortunately for O'Dwyer, she had more adept avengers than Willox batting for her within News Corp.

---

3 Just as an aside: this metaphor gets used a lot by conservative politicians, despite the fact that pies do not grow. The only way you make a larger pie is by using more resources and a greater amount of energy, as any baker will tell you.

Its journalists dug into Storrar's past—which had included jail
time, a hostile relationship with his oldest son, and a history of
drug use and mental health problems, all of which one might
think were interconnected issues—to eviscerate him. Q&A
STAR EXPOSED AS THUG read the *Herald Sun*'s headline, while
The Australian tutted ABC's 'BUDGET FAIRNESS' VICTIM PAYS
NO NET TAX and columnists like Rita Panahi, Tim Blair and
David Penberthy slammed him for daring to suggest that poor
people have it tough for reasons that aren't entirely their own
doing. Storrar, unsurprisingly, found the venom terrifying—
but that didn't stop him putting his head back above the
parapet to publicly endorse the Australian Progressives ahead
of the election.

In this atmosphere it's no wonder more experienced public
speakers still avoided the dangers of substantive policy discussion. Attempts to get the leaders to participate in a proper
election debate were continually rebuffed by the Liberal camp,
reportedly due to the PM's hectic schedule. And when one
was finally agreed to, it was on 13 May, on the PM's chosen
battleground and at his chosen time—on Sky News at 5 pm
on a Friday, thereby guaranteeing that the leaders would clash
on a station no-one watched at a time when no-one would
be watching.

Even so, the debate was a dull affair, with little more than
a repetition of established talking points. A second debate at
the National Press Club on 29 May was similarly content-free,
although memorable for watching the *Australian Financial
Review*'s exasperated Laura Tingle roll her eyes at yet another
question-avoiding sound bite. By the time the third and

final 'debate' came around, on Facebook on 17 June (another Friday—but now at 6 pm!), no-one gave a damn, not even the candidates themselves. When Turnbull confirmed that there would not be any further debates, the public's sigh of relief was audible nationwide.

The election campaign was to have several colourful battles, including the return of two Gillard-era independents having one last bash at this politics game: Tony Windsor had announced his plan to run against Barnaby Joyce in his old seat of New England, and Rob Oakeshott made a surprise last-minute announcement that he'd contest the seat of Cowper (which now contained a good chunk of what was previously within the boundaries of Lyne, the seat he'd held until 2013).

One of the more entertaining challenges, however, was for the seat of Indi, in which the Liberal candidate, former rising star of the party Sophie Mirabella, was determined to right what she saw as the hideous wrong done to her when an ungrateful electorate sent her packing at the previous election.

Mirabella was not a well-loved politician; Windsor had once described her as being the 'nastiest' person in parliament. As the member for what she regarded as a nice safe Liberal seat, she'd felt she could afford to do things like stomping out of the parliament during the Apology to the Stolen Generations, or demanding that Muslim women be forced to remove their headwear for ID, or mocking then-Prime Minister Julia Gillard for not having had children, sneering, 'You won't need [ex-PM Kevin Rudd's] taxpayer-funded nanny, will you?' But those sorts of colourful, charming antics had helped her turn a safe 10 per cent margin into a loss to independent candidate

Cathy McGowan in 2013. So beloved was Mirabella in her own community that she not only defied the massive swing to the Coalition that all their other incumbent MPs enjoyed, she became the only sitting Coalition member to lose her seat outright.

It's fair to say Mirabella didn't take this loss well. Not only did she refuse to concede the close result for well over a week—until the day Abbott announced his ministry, without her in it—she also missed few opportunities to backhand McGowan. This less-than-entirely-gracious behaviour was laid bare during 2016's phantom election campaign, when the *Benalla Ensign* reported that Mirabella had pushed McGowan out of the way in order to prevent the sitting member from having a photo taken with Assistant Minister for Health Ken Wyatt at the launch of the new wing of the Cooinda Village aged care facility on 15 April.

The story was printed five days later and was predictably (and angrily) denied by Mirabella—though McGowan confirmed that something aggressive took place and that witnesses had been shocked: 'I was very surprised by the reaction from the Liberal Party candidate,' she told *The Guardian*. 'It was aggressive, it was rude, it was disrespectful.'

Any other candidate would have taken this as their cue to embark on a charm offensive, but Mirabella decided to leave out the charm bit and concentrate entirely on being offensive. And she did so in a way that couldn't have been more effective if Labor had been running her campaign.

Sky News held a town hall meeting with the leading candidates for Indi on 21 April, at which McGowan spoke about her achievements during her three years as the electorate's MP. But this was overshadowed by Mirabella's mighty contribution—or, more specifically, the contribution that she would have made had the people of Indi not been such a bunch of McGowan-voting idiots.

'I had a commitment for a $10 million allocation to the Wangaratta Hospital that, if elected, I was going to announce the week after the election,' Mirabella declared on camera in a room full of locals. 'That is $10 million that Wangaratta hasn't had because Cathy got elected.'

It's impossible to imagine how Mirabella thought this news would go down, because she seemed genuinely shocked by the level of vitriol it inspired. People lined up on one of two sides: either Mirabella was lying, in which case this was an astonishingly barefaced piece of historical revisionism; or, far worse, she was telling the truth, in which case she and the party of which she was a member deliberately withheld hospital funding from a regional community out of pure spite.

If she was hoping that her party would back her up, she was to be disappointed. Health minister Sussan Ley issued a statement declaring that 'neither I, nor my department, is aware of any public commitment to give Wangaratta Hospital $10 million', and Barnaby Joyce rather cattily told the ABC that Mirabella was in no position to know what the situation was with hospital funding since the only person authorised to make such a statement was the relevant minister—'It's certainly not someone who's not actually in politics.'

Bill Shorten, meanwhile, didn't miss an opportunity to tie the Coalition to poor health funding: 'It is not the Australian way to say to a section of the population that, if you don't do what we say, we will punish you and withdraw vital health-care,' he thundered to the media. 'That's the sort of thing you see in a banana republic, not a functioning democracy.'

Thus, by the first week of the campaign going live, Mirabella's hopes of reclaiming the seat were basically over. Reports came through that the Liberals had withdrawn support for her campaign, thereby reducing her to local fundraising only. Just in case that looked like scurrilous gossip, she all but confirmed it on the ABC's *7.30* when she accused her party of leaking against her with a blithe, 'What do they say? If you want a friend in politics, get a dog . . . Let others be concerned about internecine affairs, I'll worry about Indi.'

And just in case the Coalition's opinion of Mirabella wasn't clear enough, Barnaby Joyce was perfectly happy to mock her at the launch for the Nationals' Indi candidate, Marty Corboy, the following night: 'I don't want to talk too much about the other candidates, they can talk for themselves and they did an *exceptionally* good job of that last night,' a jovial Joyce said of Mirabella's ABC performance. 'What I can say is the more they talk, the better you look, Marty.'

But in many ways, the real stars were the less experienced candidates.

———

An eight-week election campaign is a big ask for any aspiring politician and there were plenty of moments on the trail when even experienced party stars didn't exactly shine, from SA Greens senator Sarah Hanson-Young providing eight seconds of dead air while desperately and unsuccessfully attempting to recall the Greens' transition-to-retirement policy on ABC radio, to Julie Bishop calling her own failure to recall the Coalition's policy on the exact same subject a 'gotcha moment', to Bill Shorten being unfamiliar with the teams playing in the rugby league State of Origin and claiming to back Melbourne Storm to win—a brave choice, since the match was actually, as is always the case, between NSW and Queensland.

But those moments, while embarrassing, are to be expected. A seasoned campaigner will grasp the gaffe, own it, and move on. But then there are the campaign geese: those glorious candidates who possess the unique power to take a moment of embarrassment and transform it into a legitimate catastrophe.

Perhaps the most magical thing about any election campaign is the way that it puts its membership on display— maybe it's the safe backbencher just making up the numbers, or a delusional independent ready to set the world to rights, or the party machine factotum plonked into a campaign because they live in a convenient suburb and who is about to discover the degree to which they are woefully out of their depth.

The Animal Justice Party, for example, had registered in 2011, ostensibly representing the interests of the nation's furred and feathered folk; by 2016 it was ambitiously fielding fifty-five candidates across the nation, although some Victorian members seemed to have some fascinating alternative areas of interest.

The candidate for the seat of Menzies, Tony Hulbert, quit his campaign three days after he told the *Manningham*

Leader that he considered gay marriage 'not natural'. Batman candidate Caitlin Evans admitted it was 'not ideal' that she'd be holidaying in Vanuatu for the last week of the campaign and returning a week after the polls but, as she explained, 'This overseas holiday for over ten family members was booked well over a year ago, at considerable expense, before I even considered running as a candidate.' She added, 'If the last week makes a critical difference that's a problem for our party, but it's not a problem for anyone else.' And to be fair, it wasn't going to be critical—or, indeed, make the slightest difference to the non-fortunes of the AJP in the seat.

But the cake was taken by Douglas Leith, candidate for the Victorian electorate of Bruce, who jumped on Facebook to claim that the horrifying shooting at Pulse, a gay nightclub in Orlando, Florida, which claimed forty-nine lives and seriously injured dozens of others, was not the work of a single gunman but was actually a plot coordinated by the FBI. 'Media will not air those who say there were many shooters,' he insisted in a series of posts that claimed the entire thing was a psychological operation in order to, um, achieve some shadowy aim or other, presumably. That bit wasn't clear. But in any case, 'These people claimed victims are being carried *towards* not away from the shooting location. This, among other evidence, shows this is a psyop. Do you really think one guy could kill fifty people and injure dozens more?' he asked rhetorically. On the plus side, he did conclude that, 'It is not okay for government agents to kill people,' which is a position that is, at least, something with which mainstream voters would most likely agree.

Believing in dangerous fantasies in the face of all evidence, it might be argued, is perhaps not an ideal quality to seek in a person scrutinising legislation at a federal level. On the other hand, it always seemed unlikely that the running battle for Bruce between the Liberal challenger and its sitting Labor MP, Alan Griffin—who retained the seat—was going to be determined by the AJP.

Or maybe that was just what They want us sheeple to think.

———

Of more concern for Labor in Victoria was the performance of David Feeney, its MP for the inner Melbourne seat of Batman.[4]

Feeney's early political career had been mainly spent behind the scenes as a strategist for Victorian premier Steve Bracks and as campaign manager for South Australian premier Mike Rann. But he was best known for being one of the 'faceless men' implicated in the knifing of Kevin Rudd and, along with Bill Shorten,[5] encouraging Julia Gillard to become leader of the Labor Party.

He'd scraped into federal parliament as a senator for Victoria in 2007, despite being given the third (and historically unwinnable) position on the state ballot, and then rose to become Parliamentary Secretary for Defence. But by 2013

———

4 As everyone knows, the seat is named after John Batman, one of the founders of Melbourne. The nearby electorate of Bruce, however, is actually a tribute to billionaire playboy Bruce Wayne.
5 Shorten and Feeney have a long and tumultuous history stretching back to their university days, during which they were factional rivals, fierce allies, mutual plotters, close friends, factional rivals, bitter enemies, mutual plotters, and expedient allies again. To work out the state of their relationship at any point in time you'll need at the minimum a flow chart, internal polling and a pack of Tarot cards.

it was clear that the party would not get a third candidate into the Senate—and with Jacinta Collins and Gavin Marshall in the top slots on the ballot once again, Feeney didn't have a hope of staying in the upper house.[6]

However, his hard-won allegiances were to prove his salvation and in June he won the preselection battle for the lower house seat of Batman with the support of Shorten and Gillard (although by the time Feeney won on 1 July, Gillard had been replaced as leader by the briefly resurgent Rudd). He held the seat for Labor in 2013, after which he became Shadow Minister for Veterans Affairs and Shadow Assistant Minister for Defence.

Thanks to changing demographics and Feeney's less-than-assiduous stewardship of his constituency, Batman was going to be difficult for Labor to hold in 2016. Support for the Greens in Melbourne was spilling out into the suburbs and Feeney knew he'd need to bring his A-game.

So forgetting to add his $2.31 million investment property in Northcote—a suburb in his electorate—to his parliamentary register of interests, as required by law, was a bit of a mistake. He did put on the register his apartment in East Melbourne, which was the family home, as well as an investment property in Seddon—but since this drew attention to the fact that he

6 In what should probably have received more attention than it did at the time, it's worth noting that the drop in support for Labor in Victoria wasn't benefiting the Liberals, despite their primary vote being in the ascendant; 2007 was the last time the majors were to win three seats each in the Senate: 2010 had Labor two, Liberals one, Nationals one, future Greens leader Richard di Natale and then-DLP candidate John Madigan; 2013 was two Labor, two Liberal, one Green and, notoriously, Motoring Enthusiast Party candidate Ricky Muir falling over the line thanks to preference deals.

was not actually resident in his own electorate,[7] it all rapidly turned into a farce.

He explained to journalists that he had every intention of moving into the Northcote house, since it had been bought specifically in order that he might dwell in his actual seat, but he was undertaking renovations to the property. The lack of any evidence of said renovations was explained by Feeney subsequently; he admitted that they hadn't yet begun, not so much because the house wasn't being prepared as the new Feeney home but more because it was being rented out.

This raised another embarrassing question—as to whether or not this and his other investment property were negatively geared, given that cracking down on the overuse of the tax advantages of negative gearing was such a key plank in the Labor platform. Feeney was unable to answer the question, explaining that his wife did all the household finances. Later he confirmed that fine, yes, they absolutely were negatively geared.

Around this time the tenants of Feeney's Northcote pad put up signage on the property provocatively promoting his Greens rival, Alex Bhathal—thereby presumably guaranteeing themselves an especially harsh property inspection next time around. So Feeney went on Sky News to nip this growing controversy in the bud . . . and in doing so, he made things much, much worse.

While offering a mea culpa for neglecting to list his property on the parliamentary register, he was blindsided by

---

7 Incidentally, candidates are not under any actual obligation to live in their electorate, although failing to do so does make it seem awfully as though no shit is especially being given.

an innocuous question about whether Labor, if elected, would continue the 'schoolkids bonus'. This $4.5 billion family payment was due to expire in July, having been axed by the Coalition with the support of PUP, back in the days when there was a PUP to lend its support to things being axed.

The correct answer, incidentally, was: 'No, we're not intending to restore the payment.' However, that wasn't the answer Feeney gave.

'The . . . well, we . . . in terms of the baby bonus?' he spluttered, before admitting, 'I've been a little distracted over the last few days.' And then, having humiliated himself on television, he scurried away from the studio—leaving behind his briefing notes, which were then splashed across the front page of the *Daily Telegraph* the following morning.

Despite this being reported as an explosive leak, there was nothing in the notes that Labor hadn't already announced; but having his crib sheets exposed didn't exactly inspire confidence that Feeney was prepared for the exam—especially as it focused attention on the pitched battle for Batman, with Bhathal's popularity surging and the Greens pouring resources into the seat.

It was a close-run thing, but despite his many goofs Feeney eventually prevailed, despite a staggering 8.5 per cent swing to the Greens. Such a victory over adversity, however, was not the experience of some of the Liberal Party's more gormless candidates.

———

The Victorian Liberals provided two of the most colourful hopefuls—one for what he did, and the other for what he failed to do.

The latter candidate was John Min-Chiang Hsu, who was trying his hand in the safe Labor seat of Calwell. His chances of victory were effectively nil, so it wasn't that big a deal for the party when it suddenly disendorsed him three weeks before the polls and just after the deadline for candidate registration, meaning that Labor's Maria Vamvakinou was able to walk it in with no Liberal challenger.

In the course of the campaign it had come to light that a man named John Min-Chiang Hsu was listed on the Australian Securities and Investments Commission's company register as being the co-owner of a business called Victoria Angels Brothel and Escort Agency, trading as Paradise Playmates—a mid-priced brothel in Frankston. Hsu vehemently denied having anything whatsoever to do with Paradise Playmates, insisting in the press that he had no connection with the adult services industry and had no idea why the person on the ASIC documents enjoyed not only the same name but also the same residential address and birthdate as him. However, despite brothels being both legal and regulated in Victoria—not to mention the Liberal Party's outspoken commitment to supporting small business—the party were less than thrilled that the candidate had forgotten to mention his titillating business interest. Hsu resigned from the candidacy and the party, thereby denying political wags the opportunity to make endless jokes about promoting 'jobs and growth'.

Just beyond Calwell's south-eastern border the Liberals were hopeful of picking up the marginal seat of McEwen from Labor's Rob Mitchell by deploying the can-do Chris

Jermyn, a tech entrepreneur with an international profile. He was exactly the sort of innovative, agile, risk-taking independent businessman that the Turnbull government was all about supporting, and given Mitchell's 0.2 per cent margin the seat seemed like an easy pickup.

But things started to get weird right from the outset, with Jermyn crashing an election doorstop by Bill Shorten on 28 May with an armful of campaign corflutes, ready to hijack the gathered media . . . which asked him about Liberal health policy. At this point he got all flustered and ran away, possibly fearing that he was about to offer something akin to the notorious sound bite given by the Libs' ill-fated candidate for Greenway in 2013, Jaymes Diaz.

However, the press smelled the tantalising scent of blood in the electoral water and started to investigate the candidate's past—and things got very silly very quickly. For a start, it transpired that Jermyn's tech business, Hot Shot Media, hadn't been quite the roaring success that had been implied; it had been implicated in the high-profile collapse of the international Shutterbug Millionaire competition, from which partner company Mooter Media had managed to misappropriate US$24 million in investments before halting its trade on the ASX in 2013. Jermyn, unfortunately, had joined the board of Mooter in 2014—for a month, before quitting to pursue politics—leaving him with some very uncomfortable questions to refuse to answer regarding where the money went.

This, however, was not really a political issue. Not compared with, for example, potential electoral fraud. As already mentioned, candidates are not technically obliged to live within their own electoral boundaries. It is, however, a big risk not to do so, since it gives one's rivals an easy line of attack based on the popular fiction that an MP's loyalties are to the community they represent rather than, more accurately, the party that gave them the sweet, sweet gig in the first place.

Jermyn, thankfully, didn't have to worry about this because his registered residential address was in the lovely little town of Christmas Hills, safely within the margins of McEwen. The problem was that the address in question was a vacant 40-hectare property that had been owned by Jermyn's father Peter until he'd sold it in 2013, a month and a half before the previous election.

For those justifiably worried that poor Chris was illegally squatting on someone else's vacant lot, presumably taking shelter under trees and running his campaign from within a hand-hewn trench lest the legal owners should happen to drive by, there was another explanation. It seemed possible that Jermyn was actually living in a man-made structure on the very swanky Queens Lane, just behind Albert Park in the heart of Melbourne: a very swish address indeed, although an inconvenient hour-plus drive from the boundaries of his would-be electorate.

This latter hypothesis was bolstered when a series of angry complaints by Jermyn on social media about the inadequacies of local fast food vendors around the CBD came to light, revealing that he was deeply concerned about inaccurate signage regarding opening hours and delivery deadlines there—an odd thing about which to vent if one was living a bucolic life in the rugged Christmas Hills.[8]

A larger and more legally complex issue surrounded the fact that Jermyn had registered his country address with the Australian Electoral Commission in 2013, both as a candidate and as a voter, which is a breach of Divisions 136 and 137 of the Criminal Code ('making any false or misleading statement in any enrolment or electoral papers', maximum penalty twelve months' imprisonment) and Section 336 of the Electoral Act ('unlawfully signing any enrolment or electoral papers', maximum penalty $1000).

It wasn't clear whether Jermyn would face any charges, but at least the Liberals didn't have to worry about a legal imbroglio engulfing its MP: Jermyn helped turn the seat from a marginal to a safe Labor win, with an almost 8 per cent swing to the incumbent.

But these were only warm-up acts before the main show— and there was to be much colour and movement there as well.

---

8   To be fair, you'd be annoyed too if you'd apparently driven eighty minutes from Christmas Hills to grab takeaway from Focaccia in Melbourne only to find it closed at 9.38 pm when the sign clearly said it was open till 10 pm. Especially if you'd been sleeping in a tree.

16
THE ELECTION CAMPAIGN, OR A NATION SAYS, 'MEH'

In which Australia's passion for democracy heats up from lukewarm to tepid

The government put a brave face on the break-even polling with which it entered the election period proper, insisting that John Howard had languished in 2001 before holding off the challenge of Labor under Kim Beazley. Of course, that remarkable turnaround hadn't been because of any great love for the Howard government so much as the one-two punch of the 'children overboard' event in October, which marked the beginning of the Coalition's love affair with treating refugees like dangerous criminals, and, rather more importantly, the global horror that followed the al-Qaeda attack on the World Trade Center in New York in September that year.

However, the Turnbull government faced a couple of large problems when hitting the familiar buttons marked National

Security and Sovereign Borders. One, as elucidated earlier, was that offshore detention was not just increasingly controversial but also looking as though its days were numbered. The other was that the minister responsible, Peter Dutton, shouldn't have ever been left near a microphone unattended.

That Dutton had once been whispered about as a potential leadership contender by the right wing of the party was testament to just how shallow a talent pool it possessed, for Dutton's time in the Immigration and Border Force portfolio had not exactly been a triumph. But at least he had shown impressive consistency: he'd previously been voted the worst Australian health minister of the last thirty-five years by the readers of *Australian Doctor*, not least because of his failed attempt to introduce a wildly unpopular GP co-payment, and his time in his latest gig had been characterised by a similar quality of leadership.

He'd overseen the collapse of Australia's deal to resettle refugees in Cambodia at a cost of $55 million; he'd had responsibility for a disastrous and humiliating operation that had attempted to check visas in the middle of Melbourne (which, hilariously, was codenamed Operation Fortitude, despite being immediately cancelled as soon as Melburnians started to protest); he'd sent journalist Samantha Maiden a text intended for Jamie Briggs, in which he called Maiden a 'mad fucking witch'; and—perhaps most magically of all— he'd decided to kill some time before a press conference by making a hilarious aside to Tony Abbott and Scott Morrison about the effects of climate change on low-lying islands, joking, 'Time doesn't mean anything when you're about to,

you know, have water lapping at your door.'[1] Abbott brayed
with laughter at Pete's killer wit, but Morrison leaned in and
muttered, 'There's a boom [mic] up there,' to his colleagues
before Dutton looked directly at the camera facing him,
correctly realising how popular this clip was about to become
on YouTube. In short, Dutton had given the distinct impression that his fondness for R.M. Williams boots was less
because they were part of the standard LNP uniform and
more because they didn't have pesky laces over which he'd
be guaranteed to trip.

But with an election to win, and the threat of terrorism
ever-present in people's minds—as horrific reports continued
of violence in France, Turkey, Pakistan and Germany, as well
as the ongoing slaughter in Iraq, Syria, Lebanon and other
Middle Eastern hot spots—it was important for the government to press home its advantage by getting the Minister
for Immigration and Border Force out before the media in
order to provide a calm and mature explanation of the threats
facing Australia and to give confidence to everybody that the
Coalition was determined to keep the nation safe.

Or, alternatively, that the immigrants were coming to take
our jobs.

'They won't be numerate or literate in their own language,
let alone English,' Dutton inexplicably decided to announce
on Sky News. 'These people would be taking Australian jobs,

---

1   Leaving aside that the premise in no way supports the punchline of Dutton's
astonishingly insensitive quip, which suggests that neither he nor Abbott know how
humour works, this event became a running joke within the party. When the new
Turnbull ministry was being photographed by media after its swearing-in in July
2016, many MPs made a point of alerting Dutton to the boom mics being held by
reporters. Yes, that Dutton fellow sure does inspire respect!

there's no question about that. For many of them that would be unemployed, they would languish in unemployment queues and on Medicare and the rest of it so there would be huge cost and there's no sense in sugarcoating that, that's the scenario.'

The government immediately snapped into damage control mode. Turnbull announced that he stood behind what Dutton in no way actually said: 'As Peter was saying earlier today, many of them come to Australia from shattered areas of the world,' he pretended. 'They are from dreadful, devastated, war-torn regions of the world.'

After Dutton angrily told the ABC that he stood by his statements, he suddenly vanished from the public eye and remained largely absent for the rest of the campaign.[2] And that absence wasn't merely from the media: Dutton disappeared so comprehensively that VICE Australia even sent a reporter to his Queensland seat of Dickson to make sure he was okay after all communication from his office halted during negotiations for an interview. The resulting article by Lee Zachariah, published on 7 July and titled 'Where in the World is Peter Dutton: An investigation', revealed that staff in Dutton's Strathpine campaign office didn't apparently have access to his diary, didn't know where he'd be from day to day, didn't know where his mobile office (a caravan he was supposedly taking around the electorate) would be, and really didn't respond well to smartarse journalists putting up HAVE YOU SEEN ME? flyers in the surrounding area.

---

2 Many, many commentators drew parallels with 'Schrödinger's Immigrant', who appears to have been first popularised via UK satire site Newsthump, which warned of immigrants who would 'simultaneously laze around on benefits and also steal your job'.

Dutton also faced a serious threat from GetUp!, the grass-roots progressive organisation that had long been critical of his record in office. GetUp! also targeted the LNP's candidate for the seat of Brisbane, Trevor Evans, who had been Dutton's chief of staff and who managed an impressive own goal when GetUp! checked his website and discovered that his bio had been lifted from a US web design company's template for political websites, on which it promoted a fictional candidate named 'Tim Hawthorne'.[3]

Border security wasn't the only topic rapidly removed from the campaign table. Housing affordability had become a major issue in the national conversation, particularly in Sydney and Melbourne, where prices had gone from 'high' to 'insane' to 'personally insulting'—thanks in no small part to almost two decades of policies that promoted housing as an investment strategy rather than grubby nonsense like being places for humans to live.

The most frequently expressed solution was to discourage investment by limiting negative gearing, a neat trick by which investors could deduct their losses on investment properties from their tax while still enjoying the benefits of owning a valuable and appreciating asset. Defendants of this arrangement could (and occasionally did) argue that it kept rents down by not forcing property owners to profit from rental properties, but this didn't often get airtime—not because it was necessarily incorrect but because, now that everyone was aspirationally upper middle class, no party wanted to be the

---

3 GetUp! got curious when some sections had left in 'Tim' rather than replacing it with the more accurate 'Trevor', demonstrating the sort of assiduous attention to detail Evans learned during his time with Dutton.

one to admit that a majority of Australians were guaranteed
to face a lifetime of renting.

The Turnbull government had briefly considered introducing some limitations on negative gearing, but any chance
of sensible concessions being made evaporated when Labor
announced it would restrict negative gearing to new properties only—thereby incentivising an increase in the amount
of available housing—while grandfathering investments
purchased before 1 July 2017. The Greens had a similar
plan, without the grandfathering clause, which gave the
government all it needed to decide that, if its opponents
were against negative gearing, then it was definitely the
greatest thing in the world and the Opposition was trying
to destroy the economy and possibly the very notion of
freedom itself.

Thus on 25 April Turnbull and Morrison headed out to
Sydney's south-western suburbs to do a photo opportunity
with Penshurst couple Julian and Kim Mignacca, the sort
of battling family who was just trying to get ahead through
using an investment property to build wealth—a road to self-
sufficiency that would supposedly become closed to them
if Labor's dangerous plans to limit negative gearing to new
properties after 2017 were to become law.

If this was the PM's attempt to show that he was connecting
with the battlers, he seemed to choose oddly well-resourced
ordinary Australians. The couple's first property purchase, as
they explained to journalists during this photo-op, was an
investment property in Cronulla, not a home in which they
themselves might live—and while they had been saving they had

lived with their parents rent-free. Which is a nice option if you have it.

They then sold their Cronulla place and bought their Penshurst home, plus an investment apartment nearby which they were renting out. Except that the reason that Julian bought the investment property was, as Turnbull announced, 'in order to buy a place for his little daughter Addison, who we just met, who is nearly one'.

So, to recap, the couple who were standing on their own two feet, thanks to negative gearing: a) had parents with whom they could live indefinitely while they bought properties, and b) were now buying properties for their not-yet-one-year-old child. In a single glorious example, Turnbull had managed to illustrate everything insane about the Sydney property market.

Strangely enough, the idea of Australians aspiring to such a glorious future—one that involved buying apartments for infants and relying on mater and pater to fund the process—didn't fill the hearts and minds of those city dwellers watching this on TV with optimism. Basically, they saw their chances of ever owning a home disappear over the horizon.

Yet on 5 May Turnbull doubled down on his new get-your-parents-to-buy-your-house-for-you economic policy during an interview with 774 ABC Melbourne's Jon Faine. When Faine pointed out that the middle-class families he knew saw no hope of their children affording their own homes and that this had the potential to turn into a boomers-versus-millennials generational conflict, Turnbull got a little bit playful: 'Are your kids locked out of the housing market?' he asked. 'Well, you should shell out for them—you should support them, a wealthy man like you.'

'That's what they say,' Faine responded with a chuckle, perhaps sensing what the headlines would look like the following morning.

Turnbull, evidently, did not. 'Exactly. Well, there you go—you see you've got the solution in your own hands. You can provide a bit of intergenerational equity in the Faine family.'

Several days ensued of the PM explaining that he was joking and that, no, this didn't mean that he didn't take the issue seriously and, anyway, Labor wanted to destroy housing prices by getting rid of negative gearing and, no, it was not just people with wealthy parents who deserved housing. At the end of all that, housing affordability was officially off the agenda too,[4] to be replaced with a new message: Shouldn't *everyone* get to invest in property, somehow?

And thus was unveiled the election's most widely mocked ad: a tradesman, holding a good honest cup o' char outside a building site, asking the camera: 'Let me get this right, Mr Shorten wants to go to war with my bank? He wants to go to war with our miners? Bill Shorten wants to go war with someone like me, who just wants to get ahead with an investment property? I reckon we should just see it through and stick with the current mob for a while.'

And the internet exploded.

The sheer parodic potential of the ad made it an immediate favourite of satirists, while the twitter hashtag #faketradie began trending almost immediately, despite the fact that the

4 Well, for everyone one year or older.

person in question, Andrew McRae, was in fact a genuine qualified tradesman—specifically, in property maintenance. However, that didn't explain why he was apparently on a construction site, outside the barrier fence, drinking from a ceramic mug, with a hi-vis vest but no other safety gear, standing in front of a trestle mysteriously set up in an alley, while wearing an expensive watch and a loose gold bracelet that was not only in danger of being accidentally damaged but would also be a legitimate safety concern for a real working tradesperson.

It did, however, provide a nice break from the otherwise ghastly advertising, whether it was the excruciating sight of Shorten being interviewed by his wife Chloe about their children, or Turnbull reminiscing about his hardscrabble life with his (comfortably well-off) father after his mother abandoned the family. Both were ill-advised attempts at spin: in the first instance, to portray the Opposition Leader as a warm family man and not just a union stooge, and in the second to show that the PM—whom Peta Credlin had accurately characterised as Mr Harbourside Mansion—was in touch with the concerns and dreams of the common people. Still, they were both better than Queensland independent Bob Katter's ad, in which it was implied he had shot the major parties dead with a revolver—although this one, at the very least, was impressively on-message.

———

The government also largely chose to avoid the issue of health funding after minister Sussan Ley revealed that she had opposed the extension of the government's Medicare rebate freeze to doctors; she'd realised that this was effectively forcing doctors to impose a co-payment in order to cover their rising costs over time, but she hadn't been permitted to do anything about it. And this wasn't a great look.

On 23 May she explained on radio, 'I understand for doctors that the GP freeze has been difficult and I appreciate they're working with us. I've said to doctors I want that freeze lifted as soon as possible but I appreciate that Finance and Treasury aren't allowing me to do it just yet', without appearing to consider the optics of such a statement. Shadow health spokeswoman Catherine King didn't miss a trick though, declaring that Ley 'has basically admitted that health policy under the Turnbull government is all about cuts and about finding savings, it has got nothing to do with the health of this nation'. Ley did attempt to walk her comments back, insisting that these Medicare savings would help fuel jobs and growth, but that was pretty much the last time Ley appeared in public during the campaign.

This conceded the ground to Labor, and it began running ads outlining the consequences of people avoiding early treatment out of financial concerns. Labor now began shaping a narrative around being the only party that would protect accessible healthcare and developed a line it would repeat over and over again: 'Healthcare should rely on your Medicare card, not your credit card.'

———

The treasurer, however, could not be sidelined—which meant he was able to do things like go on the ABC and announce that he, as a straight, white, middle-class man, was a victim of persecution.

To put his claims in context: on 12 June a gunman entered a gay nightclub in Orlando, Florida, and opened fire, killing forty-nine people and wounding a further fifty-three. It was the largest single-shooter massacre on US soil and the greatest act of domestic terrorism since September 11.

On 21 June Labor's Penny Wong gave a speech about the persecution that LGBTI Australians faced on a day-to-day basis. 'Mr Turnbull, and many commentators on this subject, don't understand that for gay and lesbian Australians hate speech is not abstract. It's real. It's part of our everyday life ... Many same-sex couples don't hold hands on the street because they don't know what reaction they'll get. Some hide who they are for fear of the consequences at home, at work, at school,' she explained, before talking about the unnecessary difficulties to which she had been subjected as a lesbian parent—particularly since she remained unable to marry her partner, Sophie Allouache, which added extra bureaucratic hurdles that straight couples didn't have to face. But most of all, she opposed the idea that people who had a problem with the very existence of homosexuality were being asked to give permission for complete strangers to live their lives.

'I oppose a plebiscite [on marriage equality] because I do not want my relationship, my family, to be the subject of inquiry, of censure, of condemnation, by others,' she concluded. 'And I don't want other relationships, other families, to be targeted either ... A plebiscite designed to deny me and many other Australians a marriage certificate will instead license hate speech to those who need little encouragement.'

The following day Morrison addressed these concerns by dismissing them, arguing that he and other anti-equality spokespeople suffered the same level of cruel persecution as, you know, *those* people: 'People of very strong religious views, they have also been subject to quite dreadful hate speech and bigotry as well. It is not confined to one side of this debate,' he blithely trumpeted on ABC radio. 'I understand the concern Penny is raising, I know it from personal experience, having been exposed to that sort of hatred and bigotry for the views I've taken, from others who have a different view to me.'

His timing was exceptional. On this very day Wong's frequent sparring partner, Cory Bernardi, took to his blog to attack Turnbull for his unspectacular appearance on *Q&A* and to dismiss a suggestion the PM had made there that words had been exchanged between him and his backbench regarding homophobic language. 'By saying he'd had firm discussions with a number of colleagues, Turnbull gave implicit support to the claim that myself and other Coalition MPs are homophobic and implied that he'd had a conversation with me about homophobia,' Bernardi sulked. 'For the record I have never had such a conversation with any of my colleagues because they know that any such claims cannot be backed with facts.'

———

One of the most frequent criticisms of Turnbull was that he was wildly popular with people who weren't going to vote Liberal in a blue fit, while not appealing to the conservative base of the party. Indeed, as Leigh Sales put it to him rather bluntly on *7.30*: 'Isn't it the case that if your colleagues had known that this is where you would be [in the polls] three weeks before an election, they wouldn't have backed you to replace Tony Abbott?'

The PM had developed a nasty flu while on the election trail, but was in no position to take any time off. This meant he was in a less-than-agile frame of mind when asked how to restore business confidence, which was being undermined by mixed messages, such as that his government would remove industrial subsidies because they unfairly skewed the operation of the free market while at the same time throwing billions of dollars at submarine building in South Australia, in what looked very like a desperate attempt to protect local Liberal candidates from the relentless march of NXT.

However, something then happened that played right into the government's narrative. On 23 June the UK stunned the world by voting to leave the European Union—a seismic change to global geopolitics that was predicted to have potentially catastrophic implications for England, for Ireland, for Scotland, for the stability of Europe, for the economies of all countries involved, for the economies of all trading partners, and for the continuation of lasting peace in the northern hemisphere.

It was a shock to everyone—including UK prime minister David Cameron, who immediately resigned—not least because the support for Brexit was largely based on a series of transparent lies regarding immigration and public money sent to the EU, peddled by the likes of former London mayor turned aspirant PM Boris Johnson and UK Independence Party leader Nigel Farage. Both men immediately denied promising the things they'd been very publicly promising, almost as though they resented the voters for believing statements that were so obviously rubbish. Johnson walked away from his dream of becoming the Tory leader but was subsequently appointed foreign secretary by new British PM Theresa May, in what was either a piece of breathtaking obliviousness or a triumph of mean-spirited cringe comedy.

Locally, however, it was a godsend for Turnbull, because it gave him a new message to hammer home: stability.[5] Only by retaining the Turnbull government could Australia hope to weather the coming storms, he argued, in what was partly a warning to the public not to risk electing any of those messy independents. 'At a time of uncertainty, the last thing we need is a parliament in disarray,' he declared. 'When it comes to the minor parties, be they Lambie, Xenophon, Lazarus or Hanson, if you only really know the leader of a minor party, but you don't really know their candidates, and you don't really know their policies, then don't vote for them.'

And to be fair, he made a decent point, because the minor parties seemed to divide into two broad categories: ones named after their leaders, or ones whose name indicated the opposite of what they actually stood for, like the Health Party (comprised of vaccination sceptics), Sustainable Australia (in favour of cutting immigration) or United Patriots Front (segregation—although so united were its members that they forgot to officially register as a political party before the deadline, probably because they had some patriotism to attend to).

However, the PM's stability message was directed far more to his backbench, which was still seething and roiling with factional discord. The election was finally drawing near, and yet there was no sign that the party was any closer to rallying enthusiastically behind its leader.

---

5 You know, the sort of stability that could only be offered by a nine-month-old government that existed because of a leadership coup.

Some were having fun with it at least, like the previous PM. He gently implied during an interview with Andrew Bolt that, sure, everyone was disgusted by Turnbull, but that shouldn't stop them voting Liberal.

As mentioned in Chapter 4, Abbott looked physically pained a week before the polls when he attended the campaign 'launch', held at the somewhat downmarket Homebush Novotel in the western suburbs of Sydney, and with a far more downbeat mood than Abbott's own triumphant bells-'n'-whistles-'n'-stupid-amounts-of-balloons event ahead of the 2013 election.

It was far less jubilant than the Labor launch the previous week, not least because all the surviving Labor PMs were present except for the one who would have made things awkward. Bob Hawke, Paul Keating and Julia Gillard were all praised as Labor heroes, while Kevin Rudd tweeted his support from Russia, where he was busily campaigning to get the job of United Nations secretary-general: a bold plan, sure, but a pretty solid excuse for not being present at an event where he'd have had to make very uncomfortable small talk with Shorten and Gillard.

Then again, the Liberal launch did have one notable absence of its own: former leader Dr John Hewson, who had fallen far out of favour with the party since his stint as Opposition Leader and, like the late Liberal PM Malcolm Fraser, had experienced more than a few epiphanies about the party he'd led once he was no longer responsible for leading it. Nothing illustrated this better than the fact that, while the campaign launch was taking place in the marginal Liberal seat of Reid, he was speaking at a rally in Double Bay, deep in Turnbull's electorate of Wentworth, about the challenges facing Australia due to unchecked climate change.

———

With the world reeling from the Brexit vote, shadow treasurer Chris Bowen did Labor few favours with those concerned about his party's economic credentials by confirming that there would be greater deficits under Labor in the short term—although it was on track to return the federal budget to surplus at the same time as the Coalition was predicting, on a similarly fantastic basis. He also revealed that he'd be sweetening the deal with, um, unpopular cuts.

'Whoever receives the treasurer's incoming brief on July 3, whether it is me or Scott Morrison, the information will be the same: action is needed to restore the budget to balance, to save the AAA [credit rating],' he told ABC 702 cheerily. 'What I also say is that we released our principles [in a 32-page economic plan booklet] yesterday . . . We are releasing more savings over the next couple of days; not all of them will be universally popular.'

This seemed like the moment when Labor might have lost the narrative; but, with the polls drawing closer, there was still time for the government to get in a couple more quick fuck-ups.

First, the notoriously forgetful Arthur Sinodinos was forced to tell the media that he'd forgotten if public funds had been poured into Parakeelia Pty Ltd as the IT platform of choice for the Liberal Party and its campaigns. The correct answer was, 'Yes, obviously, because there are specific allowances for computer and data infrastructure and training and Parakeelia was the party's nominated company.' But that would have looked a little dodgy, given that it was a private company whose directors included Liberal Party federal director Tony Nutt and president Richard Alston, and, as luck would have it, Parakeelia had donated a very generous $500,000 to the Coalition.

However, even more forgetful was arts minister Mitch Fifield, who mistakenly turned up at a debate on arts policy in Melbourne without remembering the need to have actually developed a policy first. His contribution to the debate on the parlous state of arts funding and the future of public policy consisted entirely of pushing jobs and growth as a solution.

That's not even an exaggeration. When asked how he sought to address the $300 million slashed from arts funding, not to mention the $105 million that former arts minister George Brandis had ring-fenced as his own private fund, the National Program for Excellence in the Arts, Fifield responded: 'I think one of the really important things government can do is make sure that we have an economy that is strong and growing, because an economy that is strong and growing means that there will be individuals and corporates and philanthropists who are in a better position to purchase artworks, to support individual artists.'

And sure, it wasn't ideal that the arts minister's approach to ensuring adequate funding appeared to extend no further than 'If everyone's got nice jobs, they might throw more change in your guitar case', but the polls were just around the corner— and who could think about policy at a time like this?

At the beginning of the campaign the polls were more or less equal. *The Guardian*'s aggregate of all of the polling calculated the Coalition at 49.93 per cent in two-party preferred terms at the time when the election was officially called, although the campaigning had started back before the budget was even announced. And those polling numbers didn't change in any substantial way during the course of the election, which made it extra hard for journalists to provide daily copy. After all, eight weeks is a long, long time in politics; but it's also a long time in, well, weeks.

One of the biggest problems with the polls continuing to remain permanently locked at around 50:50 was that the media was forced to run stories about the likely safe-but-reduced return of the Turnbull government, based more on a gut feeling than any evidence. The *Sydney Morning Herald* ultimately backed a Turnbull return, following a similar, if more predictable, editorial from *The Australian*. This inspired many pundits to dredge up the *Herald*'s retrospectively hilarious assertion in 2013 that only the election of the Abbott government would produce the stability and economic management that the country so desperately needed.

Despite the national polls pointing towards a hung parliament, MPs from both sides declared confidently that their own internal data suggested they were on track to win. However, the media reflected a general confidence that Turnbull would be returned with ease—perhaps with a small, but manageable, swing against him.

Discussions among the cognoscenti centred around how many seats either party might gain or lose before its leadership would be called into question—the consensus being that Labor would probably pick up eight seats, which was thought not enough to prevent Shorten from facing a leadership challenge, and that Turnbull would be in serious danger in the unlikely event that the Coalition lost more than ten.

Who would challenge Shorten for the Labor leadership following his inevitable loss? pundits asked. Would Anthony Albanese make an immediate move, or would there be competing challenges from Chris Bowen and/or Tony Burke? Would Tanya Plibersek make a run for it? Was Albo even safe in his seat of Grayndler, given the resources the Greens were throwing at it? How would the party cope with its disappointment after this expected loss despite party unity and all its positive policies?

Since Labor's fate was evidently sealed, speculation turned instead to what would happen to the Liberal Party and the Coalition once Turnbull ushered them to the victory Abbott would have denied them. Sure, it was accepted, there would be ungracious members of the conservative right who would huff and puff about how Abbott would have somehow turned it all around before the polls, but they'd surely be placated— if not actively sidelined—by the impressive victory that awaited Turnbull.

Maybe, as many optimistic observers speculated, The Real Malcolm Turnbull would appear, buoyed by an election win in his own right. He'd sweep back into Canberra, challenged but re-energised, ready to silence the DelCons in his party, to renegotiate the Coalition deal from a position of strength and be the economically savvy, socially progressive leader of Australia's aspirational upper-middle-class dreams.

Others crunched the marginal seat numbers and worked out which MPs were most likely to be removed at the polls and concluded they were largely the same team who had thrown in their lot with Turnbull in 2015 in order to avert exactly this fate. That, they figured, would leave Turnbull with less support within his party and mean that any chance of the renewable-energy-lovin', marriage-equality-supportin', Australian-republic-advocatin' firebrand suddenly bursting forth was basically nil.

But either way, the answers would come shortly and the implications would gently unravel over the subsequent months as the Turnbull government settled into turning its inevitable easy victory into a mandate for change. And then, everyone seemed to think, we could relax and get back to ignoring politics altogether, the way we used to.

———

All the networks gathered together their favourite Labor and Coalition personalities for the election night broadcasts and settled in for what was predicted to be a fairly uneventful reporting of the polls.[6] Jokes about sausage sizzles and the sheer length of the campaign were shared as everyone settled in for what, if history was any guide, would probably be about three or four hours before the result would be known. Elections,

---

6 Channel 7 had clearly assumed there'd be no drama in the actual polls and had therefore gone to great lengths to create cute animations of losing candidates being strapped to rockets and fired towards the moon. Incidentally, Channel 10 didn't bother with an election special and screened *Mission: Impossible* instead. [Insert your own political joke here.]

after all, are settled in the eastern states—specifically, in New South Wales and Queensland—and it wasn't unheard of for the election result to be called even as Western Australia was closing its polling stations.

However, despite the somewhat forced camaraderie, it didn't take long for the smug confidence of the Liberal candidates to evaporate, or for the brave-faced resignation of their Labor counterparts to turn to surprise, incredulity and, finally, actual glee as the numbers started to trickle in. That reduced-but-comfortable victory for the Coalition was not appearing in the early results; as the percentages of counted votes grew, it slowly dawned on everyone that this was looking less like a skirmish, and more like a bloodbath.

Veteran ABC reporter Barrie Cassidy was the first to identify the pattern: the states that had Labor governments were not exactly falling to the Opposition, but showing signs of a small and patchy swing to Labor. This was a problem in Queensland, where the Opposition needed to pick up a number of seats in and around Brisbane if it was to be a serious contender for government, and in Victoria, where it seemed in danger of actually going backwards. South Australia wasn't looking promising either, although that was largely offset by the NXT vote disproportionately pulling votes from the Liberals—but even so, several historically safe Labor seats seemed remarkably resistant to leaving their 2013-era Liberal stewards, most notably the historically working-class seat of Hindmarsh.

However, in the states with Coalition governments, the picture was very different. There the swings to Labor were far beyond expectations.

In Tasmania Labor picked up four of the five seats, routing the sitting Liberal members in Bass, Braddon and Lyons and leaving the Coalition without a single MP in the state. In New South Wales it cut a swathe through the western suburbs. In the Northern Territory the seat of Lingiari stayed in Labor hands, to be joined by the electorate of Solomon. In Western Australia early counting had Labor making inroads in safe National seats like Durack and O'Connor.

It turned out that the national polls had reflected the national picture accurately—with both parties more or less balanced—but only because the states and territories were cancelling out each other's local swings.

The national picture was further complicated by other factors, like the rise of NXT, especially in South Australia, the sudden absence of Palmer United, and the unexpected return of One Nation. In all, Labor picked up eleven seats from the Coalition on the night, and many were still in doubt days later.

By that stage, of course, the recriminations had begun.

17
WALKING THROUGH
THE RUBBLE

The election is won . . . but at what cost?

The sun rose on a nation without a result on Sunday, 3 July 2016. And Monday. And for most of the week, as the sheer size of the government's losses became more and more clear.

To be fair, that had been evident on election night itself as the media waited in vain for the prime minister to appear and make a statement. Live television crosses to the Liberals' election night party at Sydney's Sofitel Wentworth hotel—showing a largely empty room with a few desultory clumps of people milling around as canapés circulated in an endless ballet—rammed home the prevailing lack of excitement on the night, while eyebrows were raised by the revelation that Turnbull was at home in Point Piper, rather than at the barricades with his supporters.[1]

---

1 So funereal had the event become that the young, well-dressed people holding canapés photographed in the *Daily Telegraph*'s post-election cover story—'Party Faithful Licking Their Wounds'—were soon identified on Twitter as journalists from Fairfax and *The Guardian*. A killer party it was not.

Eventually Shorten took the initiative and appeared before the Labor faithful to deliver what sounded for all the world like a victory speech. 'Friends, we will not know the outcome of this election tonight. Indeed, we may not know it for some days to come,' he began. 'But there is one thing for sure—the Labor Party is back!'

Never before had someone who had known that their chances of victory were somewhere between slim and nil sounded so downright jubilant—although that seemed less because of Labor's result than the Coalition's.

'We have argued for our positive plans and, three years after the Liberals came to power in a landslide, they have lost their mandate. And Mr Turnbull's economic program, such as it was, has been rejected by the people of Australia. Whatever happens next week, Mr Turnbull will never be able to claim that the people of Australia have adopted his ideological agenda. He will never again be able to promise the stability which he has completely failed to deliver tonight. Friends, whatever happens next week, whether we are in government or in opposition, the Labor Party is re-energised, it is unified and it is more determined than ever!' As concession speeches go, it sounded more like a declaration of war.

At around 12.30 am reports came through that Turnbull had left his mansion and was on his way to the Sofitel Wentworth. And when he arrived, he was not in a good mood.

He began by admitting that there was not and would not be a result on the night, beyond being confident that the Coalition would be able to form majority government in its own right—which, admittedly, didn't exactly indicate a ringing endorsement from the Australian people. However, after beginning in this way, a confident leader who was seeking to rally his battered troops and bolster his claim to authority might have said something along the lines of: 'We have heard the message, we have taken up the challenge, and we will repay the people's trust'—rather than, say, angrily making excuses for how unfair everyone had been.

'The Labor Party ran some of the most systematic, well-funded lies ever peddled in Australia,' Turnbull complained, adding that 'the mass ranks of the union movement and all of their millions of dollars, telling vulnerable Australians that Medicare was going to be privatised or sold, frightening people in their beds and even today, even as voters went to the polls, as you would have seen in the press, there were text messages being sent to thousands of people across Australia saying that Medicare was about to be privatised by the Liberal Party ... An extraordinary act of dishonesty. No doubt the police will investigate.[2] But this is the scale of the challenge we faced.'

These angry, defensive words were not those of a man secure in his leadership. Yes, it looked like the Coalition would be forming government one way or another, but in some respects this was the least satisfactory situation of all for Turnbull: a comfortable win would have been a mandate for the new leader and his government, while a resounding loss could have been blamed on the legacy of Abbott. Just squeaking

---

2   They did, sort of, at least to confirm that no laws had technically been broken and therefore there was no ground on which to prosecute anyone.

over the line left everything to individual interpretations, of which there would be many.

And the interpretations were not flattering.

Veteran political commentator Laurie Oakes was the first to slam the PM's less-than-gracious speech. 'It is the first time that I have seen a bloke who has won the election give a speech saying that we were robbed,' he tutted on Channel 9. 'I thought that was pretty pathetic. It was an angry speech from a guy who two days ago promised a different kind of politics because Australians were sick of this stuff ... It's going to be a pretty nasty few years.'[3]

Some from the more conservative end of the media began running hopeful stories about a challenge to the Labor leadership, suggesting that perennial left-faction leadership aspirant Anthony Albanese was poised to launch a challenge against Bill Shorten.[4] Sky News presented the challenge as being imminent in the days after the election, despite eleven seats having definitely fallen to Labor and there being a slim, but still live, possibility of Shorten ending up as prime minister. In any case, this insane party-levelling event didn't eventuate—and Albanese went on ABC TV's *7.30*

---

3 Which was downright flattering compared with a tweet by fellow politics veteran Mike Carlton: 'I have known Malcolm Turnbull for 40 years. Tutored him in journalism. What a flabby failure he is tonight.'
4 Traditionally the Labor leadership positions become vacant following an election loss, but the elaborate and time-consuming process of running a ballot of both the parliamentary party and the rank-and-file membership would only come into play if challengers appeared. Sure, there was the possibility that Labor would want to throw its hard-forged unity and newly ascendant fortunes away on a ballot that would almost certainly return Shorten and Tanya Plibersek as the leadership team, but it seemed more like wishful thinking by the terrified right.

to quash the rumours, confirming that Shorten had his full support.

A far bigger question mark hovered over Turnbull. The day after the election an anonymous 'senior Liberal' told Fairfax that there was a 90 per cent chance of Turnbull being removed during the government's next term, adding that the only factors in his favour were the lack of an obviously acceptable replacement and a general unwillingness to replace yet another leader.

The greatest criticism, however, came from the right of the Liberal Party, which saw all its nightmares coming true. Having been robbed of its influence under Tony Abbott, it now saw oblivion beckon and wasted no time in making its voice heard. Predictably, South Australian Liberal senator Cory Bernardi slammed the government for the 'very disappointing' result, declaring that it represented 'a product of the contempt shown by senior Liberals and so-called Liberal strategists for conservatives and the Liberal base. This has done enormous damage to the Liberal Party.'

He added darkly that people would be 'held to account' and explained: 'I think in the end [Turnbull] should be asking himself if he has done the Liberal Party a service or a disservice. The conclusion that I come to is we went down the same path that Labor did during the Rudd–Gillard years. We made a decision, which was incorrect in my view, to change leaders in the first term and the transaction cost of that has been felt at this election.'

It was a position echoed by conservative commentator and human-shaped tantrum Andrew Bolt, who didn't wait for the results on election night before demanding that Turnbull resign, even if he ended up winning the election. Turnbull couldn't 'seriously claim that this result is better than anything Abbott could have achieved', he wrote on his blog in an open letter to the PM, seemingly positing that the run of Newspolls that had Abbott easily losing to Labor had been on the cusp of turning around when Turnbull had challenged: 'You assassinated a Liberal prime minister, Tony Abbott, who'd won an election by a huge margin. You promised to do even better than him. You then treated the Liberal base like dirt, smashing it with a huge super tax, refusing to speak to conservative journalists, repeatedly humiliating Abbott. You have been a disaster. You betrayed Tony Abbott and then led the party to humiliation, stripped of both values and honour. Resign.'

Peta Credlin, Bolt's fellow Sky News commentator and Abbott's former chief of staff, politely twisted the knife: 'I would have backed [Abbott] in this time round,' she stated, 'because he knows how to campaign, he resonates in those regional seats, he resonates in western Sydney, and in the places where Labor has made ground tonight, but you'll never know because he's not in the race. One thing that can be said is no one can blame this result on Tony Abbott, who played I think a very fair, a very dignified team game.'

According to other key Liberal figures, however, the problem was that there hadn't been enough time for Turnbull to establish himself as being more unlike Abbott. 'At this stage I have to say anybody in the Liberal Party who thinks they faced a better future under different circumstances is not living on the same planet as the rest of us were last year,'

Cabinet Secretary Arthur Sinodinos told Channel 9. 'That is the reality and we spent nine months clawing back, trying to get the trust of the Australian people after some of the events of the early part of the term. That is the truth.'

This echoed what treasurer Scott Morrison said during the ABC's election coverage, long after his quiet confidence at the beginning of the night had been replaced by a simmering defensive fury as he insisted that the Coalition was still 'on track to win this election . . . a situation that a year ago was not looking like that at all' and 'I think it's highly unlikely [that Abbott would have won]. I think the party room made its own judgement on that last September.' And with that, Morrison pretty much ended his leadership hopes as far as the right of the party was concerned.

As the counting continued, the Liberal Party was still bickering over whose fault it wasn't. Minister for Resources Josh Frydenberg reiterated Morrison's point on ABC TV's *Q&A* on the Monday after the poll, insisting that 'it was a decisive victory for Malcolm Turnbull and he got us back to a competitive position in the poll. I don't think he should stand down at all.'

Hours earlier, Bernardi had been continuing his anti-Turnbull tour on *7.30*. 'I think the conservative wing of the Liberal Party were very, very disciplined. We offered nothing but support to the prime minister, we provided advice behind the scenes when we can. That advice was seldom listened to,' he sniffed.

At around the same time Credlin went on Bolt's show in a glorious cavalcade of internal Sky cross-promotion. As Bolt continued his crusade to return Abbott to the leadership—and thereby return Bolt himself to any degree of influence—Credlin gave a trenchant real-time assessment of what was going on within the Sky studio and the Liberal Party more broadly.

'I think the result on Saturday night reflects where the Liberal party is at,' she sighed. 'That wonderful victory they had in September 2013, when they had the faith and the trust of the Australian people behind them, has been squandered in a term of in-fighting. We watched Labor do that to themselves. We all laughed and guffawed and manufactured opportunity out of that. We swore it would never happen to us, and it took two years for us to pull ourselves apart. Mainstream parties wonder why people are leaving them in droves. This is why.'

———

While the previous PM was publicly refusing to comment beyond a general appeal for calm, the pro-Abbott forces were jockeying to retain influence. WA senator Chris Back became the latest of the Coalition agitating for Abbott to be promoted to the front bench as soon as the government was returned.

'The prime minister of the day has got to appoint those people who he believes have the best set of skills, and I would be very surprised if Malcolm did not believe that Tony has the skills needed for the front bench,' he said innocently. 'Look at his background—he has been the prime minister, he has been one of the most successful health ministers we have had. We are the party of business—in business you appoint the most skilled people, and there will be gaps on the front bench.'

Arthur Sinodinos attempted to downplay the internal unrest by presenting Turnbull as the uniter of the diverse elements in the Liberals, telling Radio National: 'The important thing to remember here is that the base of the Liberal Party is quite diverse—it's not owned by any one branch or section.' Even so, *The Australian* reported that there was a push for all Coalition MPs to return to Canberra on the Tuesday for a joint party room meeting, either to begin the process of replacing Turnbull as leader or to prevent him from making any move to push through dangerous deals with the independents. According to the story, certain elements in the party—or, to put it another way, the DelCons—were keen that the party 'avoid crossbench agreements they would later regret', which seemed like code for 'embrace emissions trading or same-sex marriage'.

Of course, there was one major problem with holding a party room meeting: no-one was sure who was actually still in the party. At this point only sixty-five parliamentarians could say with any certainty that they still had a job, and Credlin didn't miss an opportunity to rub it in by castigating the 'hapless group of bedwetters' who'd supported Turnbull and been rewarded with political oblivion. 'Malcolm Turnbull, you are the man that broke the Liberal Party's heart,' she declared on Sky News, adding 'Everyone has had a crack at me and the advice I gave the prime minister, Tony Abbott, but at least he won an election.'

Then there were the odder theories about why the government hadn't galloped home to a triumphant victory. Attorney-General George Brandis, never the greatest supporter of that new-fangled internet technology, blamed Twitter and argued that social media had led to the 'trivialisation of political discourse'. Meanwhile, billionaire Harvey Norman co-founder

Gerry Harvey went in a different direction: he contended that Australia had become ungovernable and argued: 'The only cure we've got is to have a dictator like in China or something like that. Our democracy at the moment is not working.'

The oddest theory, however, was one beloved by several right-wing commentators, who declared that the voters had favoured established (and mainly conservative-leaning) Liberal figures and turfed out a disproportionately high number of those who supported Turnbull. This interpretation relied on some implausible-sounding premises: one, that a significant number of Australian voters were aware of the factional leanings of their MP within the Liberal Party; two, that they knew how individual MPs and senators had voted in the leadership spill and had been seething for nine months, just waiting for the chance to exact their revenge at the ballot box; and three, that voters across the nation were somehow shrewd enough to strategically target such Turnbull supporters as Wyatt Roy and Peter Hendy, yet also accidentally take out outspoken Abbott supporters like Natasha Griggs, Andrew Nikolic and Jamie Briggs in the process. A more plausible interpretation—that those in vulnerable marginal seats had more strongly backed Turnbull's challenge for fear of losing their gigs in the predicted Abbott wipeout and still lost their seats with the Coalition's reduced majority—didn't seem to get as much play, probably because it wasn't nearly as excitingly conspiratorial.

Also, it wasn't as though the pro-Abbott camp was sitting pretty in the new parliament. *The Australian*'s Sarah Martin crunched the numbers and concluded that retirements and seat losses meant that Abbott's rump of support had shrunk from forty-four to thirty while Turnbull had lost sixteen of his fifty-four supporters, thanks to pre-selection stoushes, retirements or electoral defeat.

Meanwhile the Nationals had a stronger hold on the Coalition, having both improved their primary vote and increased their number of seats. An emboldened Barnaby Joyce merrily announced to the media that he would be keeping the result of their strong-arm negotiations on the down-low, telling Sky News: 'The first aspiration is the agreement remains confidential. That's aspiration one, two, three, four, five and six.' This immediately signalled to all observers that the deal would contain details that would neither enchant nor delight the general public.

There were farcical scenes too. In what could well be the first instance of fractal politics, reports emerged from Tasmania that the annual general meeting of the Australian Liberal Students' Federation, the peak federal body for the different Liberal clubs in Australia's universities, had turned into a pitched battle between the conservative right and the moderate centrists, with the former quietly changing the cut-off date for AGM registration. In what was an impressively authentic echo of the goings-on in the federal body, staffers for conservative MPs— including Jack Morgan, adviser to Alex Hawke, and Ananija Ananievski, who'd been forced to leave Kevin Andrews' office after allegations of branch-stacking—prevented their factional enemies from entering the AGM, explaining that they'd missed the deadline and therefore couldn't vote to change the (under-pressure-to-resign) executive. Their unconstitutional authority was bolstered by the presence of private security guards. While Morgan was elected president, the delegates who had been refused entry—plus about sixty other members who had left in protest—held a meeting of their own. They elected their own president, Jack McGuire, before pondering whether to form a breakaway organisation, to commence legal action against the Australian Liberal Students' Federation, or to complain to their federal dad, Liberal Party director Tony Nutt, and make him sort the mean bullies out.

Eric Abetz—who had himself been president of the ALSF in the 1970s—had been scheduled to speak at the concluding gala dinner, but he withdrew in disgust.[5] In his defence, of course, he'd had enough of this sort of childish factional self-harm at work in Canberra without also having to put up with it at home in Hobart.

———

By 7 July there were legitimate fears that Australia might have to hold a second election. The Coalition was confident of winning seventy-three seats, Labor had a safe sixty-six, and five seats had gone to independents. Six seats were still too close to call, and the postal and pre-poll votes were not quite favouring the Coalition to the degree to which the government had become accustomed. History suggested three seats each, which would give the Coalition the seventy-six seats necessary to govern in its own right, but there was still the strong possibility of a minority government.

Given that, Turnbull set about ensuring he could at least secure some form of arrangement by which he'd be able

———

5 He was replaced by a different religious conservative with a bee in his bonnet about marriage equality: Hobart's Catholic archbishop Julian Porteous who, it's fair to say, would have been equally riveting an after-dinner speaker.

to govern. Thankfully, given the fiery rhetoric both he and most of the crossbenchers had previously dispensed regarding their refusal even to countenance some sort of government-guaranteeing deal with the independents, all he needed to convince the governor-general that he was capable of forming a new government was an assurance that the independents wouldn't block supply bills or move a motion of no confidence.

While those were small concessions to make, the cross-benchers were under no compunction to comply. So Turnbull began a campaign of sweet-talking the independent MPs— or, more accurately, the ones he could at least stand to talk to.

Greens MP Adam Bandt, who had increased his lead in Melbourne, and NXT's Rebekha Sharkie, who had sent Jamie Briggs to political oblivion in Mayo, were put into the 'later' pile, while Queensland's colourful Bob Katter was the first port of call. And it went well, sort of.

In a typically long and rambling speech to the press, Katter eventually confirmed that yes, he'd begrudgingly agreed to support the Turnbull government. 'We do not want to go back to the polls, that should not be imposed upon the Australian people,' he explained, 'so today we are announcing our support by supply and confidence for a Turnbull government. I do so with no great enthusiasm.' He emphasised that his support was provisional: 'If there is the slightest hint of union-bashing, I can assure you all bets are off,' he declared, which was somewhat problematic given that the entire basis of the election—the reintroduction of the Australian Building and Construction Commission—was arguably a major union-bashing exercise.

Tasmania's independent MP for Denison, Andrew Wilkie, confirmed he would also give the Turnbull government his qualified support, as did Cathy McGowan, who had retained her Victorian seat of Indi and also increased her lead over the hapless Sophie Mirabella, who refused to concede that she'd lost long, long after everyone else had moved on. Indeed, it wasn't until 25 July that she publicly acknowledged she'd failed to get her old seat back, going on Sky News to tell Andrew Bolt that she would be quitting politics altogether for a new life as a commentator. Her syntax suggested that too might be tricky though, as she rhetorically and confusingly asked Bolt: 'When the left-wing media and GetUp! and the unions get together with the Melbourne-based feminists to have a go at you and they've had a go at you, what more can they do?'[6] Few were surprised when she took a different job in August, that of 'government and media relations' (a lobbyist, in other words) for Gina Rinehart's Hancock Prospecting.

And Mirabella wasn't the only Liberal who felt that reality wasn't portraying the party in a flattering enough light: barely had the polls closed than there was some frantic rewriting of history.

———

'I want to make it quite clear that, as prime minister and leader of the Liberal Party, I take full responsibility for our campaign—absolutely full responsibility for the campaign,' Turnbull announced on the Tuesday afternoon after the election. 'We have found the result disappointing; we accept

---

6 Oddly enough, she failed to call her two greatest election campaign foes to account: her own mouth and brain.

the verdict of the people. We put forward a very positive agenda, based on my continued belief that the best days are ahead of us as Australians and that we need to build a strong economy as the foundation for our success, for the foundation of our security.' And this was to be the new take on the situation: that the Coalition had only ever wanted to inspire and delight the nation with a jolly message of positivity, but then Labor came along with its big scary negative campaign and ruined everything.

In the days that followed the election, Turnbull and the more Turnbull-sympathetic elements of the media maintained the line that the swing to Labor had been because of the 'grotesque lie' that the government planned to privatise Medicare. Two things were largely overlooked: first, that it wasn't really a lie; and second, that there wasn't that big a swing.

The debatable point regarding the 'lie' claim depends on whether you believe that 'privatising Medicare' was something that the government planned to do lock, stock and barrel—which was unambiguously not the case—or if the government was 'privatising Medicare' by embarking on a process of offloading elements to the private sector, which was equally unambiguously true.

The decision to freeze Medicare rebates to doctors and cut rebates for diagnostic tests and scans indicated that the Coalition didn't consider Medicare to be immune to cuts, but there were other ways in which the government deliberately undermined it for the benefit of private enterprise. This manifested itself in increases to the Medicare Surcharge, paid by those Australians who don't have private health insurance, which was intended as an incentive to move people off the public system and into the private one—and which had the added effect of removing tax money from the health system and putting it into the hands of the for-profit insurance industry.

However, there had also been a plan to take the Medicare payments system and hand it over to a private organisation, citing the need to update the current system to something more 'geared for instant online transactions using smart phones and contemporary digital applications'. Who would provide this zippy new digital future wasn't made clear—although one of the rumoured frontrunners was Australia Post, which the government was also reportedly making plans to sell. This looked awfully like an attempt to artificially fatten the calf before dragging it to market.

That being said, this could have been spun as a necessary and responsible move to create a user-friendly system that was quick to access and abolished the unnecessarily long wait between paying for a service and receiving one's Medicare rebate. However, when the plan was announced in February—amid talk of an early election, a tight budget and the looming return of the debt 'n' deficit monster, which had last lumbered through the political landscape before the 2014 budget—health minister Sussan Ley was unable to answer simple and fairly important questions such as how a private company could guarantee the security of deeply sensitive medical data.

Handing the payments system over to a business better placed to develop the necessary tech might have been a really good idea both financially and practically; but, because of the context in which the idea was presented, it looked awfully like the thin edge of a wedge propped into Medicare's funding. For this reason, the government was forced to abandon the proposal during the election campaign. Turnbull actually acknowledged that the 'Mediscare' campaign couldn't possibly have worked if voters hadn't thought Labor's assertion that the Coalition was waging war on accessible healthcare was not just plausible, but already apparent. 'There was some fertile ground in which that grotesque lie could be sown. There is no doubt about that,' Turnbull conceded.

As for the question of the swing to Labor, this seemed to manifest itself in subtle ways, as opposed to issuing some sort of clear signal—such as, for example, people actually voting for Labor. In 2013 it had garnered a pitiful 33.4 per cent of the vote; in 2016 this crept up to 35 per cent. The seats Labor won were less a result of the public enthusiastically supporting the party than that voters were leaving the Coalition in droves.

But as to the final point, about the effect of Labor's scare campaign on the voting public, the weekly polling told an important story: while all this frantic activity was going on between the major parties, the two-party preferred vote didn't move significantly in either direction.

When the Coalition declared that it was about jobs and growth? No movement. When Labor unveiled its 100 Positive Policies? No movement. When the Coalition attacked Labor's negative gearing proposals with the #FakeTradie campaign? Stability? Labor's War on Business? Stick to the Plan? No movement for any of them—nor for the Mediscare campaign. The polls stubbornly reported a two-party preferred vote that hovered around 50 per cent for each side from the start of the campaign to the day of the polls, with tiny individual fluctuations that looked more like statistical errors than any sign of a sudden galvanisation of support for either party.[7]

There are a couple of ways to interpret this. One is that the parties were so perfectly matched that their campaigns were essentially countering one another blow for blow, with every successful strike for the hearts and minds of the voting public being matched and equalled with a perfectly timed counter-strike by the other side. In this reading, the election portrayed a savage battle of ideas smeared out across the greatest canvas of all: the fabric of Australia itself.

There's an alternative reading, which is this: pretty much no-one gave a shit. In this interpretation, both the major parties were largely preaching to their rusted-on bases while anyone not blindly committed to them was contributing to the record vote for 'others', which looked on track to deliver the most unwieldy Senate in Australian history. This theory also suggests that the media were not the arbiters of popular opinion they might have thought they were, and that no amount of *Daily Telegraph* anti-Shorten Photoshopped front pages or Turnbull-endorsing editorials (which just about every masthead chose to publish, for reasons that appeared obscure)

---

7   Crikey's Poll Bludger blog did an analysis of the polling after the election results were finalised and concluded that Australia's polling companies did an exceptionally strong job: all the big companies accurately predicted the result (Newspoll got it bang on; Fairfax-Ipsos overestimated the Greens' support by a single percentage point; everyone else was largely accurate), adding however that the electorate-level polling was all over the place—which might explain much of the false confidence the parties exhibited about the presence or absence of swings.

was going to change the minds of those who had already written off both parties.

This interpretation also implies that maybe the issue wasn't really what the parties were saying and doing during the campaign so much as what they'd done in the lead-up. Labor was clearly still dogged by the embarrassments of the Rudd–Gillard–Rudd era and a leader who had taken a long time to get into his stride; the Coalition only grudgingly acknowledged that it probably didn't help the Liberal cause to have had its previous prime minister make a lot of very explicit, unambiguous promises—such as 'no cuts to health, no cuts to education, no changes to pensions, no changes to the GST, and no cuts to the ABC and SBS'—and then to have either broken or made plans to break every single one of them. Abbott might have thought he outsmarted everyone by cleverly arguing that slashing the ABC's budget was actually an 'efficiency dividend' and proposing an upfront payment to see GPs was actually a 'price signal', but for some reason the electorate seemed not to have been convinced, much less charmed by his condescending rhetoric on such matters. In any case, the unified-looking Labor at least appeared to have learned something from its mistakes; the Coalition appeared determined to double down instead.

———

Finally, on 10 July—eight days after the polls closed—Turnbull felt confident enough to declare victory; or, more accurately, Shorten felt confident enough to concede defeat, thereby leaving only one option for the prime ministership. A visibly relieved Malcolm celebrated 'the first time since 2004 an Australian government has been returned with a majority' and drew a somewhat hopeful comparison with the near-wipeout that Robert Menzies experienced in 1961. It was slightly rich of him to claim that this was the 'return' of a government—this was, after all, the first election the Turnbull government had ever faced—but, as his supporters kept insisting in the press, a win is a win.

The actual final result would not be known for a month, until the final count in the Queensland seat of Herbert determined whether the government could afford to appoint a member of the party as speaker—but even with disaster so barely averted, the DelCons didn't miss an opportunity to throw their weight around.

Eric Abetz told ABC radio on 14 July that the Coalition had won 'the barest of victories . . . if we can call it a victory' and that clearly this less-than-stellar result indicated the public's unhappiness with the government's planned superannuation changes—while also indicating that, really, the whole same-sex marriage plebiscite thing should probably be put on the back burner too. You know, because he'd *hate* for it to be rushed. While Turnbull had indicated that the plebiscite would be held by the end of 2016, Abetz had other ideas.

'I would hope the question is properly ventilated and considered, that the underpinning legislation is considered by the House of Representatives, by a Senate committee et cetera, so I think due process has to take place. And then of course we need a proper period for the varying views to be canvassed in a campaign, and so whether we can still sneak that in before the end of the year, I think that will be difficult.'

Before too long the plebiscite timetable was being pushed back into 2017, with serious question marks hanging over how it was to be implemented—not helped by the newly re-relevant One Nation insisting that the vote be a referendum, with marriage defined under the Constitution rather than by legislation, which suggested that Pauline Hanson's grasp of how parliament worked was as rock-solid as ever.

Kevin Andrews, meanwhile, was still doing his job as the ex-PM's head cheerleader, telling a sympathetic Andrew Bolt that Turnbull should put his defeated rival back in the ministry. 'It would make sense to me to reappoint Mr Abbott. I mean, he's a man who's been prime minister of the country; he's got a lot of experience, he's seen as a figurehead, I think, of conservatives within the parliamentary party.'

While Abbott supporters were happy to maintain the fiction that they'd have enjoyed a comfortable win under Tony's leadership, it turned out that there was one very important and unique quality Turnbull possessed that had provided a decisive advantage to the Coalition: millions of dollars.

On 15 July *The Australian*'s Sharri Markson reported that Turnbull had ponied up a massive personal donation of a million dollars to cover the final week of TV advertising. That the leak was calculated to define Turnbull's point of difference from the previous PM was not in doubt—Abbott certainly didn't have that much sweet, sweet scratch to splash about—and some subsequent reports indicated that the final amount may have been even higher. But given the financial shortfall the Liberals faced, both through circumstance and their own doing, having a well-heeled daddy to bail them out of trouble was clearly exceptionally useful.

———

On 18 July the new ministry was revealed, the fourth in less than three hundred days,[8] and those hoping for the return of a certain former prime minister to the frontbench were, well, disappointed.

They weren't the only ones—in fact, it was hard to see the Cabinet reshuffle as anything other than a warning to the DelCons to pull their heads in.

Abbott was not returned. Neither were Abetz nor Andrews—and, obviously, Bernardi and Christensen weren't about to be given any big boy responsibilities. The only outspoken Abbott supporter to get a bump was Canberra senator Zed Seselja, who entered the junior ministry as Assistant Minister for Social Services and Multicultural Affairs. There was one other semi-nod to the Monkey Podders, with immigration minister Peter Dutton restored to the National Security Committee, so at least Abbott had a man on the inside again.

Christopher Pyne's transformation from Abbott loyalist to Turnbull herald was recognised with the Defence Industry portfolio, responsible for overseeing the nation's mighty ship- and sub-building projects, while Marise Payne remained as defence minister with the boring oversight-of-the-actual-armed-forces stuff. Pyne was, however, warned that he was not to favour South Australian companies—after

---

8   The first Abbott ministry in September 2013, the second in December 2014, the first Turnbull ministry in September 2015, and then this one. That'd be the 'stability' they were so keen on.

which, presumably, he and everyone else burst into peals of delighted laughter.

Greg Hunt was shunted into Pyne's former gig as Minister for Industry and Innovation, in which he could do precisely as much for the environment as he did when environment minister. Environment, meanwhile, was rolled into the Energy portfolio of Josh Frydenberg, showing just how important an afterthought it was for the Turnbull government.

In what was definitely not a slapdown for her less-than-stellar performance in the portfolio and the election campaign, Assistant Treasurer Kelly O'Dwyer found her gig renamed Revenue and Financial Services, with Small Business removed from her hands into the bargain. And Richard Colbeck was dropped from the Tourism portfolio even before he'd failed in his attempt to win the fifth Liberal Senate slot in Tasmania, after being shoved down the ballot by the conservative, Abetz-aligned factions in that state's party.[9]

The Nationals got a bunch of presents, though: deputy leader Fiona Nash's portfolio stash now included Local Government and Territories, hardline right-winger Matthew Canavan got Northern Australia and Resources, and Michael McCormack got the Small Business gig retrieved from O'Dwyer. In recognition of the improved standing of the Nationals in the Coalition, Luke Hartsuyker and David Gillespie got assistant ministries.

---

9 Eric Abetz also had the impressive gall to issue a statement on the day the new ministry was announced complaining about how his state hadn't been given a ministerial berth despite losing Colbeck. To be fair, thanks to the Tasmanian Liberals' virtuoso seat-losing performance, there was hardly anyone left to promote.

The downside was that this meant a huge Cabinet—thirty ministers, in fact, expanding to forty-two when the outer ministry was included, making it the largest ministry since that of Gough Whitlam. Many accurately figured that the PM had had to give more than half the Coalition some busy work so he didn't alienate any of his much-needed supporters, while also giving obligatory representation to the Nationals. Or, as Tanya Plibersek put it, 'He has just won an election, but the makeup of his front bench shows that he is worried that his colleagues are coming after him. He has to give jobs to the enemies as well as friends.'

While it looked as transparently strategic as it was, Turnbull had made clear to his established critics that they could either get with the program or face irrelevancy. The elevation of Canavan and Seselja meant that the right of the party couldn't even complain about this being a rejection of conservative values, since ambitious right-wingers were clearly being rewarded and the Nationals placated. Suddenly the DelCons looked very, very lonely indeed.

But just when it seemed as though he was starting to get the hang of this prime minister thing after all, there was a challenge from the north that threatened to rend the already-tenuous government in twain.

Because now the LNP decided that it wanted some attention.

———

As we explored at irritating depth earlier in this very book, the Coalition of the Liberal and National parties is a marriage of convenience entered into because the Nationals are irrelevant in most of the nation, but would absolutely eat the Liberals alive in Queensland.[10] However, since 2008 neither the Liberals nor the Nationals exist in that state, replaced by the merged creation called the Liberal National Party. Neither Liberal nor National (nor, for that matter, liberal or national), all federal members are assigned to either the Liberal or National party rooms in Parliament House by whatever is the conservative political equivalent of the Sorting Hat from Hogwarts.

However, the LNP parliamentarians weren't all entirely delighted to be divided between Slytherin and Hufflepuff, and periodically would make public statements insisting that there were actually three parties in the Coalition: the Liberals, the Nationals, and the LNP,[11] and maybe the latter should get its own party room and frontbench representation.

This suggestion was first mooted two months after the 2013 election, before being very firmly quashed by Tony Abbott. And the reason it came up was Senator Ian Macdonald, who was a member of the Liberal party room but was sick and tired of not being taken seriously anymore, goddammit. He'd last held a ministerial position in the final Howard term, as Minister for Fisheries, Forestry and Conservation, until getting kicked to the backbench in a ministerial reshuffle in January 2006. He'd held a couple of shadow parliamentary secretary positions while the Coalition was in opposition and had assumed that he was going to waltz into the Science portfolio after the 2013 election victory, until he got the call from Abbott saying that a) there was no Science portfolio anymore, and b) he wasn't getting a frontbench spot in any case.

10 Not a metaphor.
11 And the Country Liberal Party, if you wanted to count the Northern Territory. Which, for the most part, no-one did.

ANDREW P STREET

He didn't hide his disappointment either. 'What should have been one of the proudest days of my life has turned into one of the worst,' he told Fairfax the week after the election. 'The ecstasy of a new government and success in the north has turned a little sad with a phone call from Tony Abbott saying he has no room for me in the new ministry.'

That soured matters between the men, but the conservative Queenslander was no fan of Turnbull's either and publicly admonished him for the leadership challenge. 'I am disappointed to hear this raised publicly a week out of the Canning by-election,' he scolded at the time. 'I personally haven't been enamoured with Abbott as a person, but I think since the spill last time, he's done a good job.'

With Macdonald not-enamoured of Abbott, nor of Turnbull, he might have looked at the inevitable resignation of Nationals leader Warren Truss as a good opportunity to improve his frontbench chances by changing party rooms— but the failure of fellow LNP member Ian Macfarlane to pull off the same trick for the exact same reason closed off that option. And so, on 22 July, the Queensland LNP executive, looking at the new, enormous front bench and deciding the LNP was not getting the respect it so richly deserved, considered a motion to have its members leave the Nationals and Liberals in order to create its own party room.

The government's response was swift—it sent Nationals leader Barnaby Joyce and Attorney-General George Brandis to quell the unrest. Statements were issued to the effect that this was just a playful misunderstanding, but *The Guardian* reported: 'Senator Ian Macdonald will bring a motion to the Liberal National Party state conference next month.'

Macdonald's argument was simple: the LNP contributed twenty-seven of the Coalition's seventy-six seats, but its contribution 'not just in this election but the last couple of decades has never been fully recognised in the makeup of the ministry'.

Liberals and Nationals rallied to insist that this definitely wasn't a thing. Mathias Cormann told Sky, 'There won't be any split ... The arrangements continue as they have been,' while Brandis emphasised that there were already four Queenslanders in the ministry of forty-two, so what were they complaining about?

Joyce declined to comment, but he presumably saw his position as deputy PM under threat, since the Nationals would have a mere fourteen seats without the LNP—a loss of constituency that would dramatically undermine his authority, although making it much easier for the Nationals to carpool.

And thus did the PM acquire another bonus post-election challenge: to placate his angry Queenslanders.

———

Labor, meanwhile, faced its own issues as it began looking at its parliamentary team. Tasmanian senator Lisa Singh had defied the factional push that put her at the unwinnable bottom of the ticket by persuading Labor voters to number the ballot below the line, allowing her to become Labor's fifth senator (thereby sticking one in the eye of supporters of union functionary John Short, who'd been plonked above her on the ballot). Factions also mobilised to move Kim Carr to the back bench after he'd been involved in disputes with Penny Wong and Tanya Plibersek, in a rift that threatened to split Labor's left. David Feeney was also shoved onto the back bench over his poor electoral performance. For all of the unity in public, there were clearly still tides drifting within Labor.

The Greens, meanwhile, were in a similarly tricky position. Unlike the other parties, they could genuinely argue that their decision to support the changes to the Senate voting system was a matter of long-held and passionately supported democratic principle rather than for any sort of grubby political gain. However, they were able to make that argument principally because they hadn't enjoyed a political gain of any kind, grubby or otherwise.

Despite giddy hopes of picking up as many as four new lower house seats in inner-city electorates of Melbourne and Sydney, the Greens ended the 2016 campaign as they had begun it, with one seat in the reps—Melbourne, held by Bandt. They suffered a narrow loss in the seat of Batman and had brief preference-based hopes that they might just squeak into Melbourne Ports, depending on how the Liberal vote shook out; but ultimately Labor held on to both seats despite truly heroic amounts of resources being thrown at the battles.[12]

However, it was in the upper house that the real effects of the Greens' support for Senate reform became clear. Without the preference deals that had previously elected South Australia's Sarah Hanson-Young and Western Australia's Scott Ludlam, both of those states suffered: SA lost Robert Simms (and Hanson-Young barely gathered enough votes for the

12 The Greens also went hard in the NSW seats of Grayndler and Sydney but didn't make much of a dent. Most strategists agree that the Greens haven't got much hope of taking these seats from Labor until Anthony Albanese and Tanya Plibersek, the respective members, resign.

eleventh seat) while WA's Rachel Siewert only scraped in to the twelfth spot. Nick McKim also barely scraped over the line for the last seat in Tasmania—thereby denying One Nation a win, as well as quashing the hopes of a return to parliament for ex-tourism minister Colbeck—thus avoiding an embarrassing loss in the party's traditional heartland.

The Greens had stalled in New South Wales, where the state party had been at loggerheads with the federal organisation since September 2015, when Lee Rhiannon, the state's sole Greens senator, had the Higher Education portfolio taken from her and handed to brand-new SA senator, the aforementioned Simms. At the time the NSW party had indicated that it would not contribute to the federal election campaign, but a détente was reached before the election. Nonetheless, the fierce undercurrents created by the notoriously hard-left NSW party, which had never been remotely comfortable with Richard di Natale's attempts to turn the Greens into a more mainstream party, were now in full view.

Di Natale put a brave face on the result, attempting to spin it as a reduced-influence-in-the-Senate-half-full situation. 'While we achieved a significant increase in the lower house it doesn't appear that increase has followed in the Senate. One possibility is that voters now perceive us as a major party and are voting for us in the lower house but then voting for a micro party in the Senate,' he rather optimistically told *The Australian*. He indicated that this would serve the party well in future elections.

Then again, with this sort of a result, it doesn't seem a foregone conclusion that he'll be around to see it.

And then there was the Senate crossbench, which promised to be even more dysfunctional than the one Turnbull had sought to clear—sorry, definitely *not* sought to clear out by holding a double dissolution election. After all, he'd said as much in his widely criticised election night speech, insisting that the double dissolution 'was not a political tactic. It was not designed to remove senators or get a new Senate because new senators are better than old senators or whatever.'

And it's a good thing that it (ostensibly) hadn't been his tactic, because if it had been, it backfired terribly. With the final counting still being conducted a month after the election, the Coalition had slipped from thirty-three senators to thirty, Labor had gained one to achieve a final count of twenty-seven, and the Greens had dropped by one to nine. With thirty-nine votes required to pass or block legislation, this posed a challenge for the government: it would need nine of the eleven crossbenchers to pass any legislation that Labor and the Greens declined to support.

The problem was the marvellous diversity of the cross-bench. With three NXT senators and four from One Nation, the government would need to depend on the support of two parties with very, *very* different agendas—and then put on its best wooing face to convince the loose-cannon broadcaster Derryn Hinch to agree, plus three of the senators Turnbull had sought to throw out from the last parliament: Jacqui Lambie, Bob Day and David Leyonhjelm. And with Hanson keen to avenge herself on the party she blamed for her twenty years in the political wilderness—and she and Lambie already throwing brickbats at each other in the press—it was looking like being a very, very, very entertaining sort of upper house.

———

While the situation in 2016 isn't quite that of 2010, there are plenty of comparisons to be made between Turnbull and Gillard: both rolled an elected PM, both saw their government's popularity briefly spike and then plummet, and both won the subsequent elections by the skin of their teeth. However, there's another point they have in common: both are moderates who were tolerated but certainly not adored by the extremes of their party.

Howard could talk about being the great conciliator in the broad church of the Liberal Party, but he didn't have to win over conservatives who were still fuming over being robbed of the glorious, entirely imaginary conservative golden age they'd be enjoying right now under a returned Abbott government. Howard's wins were sometimes close, but always decisive— and since he was of the right, whatever concessions he handed out were to the grateful moderates.

Turnbull is in a very different position: whatever progressive policy he might want to put forward is off the table and any conservative concessions he makes to the DelCons will be insufficient to meet their demands. Even complete surrender isn't enough, as the furore over Safe Schools demonstrated.

How would that play out, in a divided party dependent on a disparate Senate? What sort of reforming legislation will be happily passed by the centrist, community-focused NXT and simultaneously the protectionist, hard-right One Nation? Is the Man in the Top Hat set to be remembered by history as the least effective Australian prime minister in history, or does he still have some clever plans and secret tricks up his sleeve?

We're about to find out.

18
THE BALANCE OF POWER GOES WEIRD

In which we are captivated by the sinuous dance of the independent parties, as one waxes influential and another wanes

When the Palmer United Party launched its election campaign in 2013, no expense was spared. Hundreds of supporters lobbed into the Palmer Coolum Resort, where the party's titular head, who was running in the lower house seat of Fairfax, flanked by candidates sporting ties and scarves in the party's trademark canary yellow, ready to represent a hot new sound in the staid political scene.

And yet, inside of three years, it was all over bar the . . . well, not even shouting. Muttering, maybe? Sighing? Tutting?

After pouring millions into advertising campaigns around the nation in 2013, Clive was rewarded with a win in Fairfax by literally dozens of votes, and the unexpected election of three senators to the upper house: ex-rugby league star

Glenn Lazarus (affectionately nicknamed The Brick With Eyes by former Triple J sports commentators Roy and HG) in Queensland, former Australian Defence Force member Jacqui Lambie in Tasmania, and Zhenya 'Dio' Wang, ex-CEO of the Palmer-owned Australasian Resources, in Western Australia.[1]

They also had a bonus senator of sorts in the Australian Motoring Enthusiast Party's Ricky Muir, who'd been accidentally elected in Victoria thanks to a labyrinthine web of preference deals and who demonstrated his unfamiliarity with the process by agreeing to vote as part of an unofficial bloc that would effectively give PUP the balance of power after the new Senate first sat in July 2014.

By that point, however, the honeymoon was already over. Muir had distanced himself from PUP, going on to be an unexpectedly thoughtful and principled parliamentarian who considered his votes carefully. The Queensland and Northern Territory branches—made up of disgruntled LNP and Country Liberal Party members who had jumped ship—were awash with members fighting with Palmer and quitting the party. Battles between Palmer and Lambie grew more frequent and public, and in November 2014 she quit the party, with Lazarus following suit the following March. This left Wang as the party's only representative in the upper house.

Meanwhile, Palmer himself earned the dubious honour of being the MP who turned up for work the least often, attending a dismal 6.2 per cent of the lower house divisions. At first this was put down to Palmer having achieved everything

1 It's never been made clear why Zhenya Wang is known as Dio, but I for one sincerely hope that it's because he drove to Canberra blasting *Holy Diver* at full volume.

he'd wanted from the creation of his party: to stick it to the Liberal National Party of Queensland, with whom he'd previously had a mighty falling-out—despite years of being one of its most ardent supporters and heaviest donors—after the newly installed state government of Campbell Newman failed to support his business projects in government. PUP had been widely theorised as an instrument of vengeance against Newman, and certainly once Newman's government was unexpectedly turfed out in January 2015 it did seem as though the wind went out of Palmer's sails.

However, it soon became clear that Palmer's absence from parliament might be because he had other things on his mind: specifically, the decline of his business empire. While Palmer had technically been obliged to give up his day job in order to serve as a full-time parliamentarian for the good people of Fairfax, he was clearly a believer in multi-tasking. And, in line with the consensus of cognitive behavioural research that it's impossible to do more than one thing at once, his performance in both roles was less than stellar.

Emails emerged showing that purchase orders and directorial duties for Queensland Nickel had been carried out by a mysterious fellow named Terry Smith, using an email address that Palmer had occasionally used for parliamentary business. There was also a twenty-six-day window when Palmer replaced his nephew Clive Mensink as director, supposedly because Mensink was on leave, during which Queensland Nickel donated $70,000 to the Palmer United Party. In fact, it was to transpire that various Palmer-owned businesses donated over $10 million to the party, including $5.9 million from Queensland Nickel itself. And that was a problem, since the last donation—of $288,516 on 31 December 2015—was uncomfortably close to 18 January, when Queensland Nickel went into voluntary administration and sacked 237 workers before closing down operations altogether, leaving around eight hundred workers without jobs and reportedly owing $74 million in unpaid entitlements.

Palmer angrily insisted that he'd done nothing wrong, that the donations were entirely above board and that the millions siphoned out of Queensland Nickel for the party had nothing to do with the company closing its refinery in Townsville (which he attributed to the falling price of nickel). Ultimately the Queensland government stepped in to pay $68 million of the worker entitlements in May while announcing plans to recover funds from Palmer personally.

Unsurprisingly the PUP campaign launch in June 2016 was a dismal affair. Held in the Brisbane office of the Palmer-owned Mineralogy—since the Palmer Coolum Resort had shut its doors in early 2016—barely thirty people showed up to watch the party launch what everyone knew was going to be its last-ever federal election campaign.[2] Zhenya 'Dio' Wang, the only one of the three 2013 senators not to have quit the party in disgust, pledged to continue to 'keep the bastards honest' in a tired line that evoked another once-powerful and now deregistered minor party, the Australian Democrats. Palmer himself looked tired and bored; he refused to take

---

2   Despite the Palmer Coolum Resort being shut, it was still Palmer's supposed 'residence' during his stint as the Member for Fairfax, suggesting that it was an uncannily authentic-looking doppelpälmer cooling his heels at Palmer's Gold Coast mansion.

questions from the apparently unquestioning media that he slammed in his prepared speech. He hadn't even bothered to wear his trademark PUP yellow tie, opting instead for a handsome burgundy number.

While Palmer claimed that the party would reclaim the balance of power in the upper house at the election, not even those on stage seemed prepared to believe it. And thus did the great PUP experiment end: not with a bang, but with a series of lawsuits.

However, while PUP was the game changer in 2013, in 2016 there was a new disrupter—and it was another party based around a single politician's name, credibility and charisma: the Nick Xenophon Team.

———

Xenophon is an enigmatic figure in the Australia politics-cape. The son of working class immigrants (father from Cyprus, mother from Greece) who worked hard to send their son to Adelaide's Prince Alfred College, he was a former Young Liberal at Adelaide Uni but grew disenchanted with the party, thereby nearly mirroring the attitude of the future NXT voting base. As a suburban personal injury lawyer, he became increasingly concerned about the effect that pokies were having on the lower-income folks who were so often his clients, and decided to do something about it.

Few politicians can parlay a successful single-issue cause into a viable political career, but Xenophon did so with the No Pokies Party. He was elected to the South Australian legislative council in 1997—the first independent candidate to manage this in over half a century—and remained there until resigning in 2007 to stand as a federal candidate for the Senate. Since that win his primary vote increased at every election and his vote was key to the passage of legislation in the crossbench-controlled Senates of 2008–11 and 2014–16.

His considered, centrist approach has been notable not only because the very idea of assessing legislation on its merits seems impossibly exotic and somewhat suspicious in the generally tribal field of Australian politics, it's also at odds with a public persona that suggests a penny-pinching goofy uncle with a death wish.

There's his much-discussed love of thrift (only ever flying economy even on official travel, only wearing $99 Lowes suits), his love of animal- and pun-based political stunts (leading a goat to the South Australian parliament to encourage the public not to 'kid around with their vote'; launching his federal campaign at the giraffe enclosure at Adelaide Zoo to indicate that he'll 'stick his neck out' for South Australia, etc.), and the fact that he underwent open heart surgery in 2002 and spinal surgery in 2010. Yet on he goes.

His decision to create a new party as the parliament made decisive moves towards changing the Senate ballot was initially seen as being South Australia specific: after all, he'd picked up almost two full quotas of votes in 2013, suggesting that running other candidates in his home state and elsewhere would provide him with multiple Senate seats in 2016. But the real shock was that he was running lower house candidates—and, as the election got closer, it started to look as though NXT could actually dislodge some Liberal MPs in South Australia and give Labor candidates a good solid scare.

In the end, despite these feverish expectations, the NXT won just three Senate seats in SA (plus the lower house seat of Mayo), but this was enough to give him a strategically powerful balance-of-power upper house bloc. A situation, in other words, that looked awfully PUP-like.

———

The problem facing NXT isn't quite the same as that faced by Palmer United. The leader of the party has proven his credentials: he is a unique figure with a trusted reputation earned through two decades of public service. So unique is he, in fact, that it has always been hard to imagine finding similar people to join the team.

At least with the four main political parties there's a clear sense of why people join: to support the working class (Labor), to promote the individual (Liberals), to protect the environment (Greens), or to hang out with rich people (Nationals). Even Palmer United had a clear and widely understood mandate: sweet, sweet revenge. With NXT the attraction seems to be . . . what, exactly? Xenophon's idiosyncratic mix of gambling reform, personal freedom, limits on deregulation and protection of the South Australian maritime industry reflect his particular beliefs and values rather than any particular overarching philosophy—but that's not the biggest threat to NXT expanding from one man to a national political force. Put bluntly: what's to stop opportunistic candidates from pulling a political switcheroo?

The problem with attracting the best and brightest for politics is that the entire system of party preselection is not entirely based on merit. As every election demonstrates, parties often find themselves preselecting candidates based on criteria like 'they live in the right area' or 'their dad was an MP' or 'there is literally no other alternative' without necessarily checking things like 'Have they forgotten to mention their criminal record?' (WA federal Labor candidate Chris Brown, 2016), 'Is their Facebook history a litany of violent and misspelled abuse?' (SA state Liberal candidate Anthony Antoniadis, 2014; WA state Liberal candidate Daniel Parasiliti, 2016; Victorian state Liberal candidate Jack Lyons, 2015; federal Labor candidate Imran Syed, 2015) and/or 'If the candidate is trumpeting a six-point plan, will they be utterly unable to name five of them and then become a national laughing-stock?' (the gold standard: Jaymes Diaz, whose federal Liberal career as aspirant MP for Greenaway in 2013 evaporated in a ninety-second interview on Channel 10 that presumably plays out in the nightmares of every political hopeful in the country). And all of those duds were selected by the biggest, most powerful parties, all of which presumably attract more viable political options than would be the case for smaller, less well-resourced organisations with fewer plausible chances for advancement.

And this is where the PUP comparison must give Xenophon pause.

There are challenges inherent in finding like-minded individuals who are determined to be part of politics but are still willing to travel a harder, lonelier road than they'd have when joining a large, more secure party. So Xenophon would be looking for candidates independent-minded enough to opt for a small party over the major parties, but still team players enough to subsume themselves to the needs of NXT.

That seems like a tricky needle to thread, and the history of small parties in Australia is not exactly a litany of triumphs.[3]

One might look at Rebekha Sharkie, NXT's successful candidate for Mayo, and figure that her history of working in the office of Mayo's previous MP—the Liberal Party's Jamie Briggs, who was not re-elected—might have given her valuable insight into the process while also fuelling her discontent with the party machine. After all, that was also the case with former Labor staffer and Liberal Party member Jacqui Lambie, who was . . . oh, yeah.[4]

At least with the Liberals or Labor there's an outside chance of one day being prime minister, or at least getting a lucrative frontbench berth. With Xenophon, you know you're not even going to be allowed to fly business class.

After all, the most familiar path for a minor party member with a taste for power is either to jump ship for a bigger party (former Australian Democrat Andrew Bartlett later switched to the Greens and—perhaps most notoriously—former Nuclear Disarmament Party leader Peter Garrett switched to Labor) or to just quit the party once in power and go independent. That can't be lost on Xenophon, since three of his recent crossbench colleagues had followed that pattern: Lambie, Lazarus and former Democratic Labor

---

3   RIP, Australian Democrats 1977–2015. After a youth of rare promise and achievement, it passed away at the age of thirty-eight after a long, debilitating GST-related illness, complicated by internal leadership haemorrhages. The party is survived by Greens candidates, high-level political strategists, and angry bloggers still fuming about internal disloyalty. Gone too soon.

4   She worked in the office of Tasmanian Labor senator Nick Sherry in 2008, but joined the Liberal Party in 2011 before quitting after a failed preselection bid for the Division of Braddon. She joined Palmer United in 2012.

Party senator John Madigan. And when assessing someone's current relationship, it's often instructive to have a little look at their exes.

On the positive side, there's John Darley, who replaced Xenophon as the No Pokies representative in the South Australian Legislative Assembly in 2007 and was re-elected in his own right (under the NXT banner) in the South Australian state election in 2014 and has enjoyed a solid, if somewhat unspectacular, state parliamentary career.

On the deficit side, there's Ann Bressington, a long-time anti-drug campaigner who was elected as the No Pokies candidate along with Xenophon at the 2006 state election, and who went rogue shortly thereafter. After introducing a successful bill to outlaw the selling of 'drug use paraphernalia' in SA, she attempted to bring in compulsory twice-annual random drug testing of all secondary students—a plan that could be kindly described as 'ambitious' (or less kindly as 'ludicrous')[5]—and a similarly failed bid to raise the drinking age in SA from eighteen to twenty-one. She also launched a savage attack on Xenophon when he first declared his intention to leave the state parliament and run nationally, accusing him of illegal fundraising, mismanaging campaign funds and ignoring her in parliament. In 2013 she announced that she was jumping ship to run as a candidate for Katter's Australia Party, although she ended up not running at all in the 2014 election.[6]

---

5 ... the descriptor chosen by Dr David Caldicott of the Royal Adelaide Hospital.
6 Without Bressington's incandescent star power, KAP drew a mighty 0.1 per cent of the vote.

So, will NXT become a powerful new force in Australian politics, or a spider's egg sac set to burst and send a new crop of attention-seeking independents scurrying everywhere after one argument too many with their party leader?

The Magic 8 Ball of parliament says: *Reply hazy, try again.*

EPILOGUE
WELCOME TO THE
NEW NORMAL

*In which we leave the Man in the Top Hat to face the
challenges of governing in a new world of compromise*

As these last words are being written, at the beginning of
August 2016, the signs for Australia aren't great. Interest rates
have been cut yet again, indicating that all those warnings
about dire consequences of Brexit/Trump/a Chinese slowdown
are not inspiring consumer or business confidence; Turnbull's
turnabout refusal to rubber-stamp the nomination of former
prime minister Kevin Rudd as a candidate for secretary-
general of the United Nations has raised even more questions
about the degree to which he is at the mercy of his right
wing;[1] the final recount of the seat of Herbert has confirmed
that the Coalition has a single-seat majority in parliament
(although the government is currently weighing up whether
or not to mount a legal challenge to hold the election in the

---

1   Is Turnbull also still bearing a grudge against Rudd over the humiliation of the
Godwin Grech debacle? You be the judge!

seat over again—hey, what does Turnbull have to lose?); and party instability is still manifesting in leaks, backgrounding against Turnbull, and public threats from MPs like George Christensen to cross the floor if they don't get their way.

And with that fragile one-seat majority—which vanishes once a Speaker is appointed—those threats can't be laughed off. As a delighted Bob Katter warned during his rambling in July, 'You try running a government with one vote up your sleeve. Don't have your mother die, because you can't go to the funeral! Don't go to the bathroom!'

And, exhaustingly, this is all before parliament has even sat. Once that happens there'll be the Royal Commission into Youth Detention in the Northern Territory, the joint sitting over the ABCC legislation, some sort of movement towards the marriage equality plebiscite, and all those still-unpassed budget details, no doubt accompanied by angry cries of 'b-b-but we have a mandate!' as the wildly disparate Senate crossbench merrily knocks them back. Given the fairly different—indeed, competing—philosophies of the South Australian Xenophon-led centrists and Hanson's regional protectionists, that, to put it mildly, is going to be a challenge.

Meanwhile, Tony Abbott took to *Four Corners* to decry the dangerous and potentially corrupt factionalism affecting the NSW Liberal Party which, purely by coincidence, is currently determined by the faction that supports Turnbull rather than Abbott, putting the PM in the invidious position of either being seen to support a dodgy system that benefits him or supporting democratic reforms that would undermine his authority.

It's fair to say that the Man in the Top Hat is in for some colourful times.

———

It's incredibly easy—and a whole lot of fun!—to predict seismic changes in the political sphere and declare that Things Will Never Be The Same. And for all of the talk that the 2016 election marks the end of the two-party system, the major parties have proven remarkably resilient in the face of confident predictions of their death.

After the 2007 Ruddslide election the papers were filled with editorials predicting that it would take a generation or more for the vanquished Liberal Party to recover from its devastating loss. Indeed, more than one pundit posited that we'd just seen the end of the left–right divide and that the future of Australian politics would be between the forces of industry and the challenges of the environment, with Labor and the Greens duking it out, while the Liberals and Nationals yelled impotently from the sidelines.

That, as you may have noticed, didn't happen.

Similarly, the 2013 Ruddrout unambiguously meant that Labor was finished, with its left-wing voter support haemorrhaging to the Greens and the centrists flocking to the sensible, responsible Coalition, in a sure sign that the nation was headed for another Menzies/Howard-style era of careful conservatism. There was no way that Bill Shorten could possibly last more than a few pitiful months as leader.

That, too, proved a somewhat ambitious reading of the situation.

So where does the future actually stand? Here's a confident guess: on the middle ground.

That's probably the single safest, smuggest prediction in the history of safe, smug predictions, because Australian politics has always been a battle for the middle. The crisis facing the major parties is partly how to reconcile their internal divisions—worker rights versus neoliberal globalisation in the case of Labor; small government liberal economics versus intrusive moral and social control for the Coalition—and partly how they deal with the question of where their middle ground support has gone. And make no mistake: neither party has won the hearts and minds of the nation. The 2016 election could be a blip, or we could be about to embark on a dramatic future of multi-party coalitions.

It's just barely possible that NXT and One Nation may make the move from being transit lounges for protest voters to becoming the established alternative parties of the grumpy centre and the furious right respectively—attracting disenchanted (mainly) Liberal and National voters to their respective camps. Then again, the pungent miasma rising from the cemetery of Australia's minor parties is a potent reminder that even the most vigorous have a sad history of being prematurely dumped unmourned into shallow graves.

Even as you read this, Coalition pollies will have already made overtures to the innocent, enthusiastic new minor party senators, suggesting that they should maybe share a drink and talk about how things work in the big, confusing upper house. And if one thing leads to another, and said senators should realise that jumping ship would give them even more legislative power, while not having to obey Xenophon/Hanson, then where's the harm?[2] After all, that line of persuasion worked for Labor with the then-leader of the Australian Democrats, Senator Cheryl Kernot, back in 1997.

Then again, that can also be a humiliating disaster for all concerned. Like with Labor and the then-leader of the Australian Democrats, Senator Cheryl Kernot, back in 1997.

———

Perhaps the most shocking thing about the current state of Australian politics is that so many of the newly divisive issues are stark reminders of everything we've lost—or, more accurately, allowed to be slowly eroded from underneath us— courtesy of economic and social forces largely directed by our governments.

The reintroduction of the ABCC reminds us of the power that unions once wielded, when the idea of constant improvements in working conditions was casually assumed and the government had to invent a construction sector Stasi to bring them down. The cruel debates we're having now over the supposed need to remove weekend penalty rates would never have gained traction in 1996. How did we end up accepting the heavily casualised, wage-frozen, arrive-at-dawn-and-leave-after-dark workforce that is so standard in Australia as to be unremarkable? When exactly did we sacrifice the working week in return for timid wage slavery?

The return of One Nation, amid discussions of Indigenous recognition, should remind us of the Australia that existed

---

2 Remember, parents of independent senators: be sure to teach your kids to advocate for themselves at such a moment. They need to know that the bigger, older senators might make all sorts of promises, but still not really have the independents' best legislative interests at heart.

before Pauline Hanson turned up—when multiculturalism was (correctly) seen as one of Australia's greatest strengths; when we were starting to regard ourselves as a player in Asia, rather than as a European afterthought; when it seemed that the Royal Commission into Aboriginal Deaths in Custody would be a game-changer that would finally see concrete steps taken towards improving the lives of our most marginalised. Hell, it was all but assumed that an honest-to-god treaty was an inevitable next step from the Mabo ruling on native title. How did we get so badly sidetracked, to the point where we are now bickering over 'recognition'?

An entire generation of Australians are about to become lifetime renters. Home ownership in our largest cities is now framed as a privilege for which great sacrifices are demanded, rather than as a perfectly reasonable expectation for a working family. There was a time when full employment was an explicit goal of every federal government, when a job for life was the norm and the idea of a quarter-acre house in the suburbs, within easy commuting distance, was so common as to be a mock-worthy stereotype. Now it seems like an idyllic fantasy to an increasing number of Australians, while the very-well-off panic about their retirement investments becoming worthless if there's a housing crash. Who's happier for it? No-one exactly seems to be winning.

So perhaps what we're going through is a (thankfully, gentler) version of what the UK and US are currently experiencing whereby our basically two-party system is being forced to rapidly evolve out of fear of being rendered irrelevant. Perhaps this is a chance for us to heed these strange policy ghosts of the eighties and nineties, and recalibrate our society accordingly. After all, we seem to have lost a lot more than we signed up for. Perhaps it's about time we called shenanigans.

———

It's entirely possible that the rest of the Turnbull epoch will be a series of increasingly bitter fights against an intractable Opposition and a Senate crossbench that knows it has the power to hold out for whatever conditions it fancies—gambling restrictions for NXT, a Royal Commission into Islam for One Nation, dry ice and Wrestlemania-style entrance music for Derryn Hinch—while support within the Coalition diminishes, with those who hoped for a brighter future under Turnbull edging away from the weakened leader and those who seek to topple him moving in for the kill. (To replace him with Abbott? With Morrison? Dear god, with *Dutton*?) This could be a hollow encore of the Gillard (or, if you'd prefer a Liberal version, Gorton) government all over again, with the same horrible sense of potential squandered, thanks to a party that couldn't put its own petty rivalries aside to focus on the greater national good.

Alternatively, perhaps Turnbull will turn out to be Howard or Hawke, grabbing a narrow victory and transforming it into a curtain-raiser to an epoch of impressively dull stability, in which no-one worries about politics for another decade.

Then again, that glorious, refreshing dream of political boredom seems unlikely. After all, as someone or other once said, there's apparently never been a more exciting time to be an Australian.

Hold on tight to one another, friends. We're about to find out just how exciting those times can get.

ACKNOWLEDGEMENTS
OR THE PEOPLE WHOSE
FAULT THIS ALSO IS

Oh sure, it looks obvious *now*—but the idea that there should be a follow-up of some sort to *The Short and Excruciatingly Embarrassing Reign of Captain Abbott* wasn't ever intended as a thing, even as politics got weirder and weirder and I kept getting distracted from another book I was (and remain) committed to completing.

So thank you, Allen & Unwin, for letting me dive headlong into this morass once again, and I promise I'll get back on to the other stuff right away. Honest.

And once again, I'm indebted to my editors, who said, 'No, definitely not,' and then, 'Okay, fine, convince us,' and then, 'You might have a point,' and finally, 'Right, you have a few months,' when I was bombarding them with emails about this book. Without the sage counsel and top-notch copy-wrangling of Richard Walsh and the steady hand of

Rebecca Kaiser this would just be another imaginary thing in my skull and a series of very boring conversations in pubs.

Three other people who had graciously lent their talents to *Captain Abbott* have returned to assist with this book, to my considerable relief: Ali Lavau was again on copyediting duties, fixing my typos and preventing me from reusing the same words and phrases all the time as though I was an unconvincing chatbot. Mad props are also due to Daniel Boud for making me look far, far better in photographic representation than I do in real life, and the magnificent Robert Polmear, whose cover design is another triumph of the graphical arts.

Enormous thanks are due to those who have allowed m'column View from the Street to be an ongoing snarky rant in the *Sydney Morning Herald* and the rest of the Fairfax family: thank you to Judith Whelan and Leigh Tonkin, and all the people who put the thing out in a way that the world can see.

And, of course, Dee Street remains the best person in the entire world, and without her love and support none of this would be even remotely worth doing.

Also, thanks in advance to the forthcoming Streetling, who provided a solid incentive to get words down: we haven't met you yet, admittedly, but we're quietly confident you're going to be pretty damn amazing. Hope you like Bowie, little one, because you're going to be hearing a lot of him.